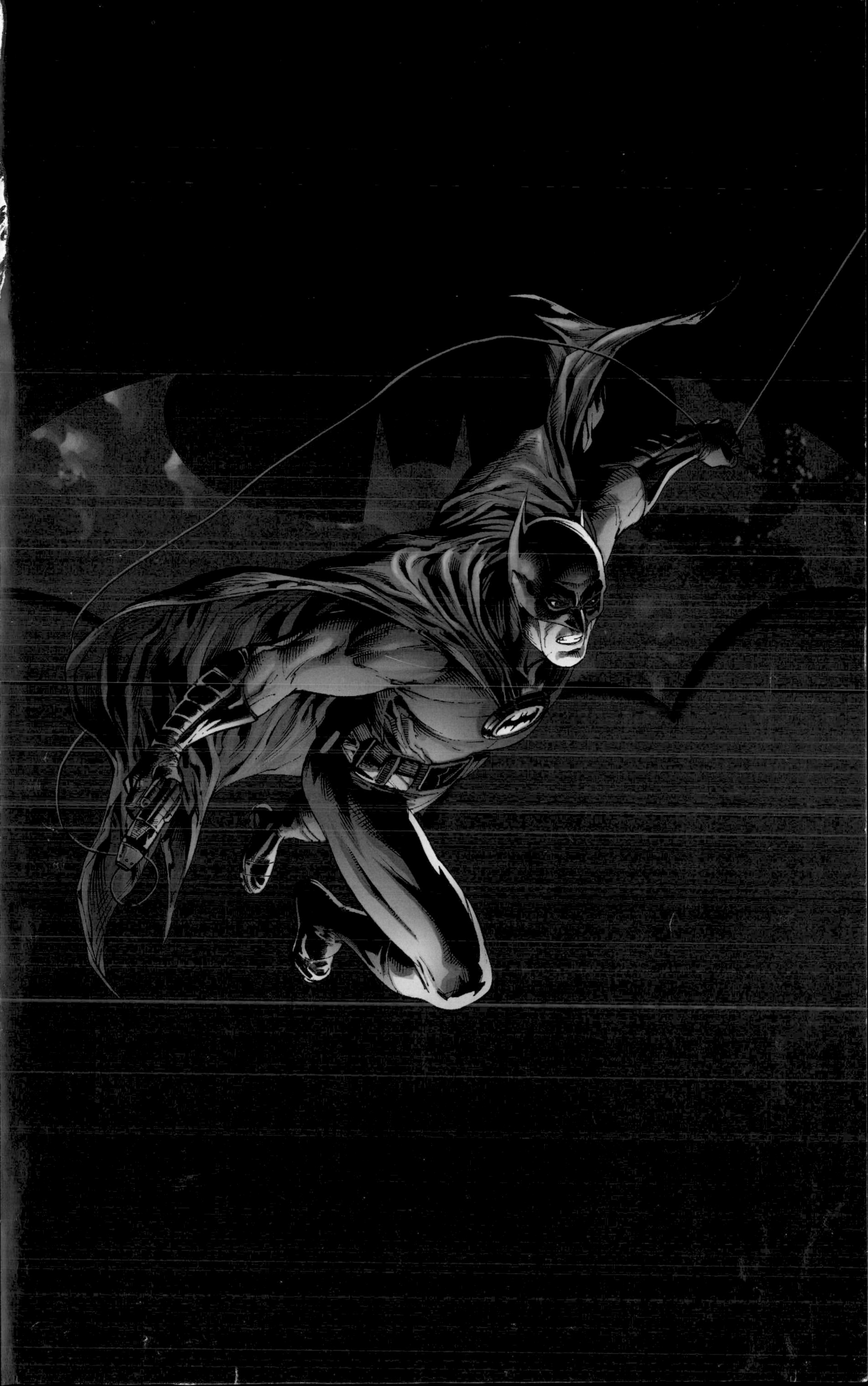

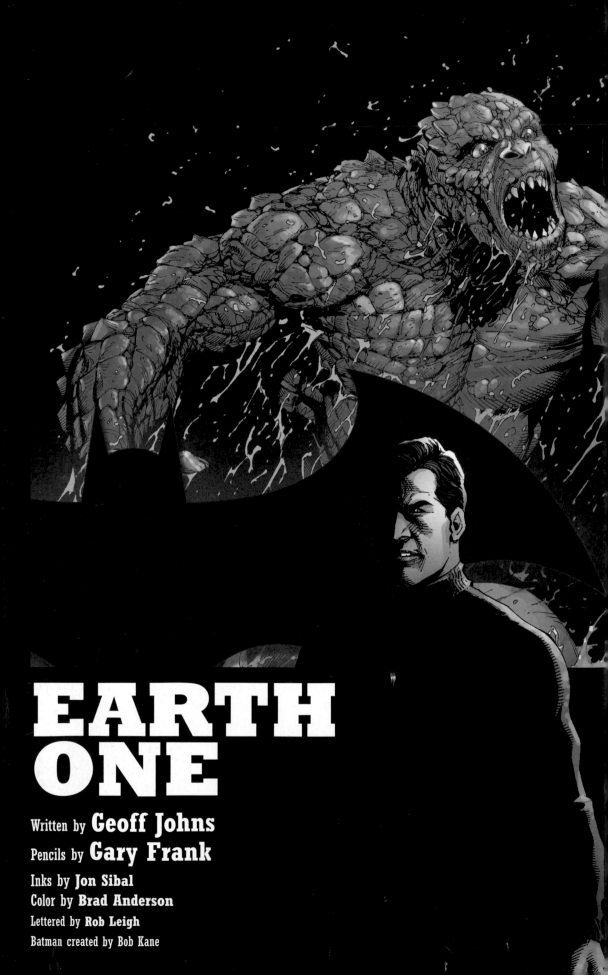

EARTH ONE

Written by **Geoff Johns**

Pencils by **Gary Frank**

Inks by **Jon Sibal**
Color by **Brad Anderson**
Lettered by **Rob Leigh**
Batman created by Bob Kane

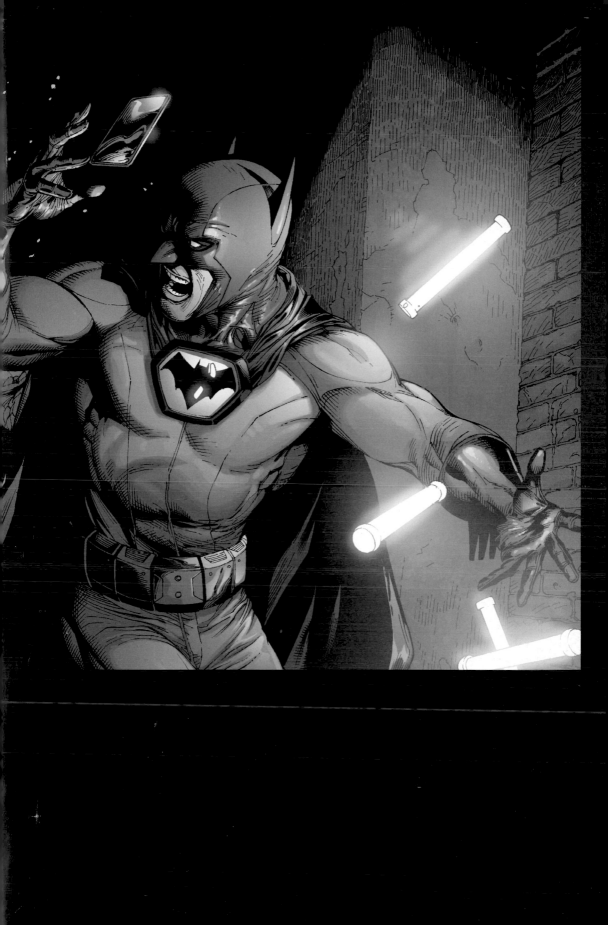

BATMAN: EARTH ONE VOLUME TWO

Published by DC Comics. Copyright © 2015 by DC Comics. All rights
reserved. All characters featured in this publication, the distinctive
likenesses thereof and related elements are trademarks of DC
Comics. The stories, characters and incidents featured in this
publication are entirely fictional. DC Comics does not read or
accept unsolicited submissions of ideas, stories or artwork.

DC Comics, 4000 Warner Blvd., Burbank, CA 91522.
A Warner Bros. Entertainment Company
Printed by RR Donnelley, Salem, VA, USA. 4/3/15. First Printing.
HC ISBN: 978-1-4012-4185-8

Library of Congress Cataloging-in-Publication Data

Johns, Geoff, 1973-
  Batman : earth one , volume 2 / Geoff Johns , Gary Frank.
  p. cm.
  ISBN 978-1-4012-4185-8 (hardback)
  1. Graphic novels. I. Frank, Gary, 1969- II. Title.
PN6728.B36J64 2012
741.5'973 — dc23
                              2012000608

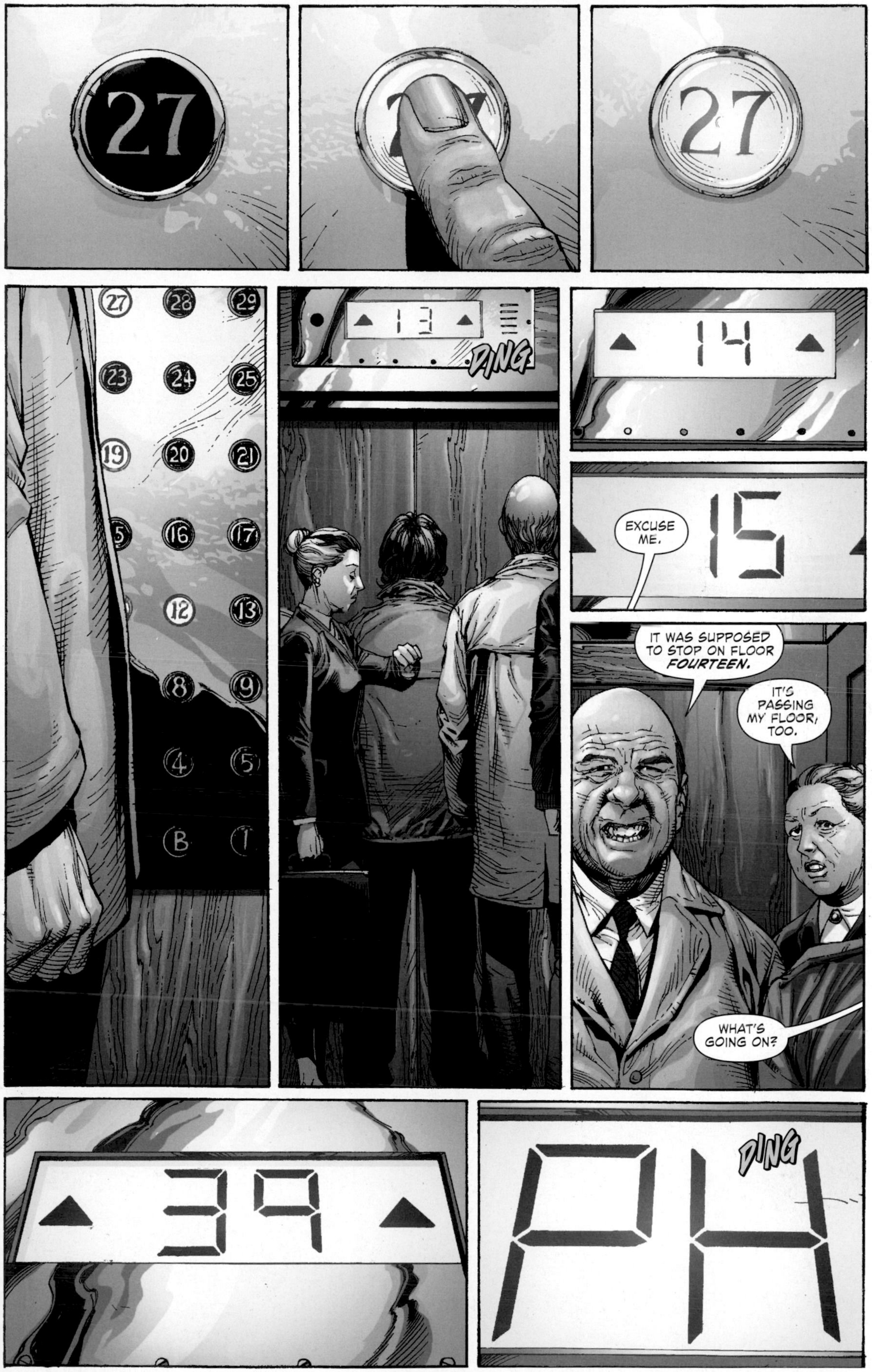
27
27
DING
EXCUSE ME.
IT WAS SUPPOSED TO STOP ON FLOOR FOURTEEN.
IT'S PASSING MY FLOOR, TOO.
WHAT'S GOING ON?
DING

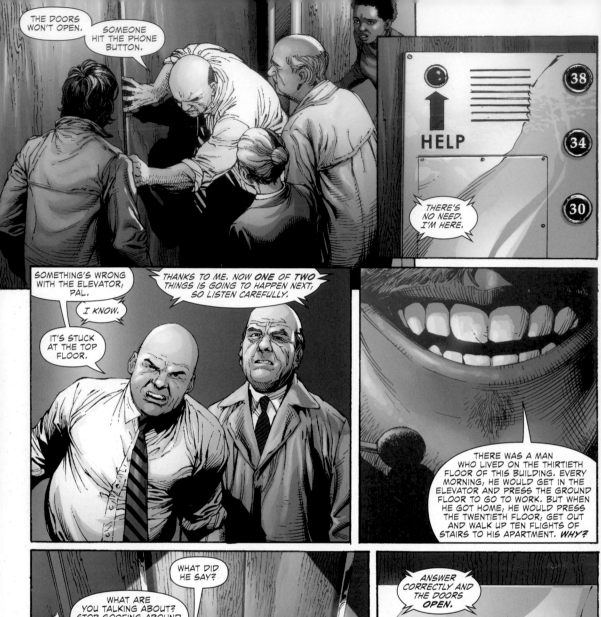

THE DOORS WON'T OPEN. SOMEONE HIT THE PHONE BUTTON.

38 34 30

HELP

THERE'S NO NEED. I'M HERE.

SOMETHING'S WRONG WITH THE ELEVATOR, PAL.

I KNOW.

IT'S STUCK AT THE TOP FLOOR.

THANKS TO ME. NOW ONE OF TWO THINGS IS GOING TO HAPPEN NEXT, SO LISTEN CAREFULLY.

THERE WAS A MAN WHO LIVED ON THE THIRTIETH FLOOR OF THIS BUILDING. EVERY MORNING, HE WOULD GET IN THE ELEVATOR AND PRESS THE GROUND FLOOR TO GO TO WORK. BUT WHEN HE GOT HOME, HE WOULD PRESS THE TWENTIETH FLOOR, GET OUT AND WALK UP TEN FLIGHTS OF STAIRS TO HIS APARTMENT. WHY?

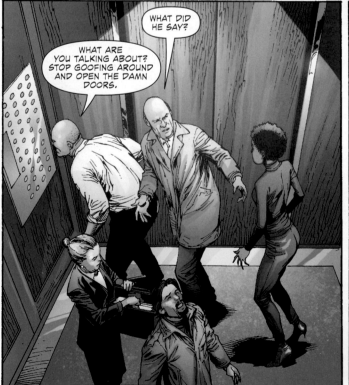

WHAT DID HE SAY?

WHAT ARE YOU TALKING ABOUT? STOP GOOFING AROUND AND OPEN THE DAMN DOORS.

ANSWER CORRECTLY AND THE DOORS OPEN.

ANSWER INCORRECTLY AND YOU ALL FALL FORTY FLOORS.

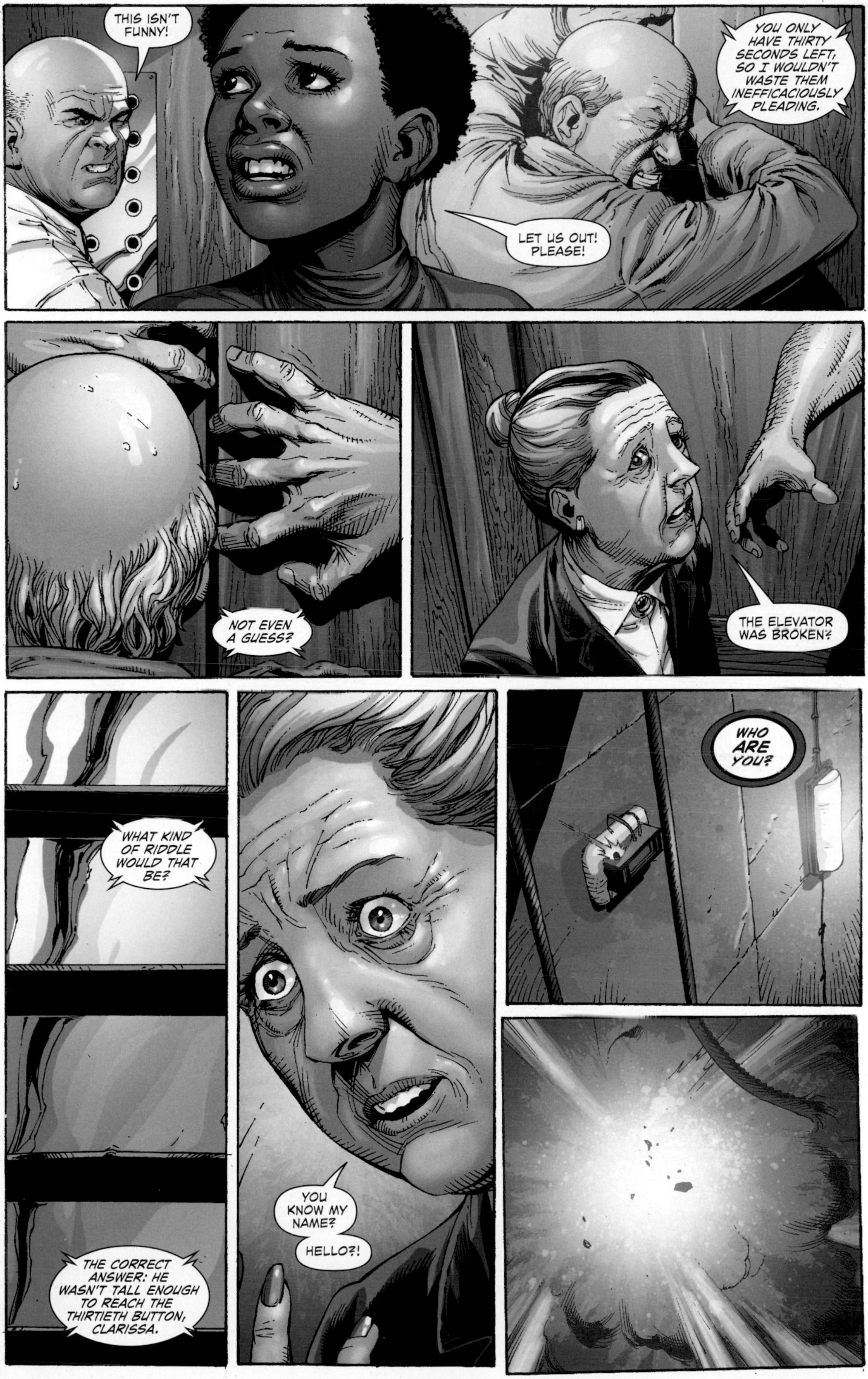
THIS ISN'T FUNNY!
YOU ONLY HAVE THIRTY SECONDS LEFT, SO I WOULDN'T WASTE THEM INEFFICACIOUSLY PLEADING.
LET US OUT! PLEASE!
NOT EVEN A GUESS?
THE ELEVATOR WAS BROKEN?!
WHAT KIND OF RIDDLE WOULD THAT BE?
THE CORRECT ANSWER: HE WASN'T TALL ENOUGH TO REACH THE THIRTIETH BUTTON, CLARISSA.
YOU KNOW MY NAME?
HELLO?!
WHO ARE YOU?

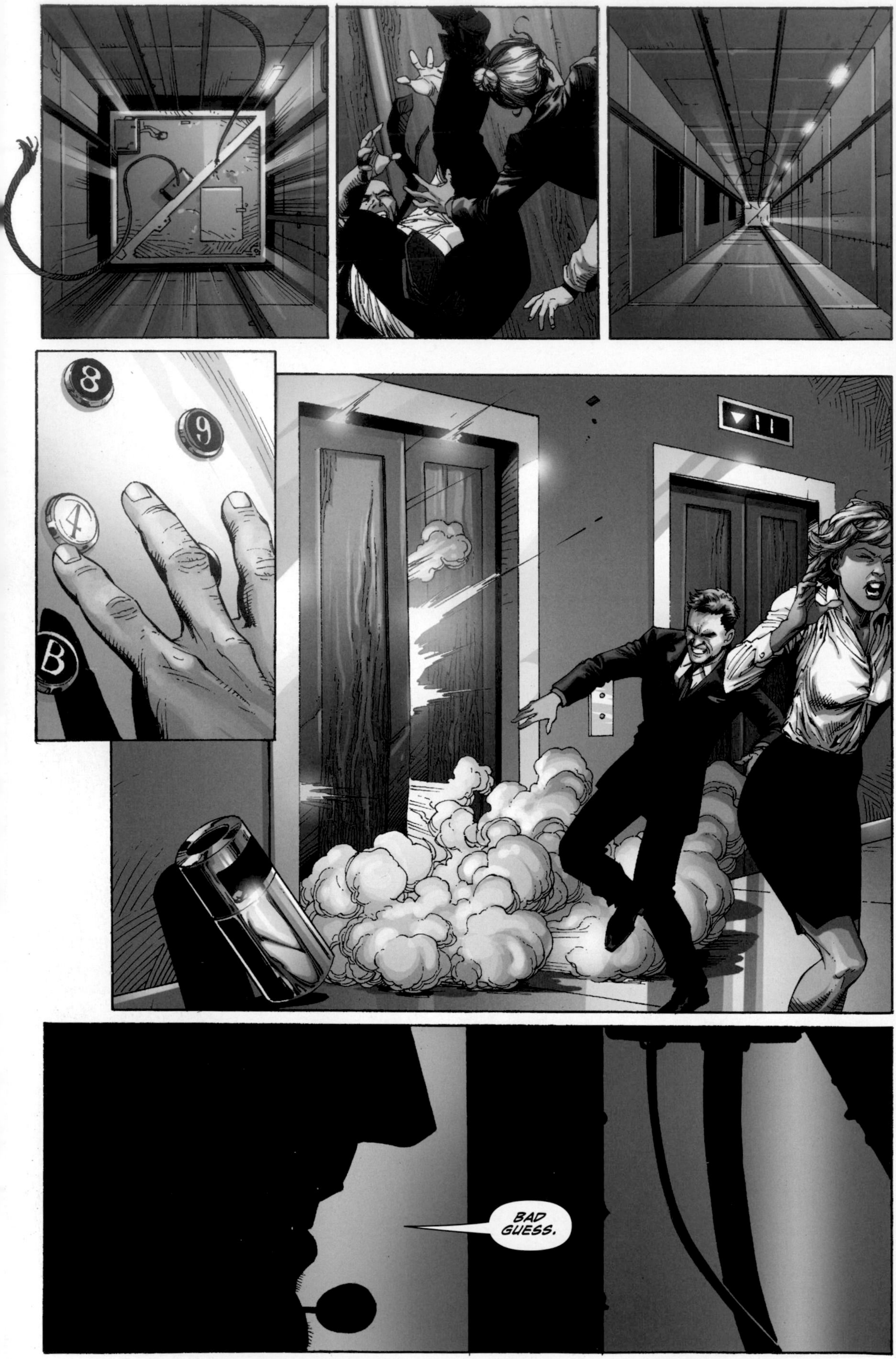
BAD GUESS.

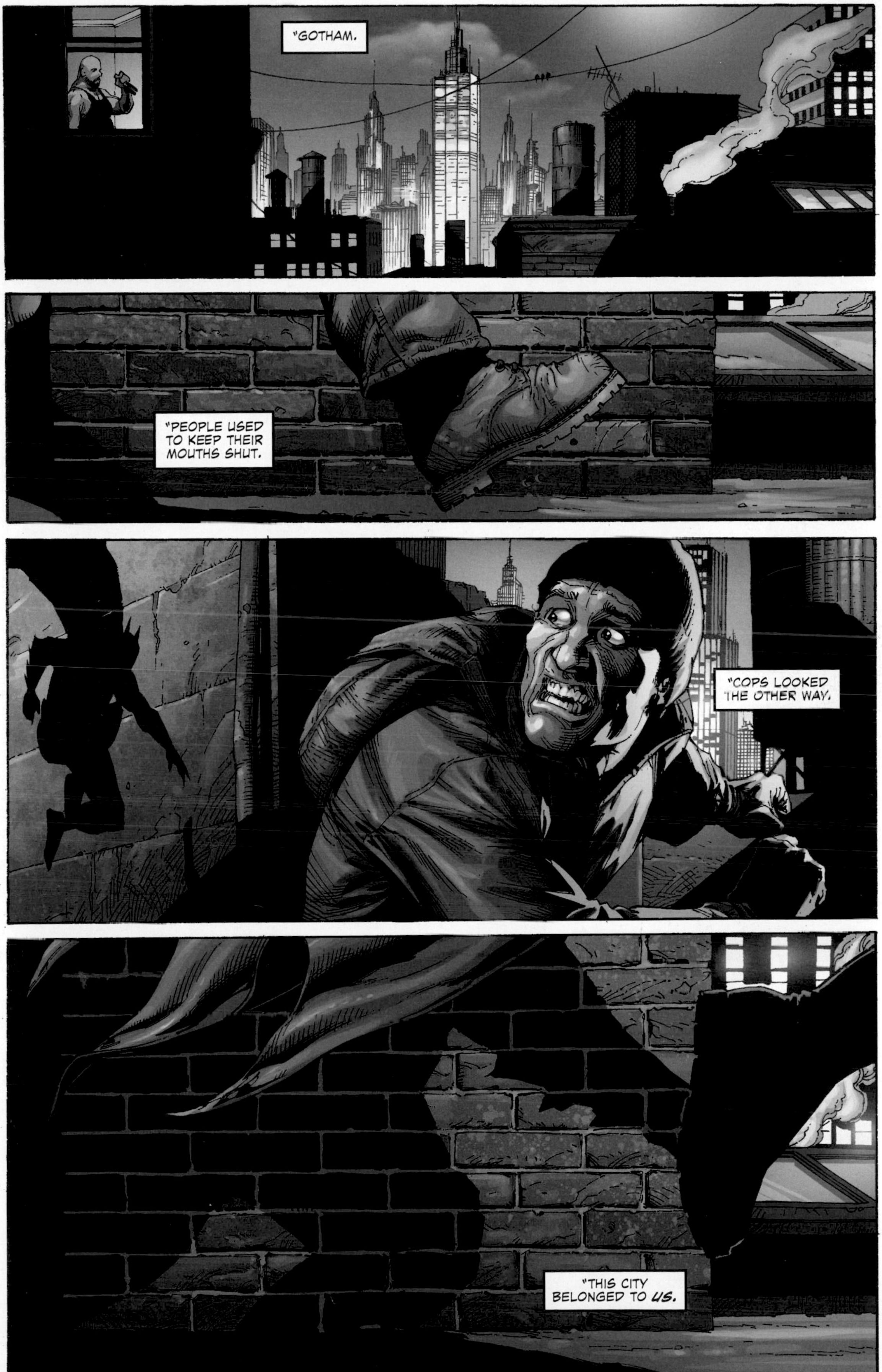
"GOTHAM.
"PEOPLE USED TO KEEP THEIR MOUTHS SHUT.
"COPS LOOKED THE OTHER WAY.
"THIS CITY BELONGED TO *US*.

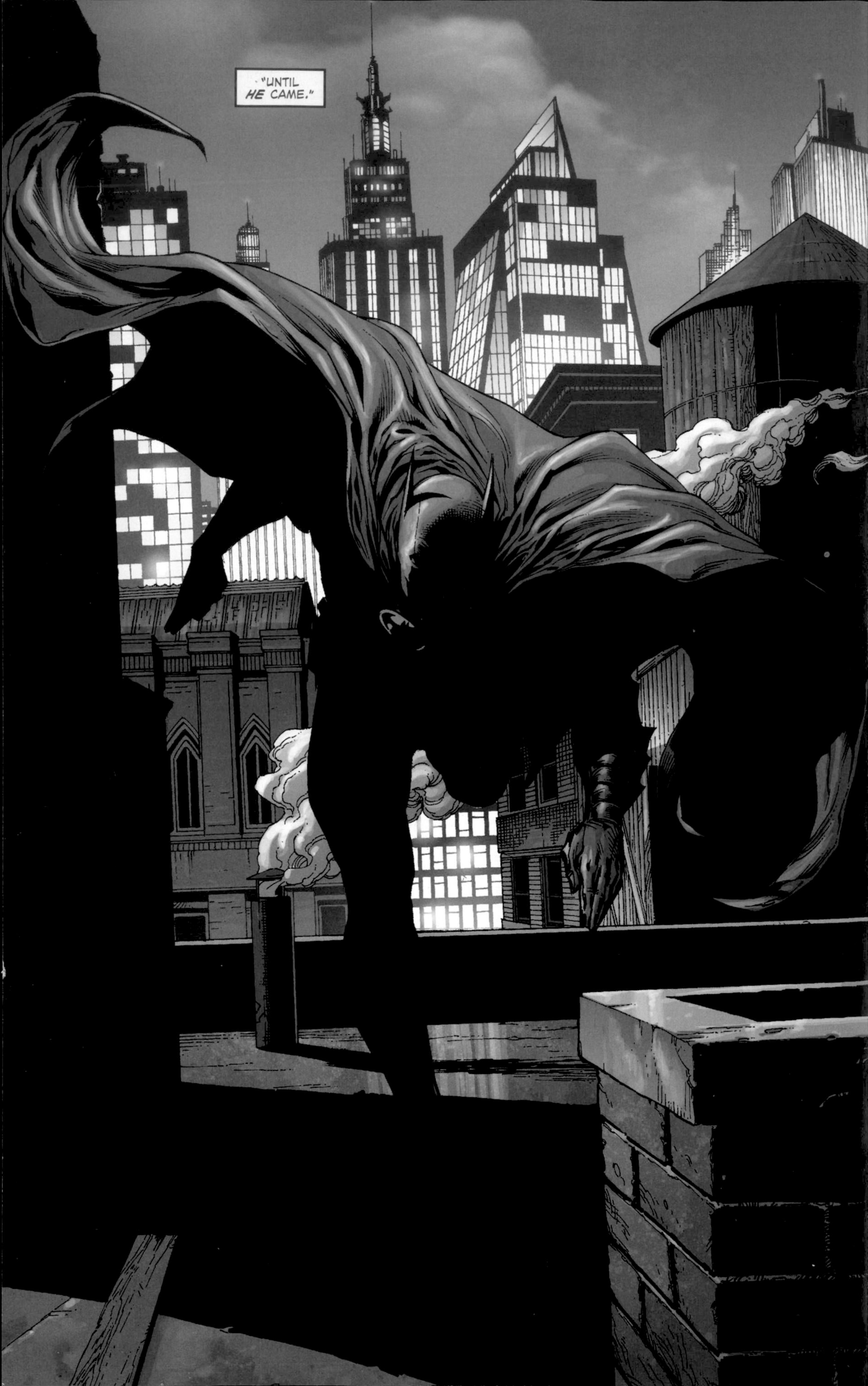
"UNTIL HE CAME."

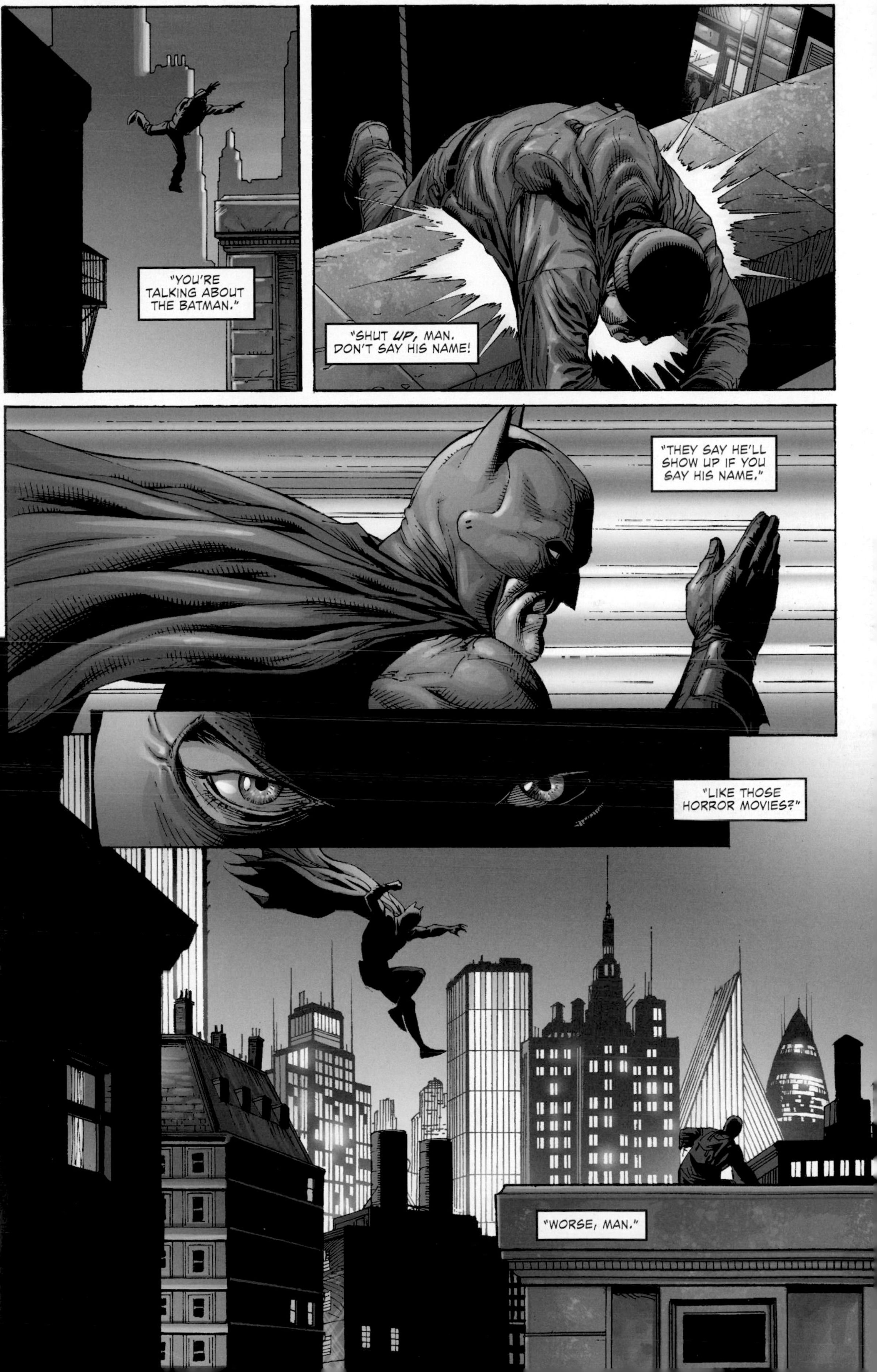
"YOU'RE TALKING ABOUT THE BATMAN."
"SHUT UP, MAN. DON'T SAY HIS NAME!
"THEY SAY HE'LL SHOW UP IF YOU SAY HIS NAME."
"LIKE THOSE HORROR MOVIES?"
"WORSE, MAN."

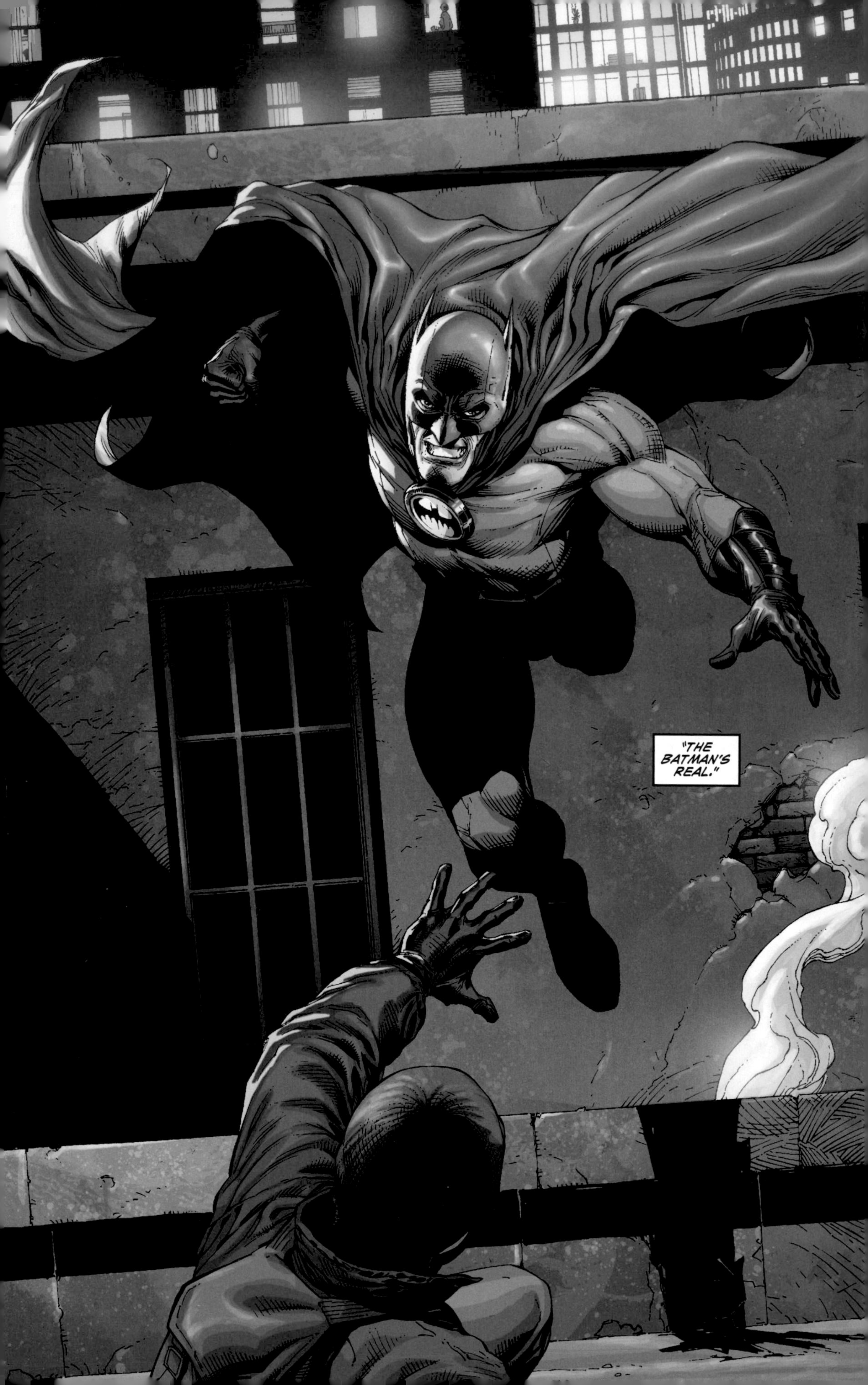
"THE BATMAN'S REAL."

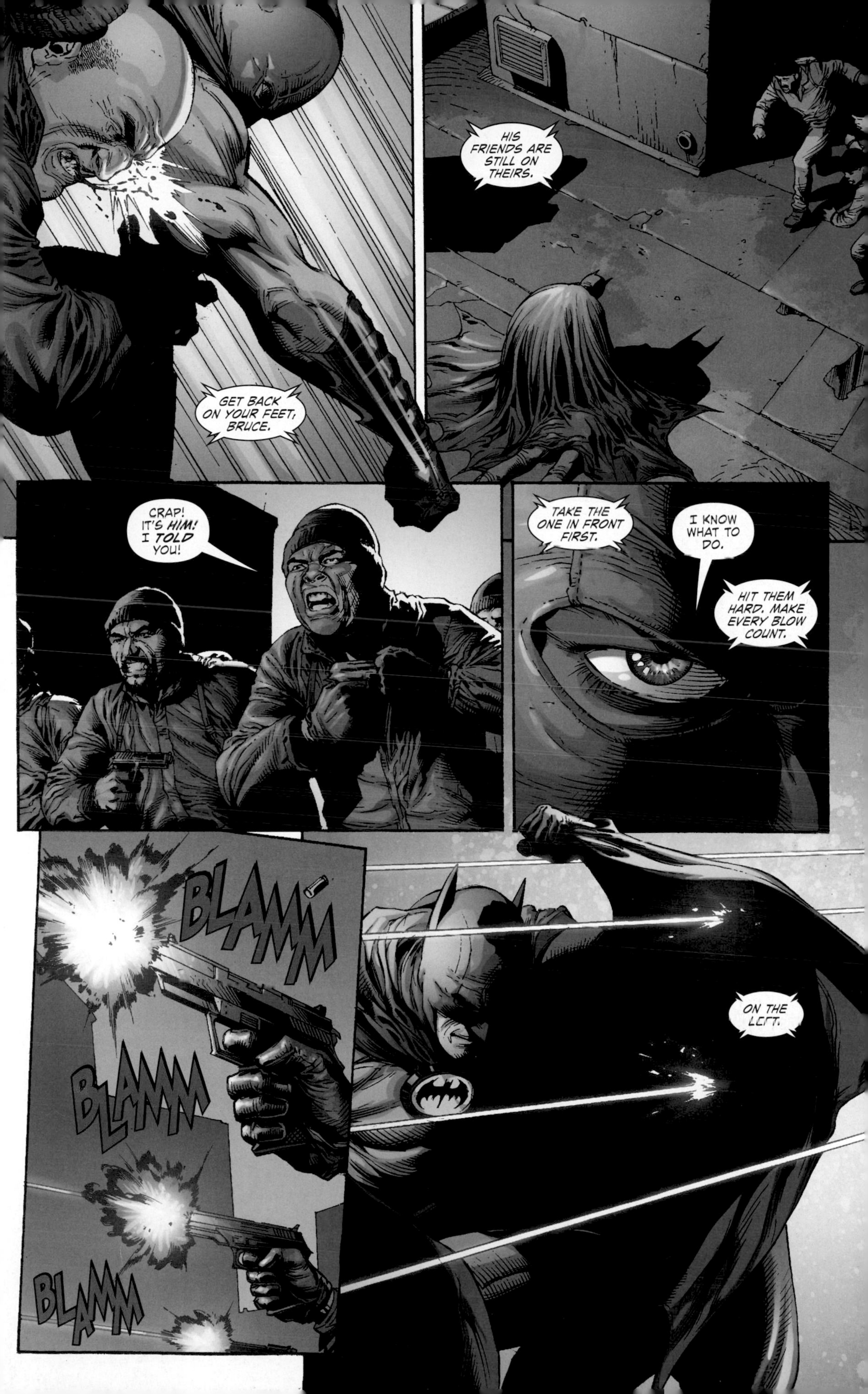
GET BACK ON YOUR FEET, BRUCE.
HIS FRIENDS ARE STILL ON THEIRS.
CRAP! IT'S *HIM!* I *TOLD* YOU!
TAKE THE ONE IN FRONT FIRST.
I KNOW WHAT TO DO.
HIT THEM HARD. MAKE EVERY BLOW COUNT.
BLAMM
BLAMM
BLAMM
ON THE LEFT.

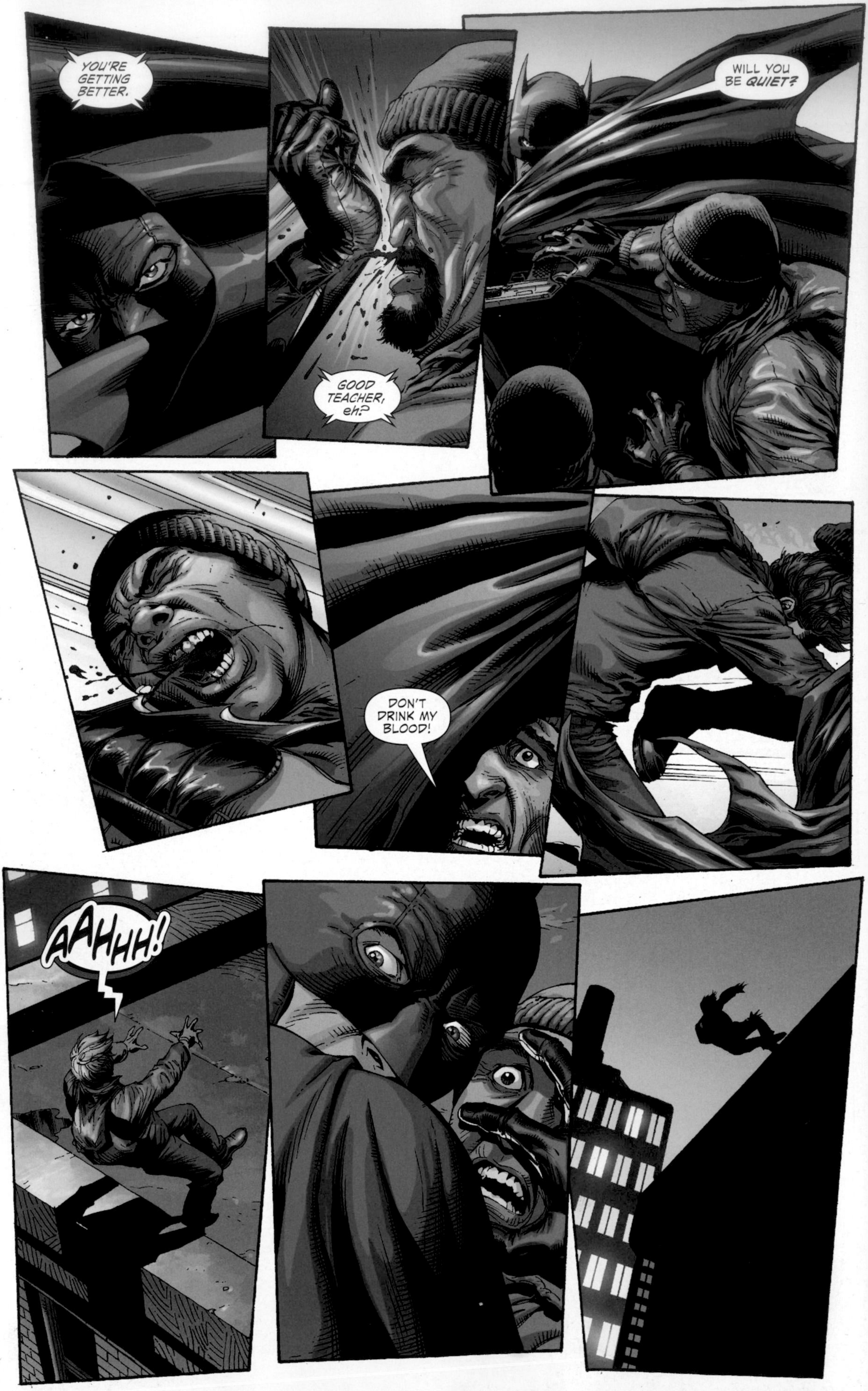
YOU'RE GETTING BETTER.
GOOD TEACHER, eh?
WILL YOU BE QUIET?
DON'T DRINK MY BLOOD!
AAHHH!

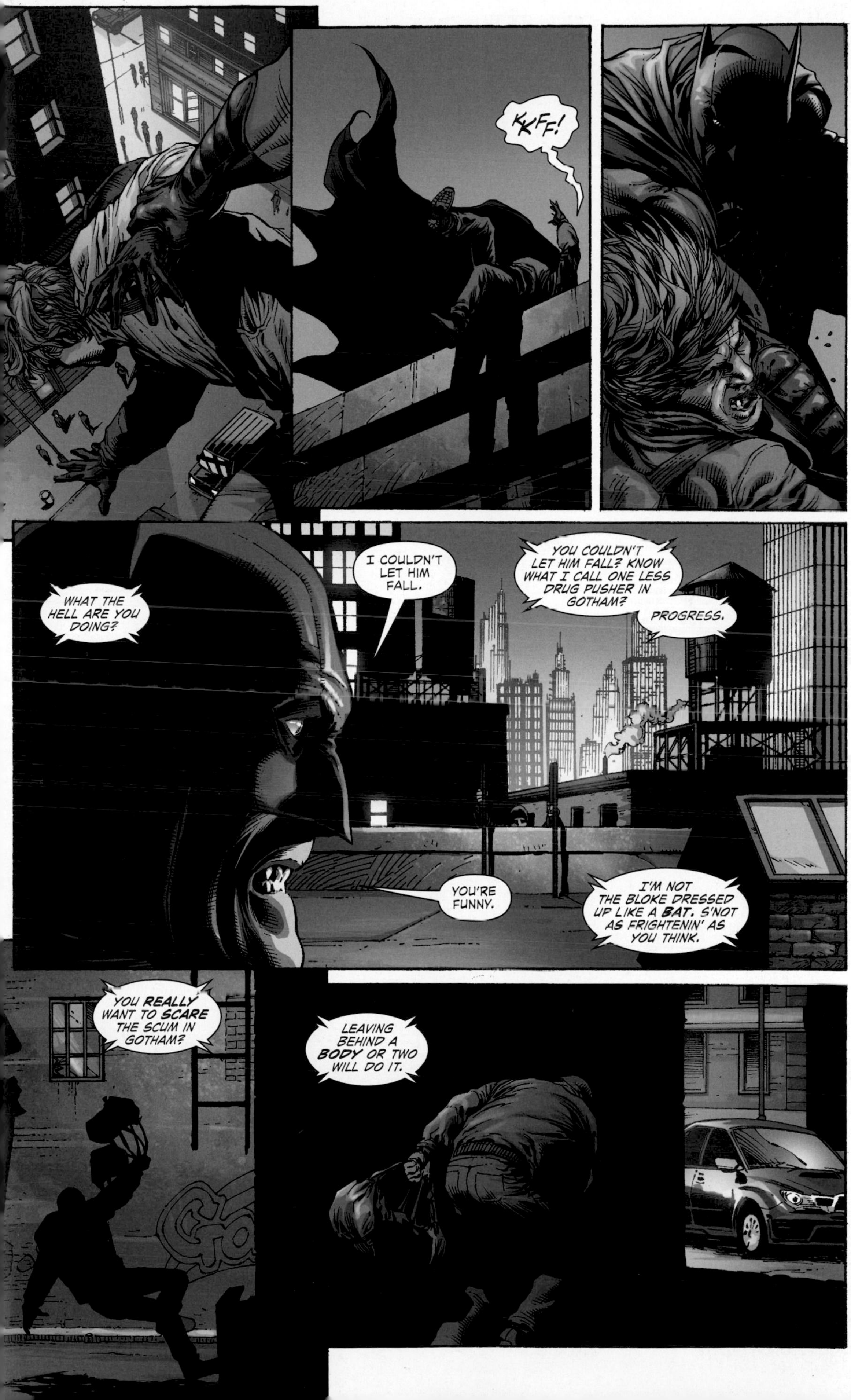
KKFF!
WHAT THE HELL ARE YOU DOING?
I COULDN'T LET HIM FALL.
YOU COULDN'T LET HIM FALL? KNOW WHAT I CALL ONE LESS DRUG PUSHER IN GOTHAM?
PROGRESS.
YOU'RE FUNNY.
I'M NOT THE BLOKE DRESSED UP LIKE A BAT. S'NOT AS FRIGHTENIN' AS YOU THINK.
YOU REALLY WANT TO SCARE THE SCUM IN GOTHAM?
LEAVING BEHIND A BODY OR TWO WILL DO IT.

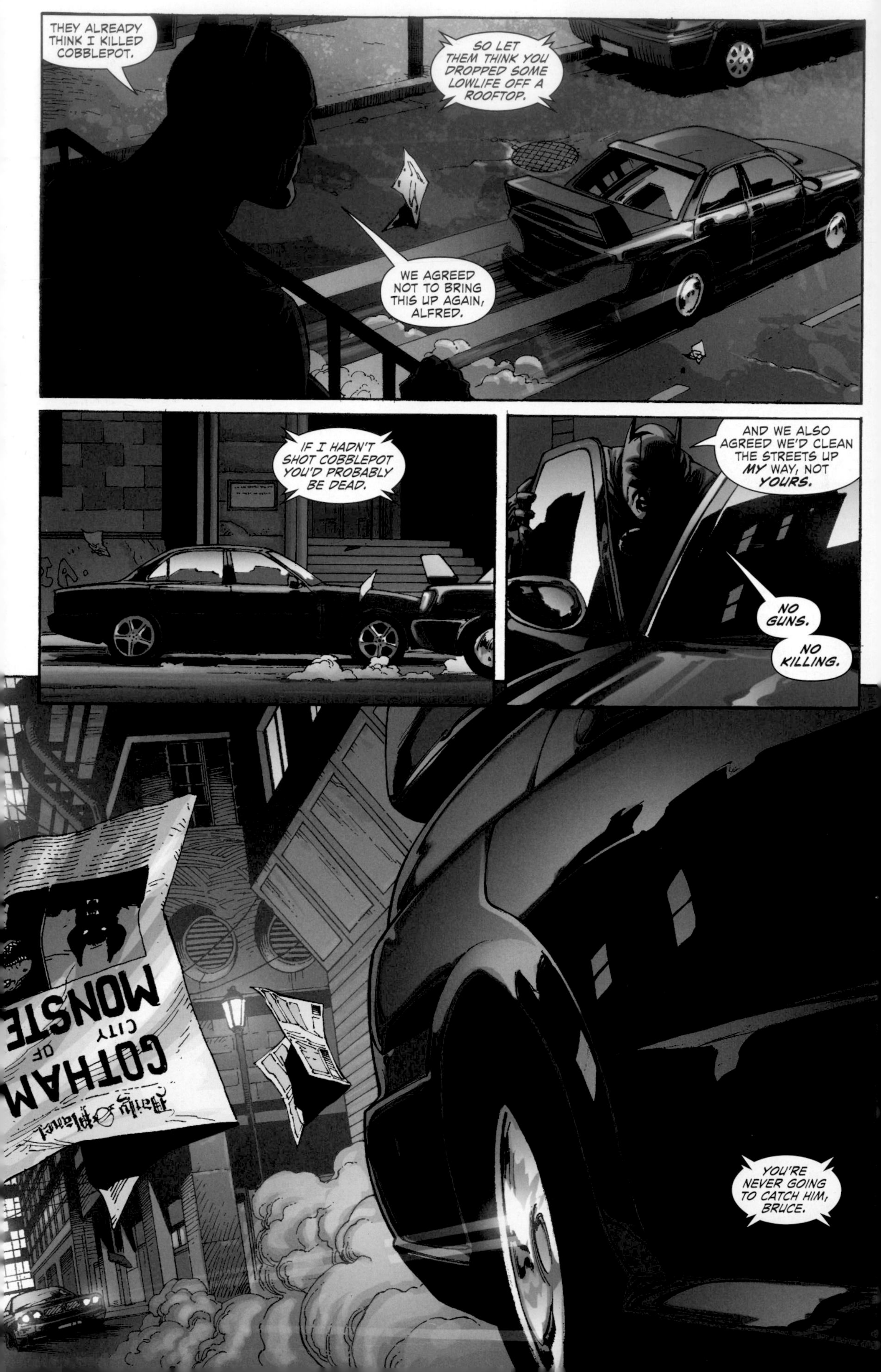
THEY ALREADY THINK I KILLED COBBLEPOT.
SO LET THEM THINK YOU DROPPED SOME LOWLIFE OFF A ROOFTOP.
WE AGREED NOT TO BRING THIS UP AGAIN, ALFRED.
IF I HADN'T SHOT COBBLEPOT YOU'D PROBABLY BE DEAD.
AND WE ALSO AGREED WE'D CLEAN THE STREETS UP MY WAY, NOT YOURS.
NO GUNS.
NO KILLING.
YOU'RE NEVER GOING TO CATCH HIM, BRUCE.

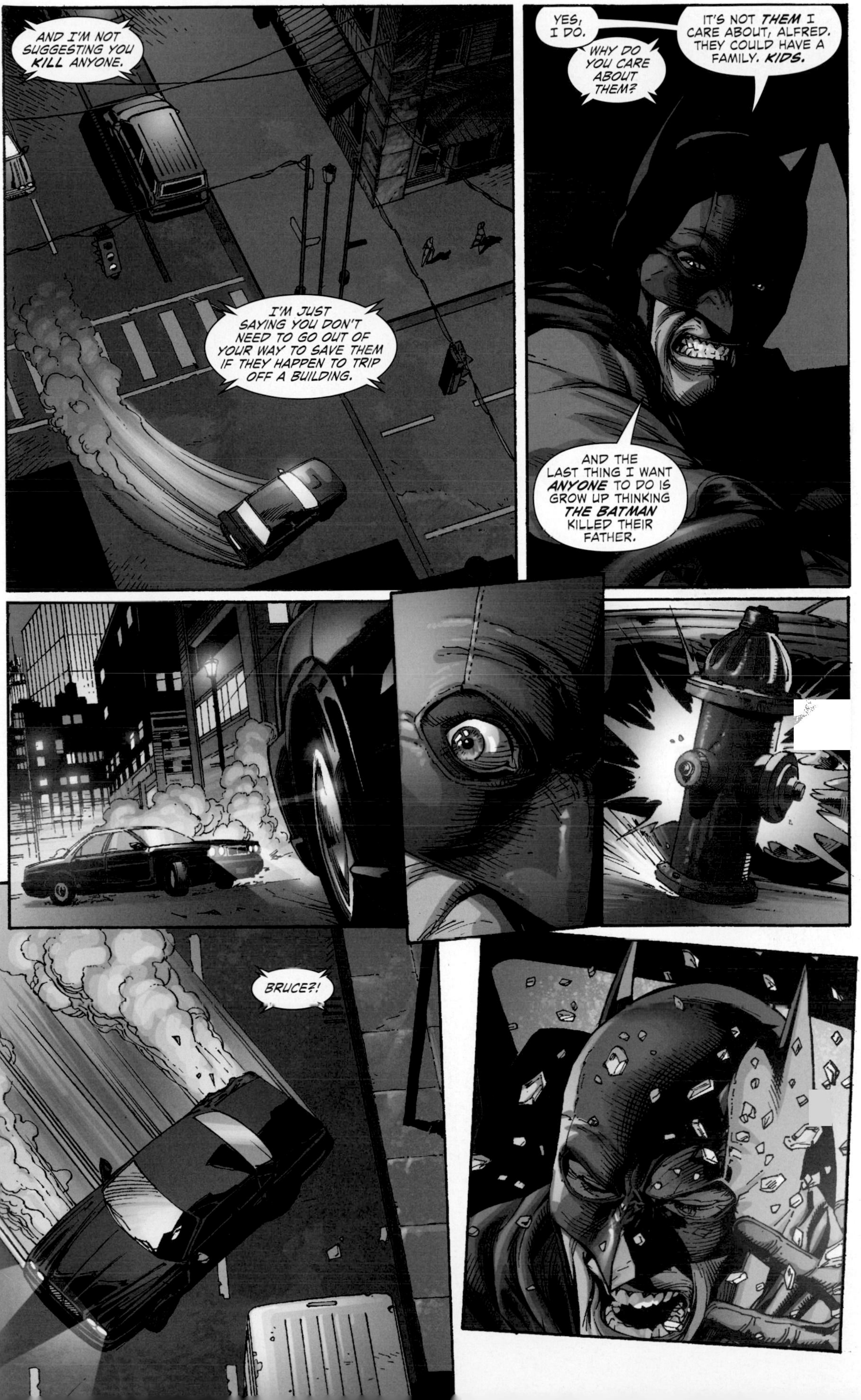
AND I'M NOT SUGGESTING YOU KILL ANYONE.
I'M JUST SAYING YOU DON'T NEED TO GO OUT OF YOUR WAY TO SAVE THEM IF THEY HAPPEN TO TRIP OFF A BUILDING.
YES, I DO.
WHY DO YOU CARE ABOUT THEM?
IT'S NOT THEM I CARE ABOUT, ALFRED. THEY COULD HAVE A FAMILY. KIDS.
AND THE LAST THING I WANT ANYONE TO DO IS GROW UP THINKING THE BATMAN KILLED THEIR FATHER.
BRUCE?!

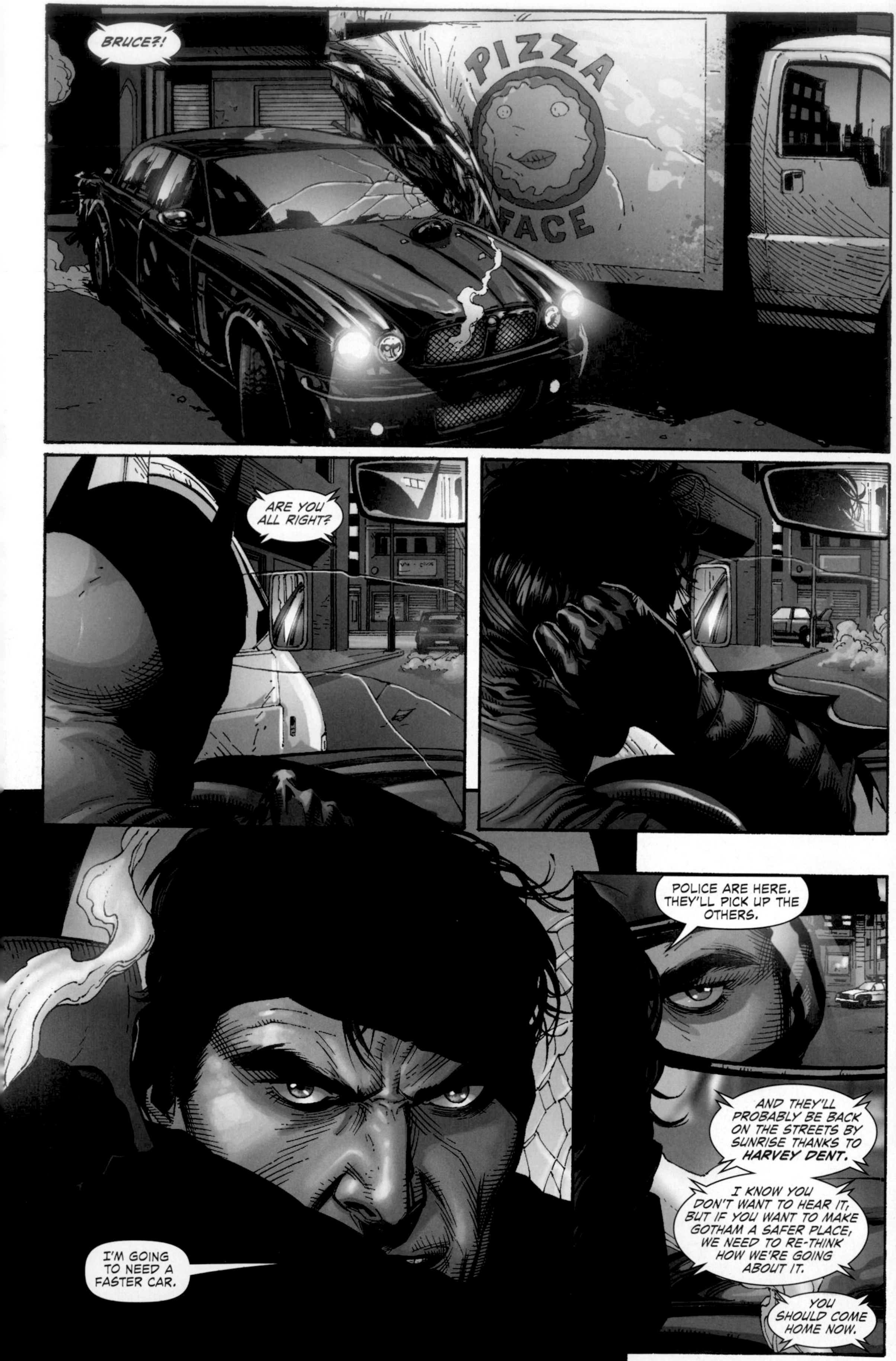
BRUCE?!
PIZZA FACE
ARE YOU ALL RIGHT?
POLICE ARE HERE. THEY'LL PICK UP THE OTHERS.
AND THEY'LL PROBABLY BE BACK ON THE STREETS BY SUNRISE THANKS TO HARVEY DENT.
I KNOW YOU DON'T WANT TO HEAR IT, BUT IF YOU WANT TO MAKE GOTHAM A SAFER PLACE, WE NEED TO RE-THINK HOW WE'RE GOING ABOUT IT.
YOU SHOULD COME HOME NOW.
I'M GOING TO NEED A FASTER CAR.

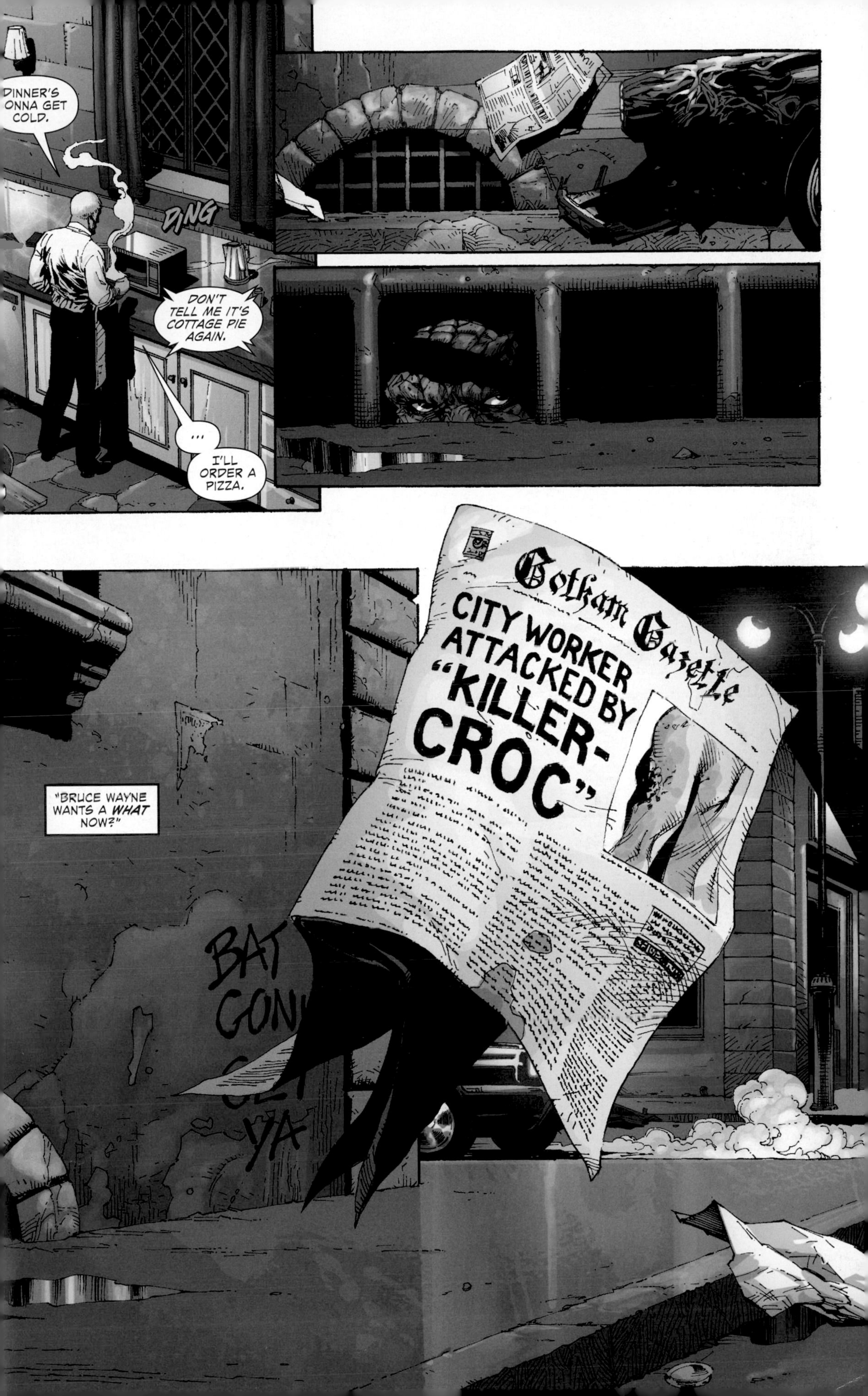
DINNER'S ONNA GET COLD.
DING
DON'T TELL ME IT'S COTTAGE PIE AGAIN.
...
I'LL ORDER A PIZZA.
Gotham Gazette
CITY WORKER ATTACKED BY "KILLER-CROC"
"BRUCE WAYNE WANTS A WHAT NOW?"
BAT
YA

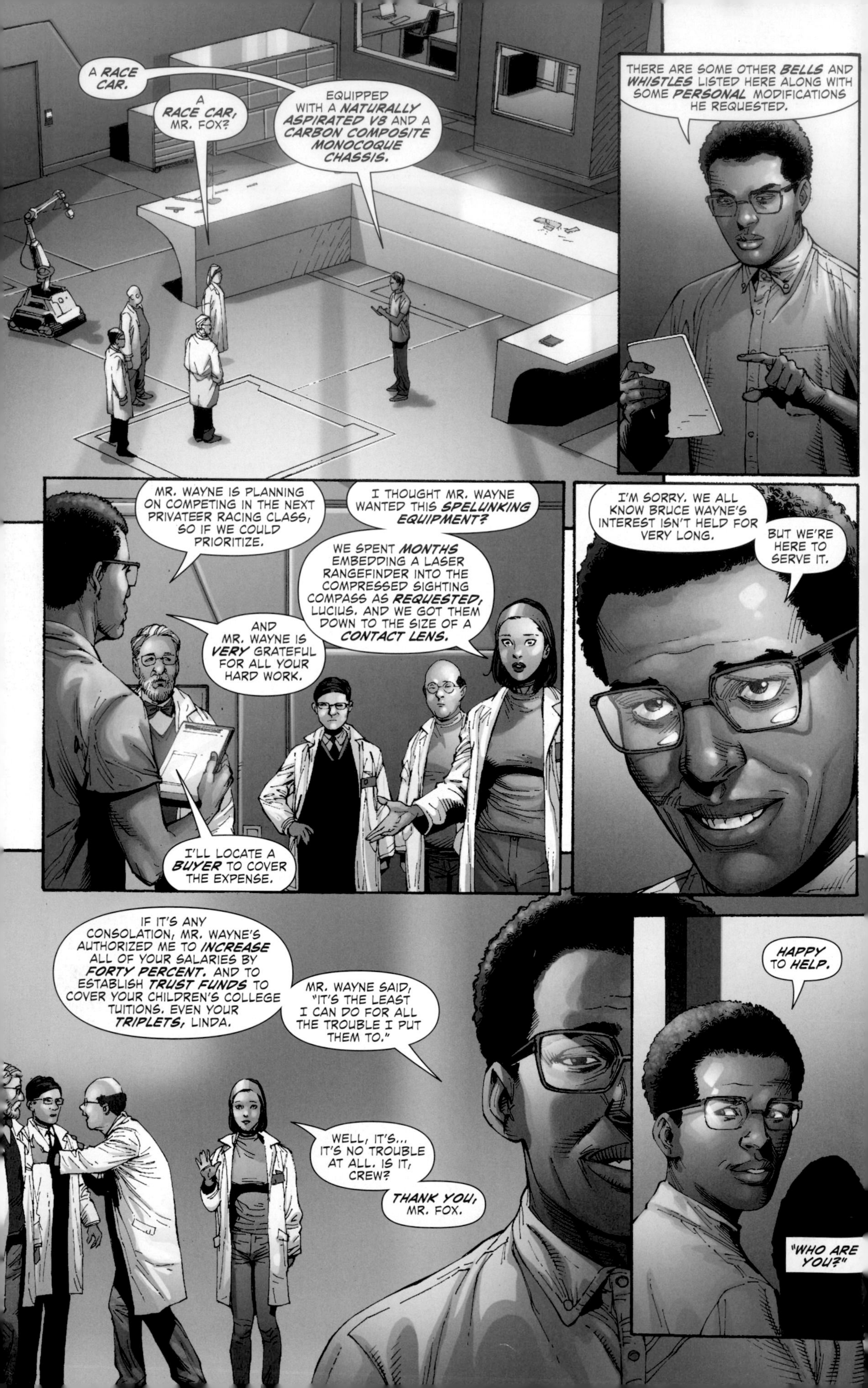
A RACE CAR.
A RACE CAR, MR. FOX?
EQUIPPED WITH A NATURALLY ASPIRATED V8 AND A CARBON COMPOSITE MONOCOQUE CHASSIS.
THERE ARE SOME OTHER BELLS AND WHISTLES LISTED HERE ALONG WITH SOME PERSONAL MODIFICATIONS HE REQUESTED.
MR. WAYNE IS PLANNING ON COMPETING IN THE NEXT PRIVATEER RACING CLASS, SO IF WE COULD PRIORITIZE.
I THOUGHT MR. WAYNE WANTED THIS SPELUNKING EQUIPMENT?
WE SPENT MONTHS EMBEDDING A LASER RANGEFINDER INTO THE COMPRESSED SIGHTING COMPASS AS REQUESTED, LUCIUS. AND WE GOT THEM DOWN TO THE SIZE OF A CONTACT LENS.
AND MR. WAYNE IS VERY GRATEFUL FOR ALL YOUR HARD WORK.
I'LL LOCATE A BUYER TO COVER THE EXPENSE.
I'M SORRY. WE ALL KNOW BRUCE WAYNE'S INTEREST ISN'T HELD FOR VERY LONG.
BUT WE'RE HERE TO SERVE IT.
IF IT'S ANY CONSOLATION, MR. WAYNE'S AUTHORIZED ME TO INCREASE ALL OF YOUR SALARIES BY FORTY PERCENT. AND TO ESTABLISH TRUST FUNDS TO COVER YOUR CHILDREN'S COLLEGE TUITIONS. EVEN YOUR TRIPLETS, LINDA.
MR. WAYNE SAID, "IT'S THE LEAST I CAN DO FOR ALL THE TROUBLE I PUT THEM TO."
WELL, IT'S... IT'S NO TROUBLE AT ALL. IS IT, CREW?
THANK YOU, MR. FOX.
HAPPY TO HELP.
"WHO ARE YOU?"

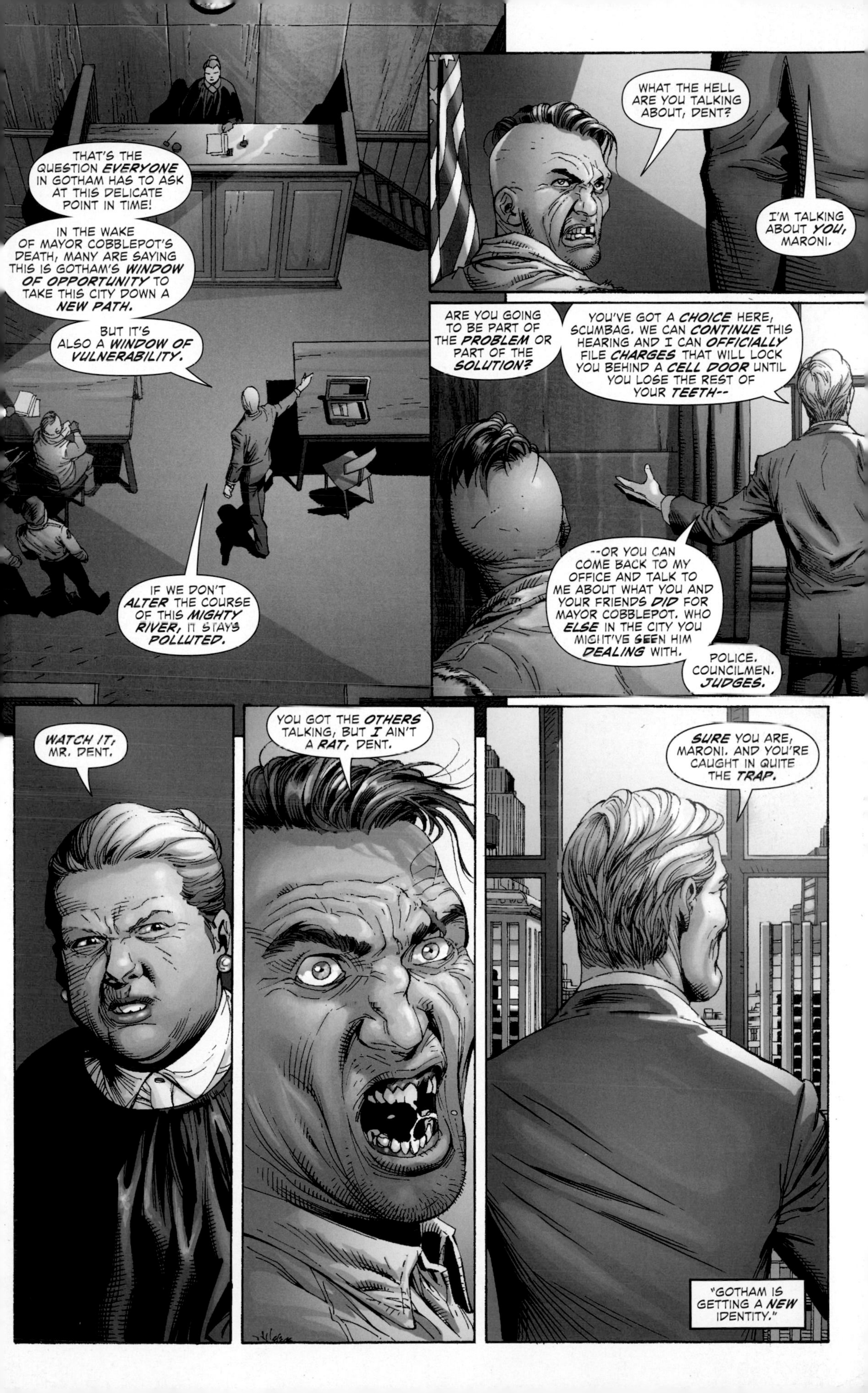
THAT'S THE QUESTION EVERYONE IN GOTHAM HAS TO ASK AT THIS DELICATE POINT IN TIME!
IN THE WAKE OF MAYOR COBBLEPOT'S DEATH, MANY ARE SAYING THIS IS GOTHAM'S WINDOW OF OPPORTUNITY TO TAKE THIS CITY DOWN A NEW PATH.
BUT IT'S ALSO A WINDOW OF VULNERABILITY.
IF WE DON'T ALTER THE COURSE OF THIS MIGHTY RIVER, IT STAYS POLLUTED.
WHAT THE HELL ARE YOU TALKING ABOUT, DENT?
I'M TALKING ABOUT YOU, MARONI.
ARE YOU GOING TO BE PART OF THE PROBLEM OR PART OF THE SOLUTION?
YOU'VE GOT A CHOICE HERE, SCUMBAG. WE CAN CONTINUE THIS HEARING AND I CAN OFFICIALLY FILE CHARGES THAT WILL LOCK YOU BEHIND A CELL DOOR UNTIL YOU LOSE THE REST OF YOUR TEETH--
--OR YOU CAN COME BACK TO MY OFFICE AND TALK TO ME ABOUT WHAT YOU AND YOUR FRIENDS DID FOR MAYOR COBBLEPOT. WHO ELSE IN THE CITY YOU MIGHT'VE SEEN HIM DEALING WITH.
POLICE. COUNCILMEN. JUDGES.
WATCH IT, MR. DENT.
YOU GOT THE OTHERS TALKING, BUT I AIN'T A RAT, DENT.
SURE YOU ARE, MARONI. AND YOU'RE CAUGHT IN QUITE THE TRAP.
"GOTHAM IS GETTING A NEW IDENTITY."

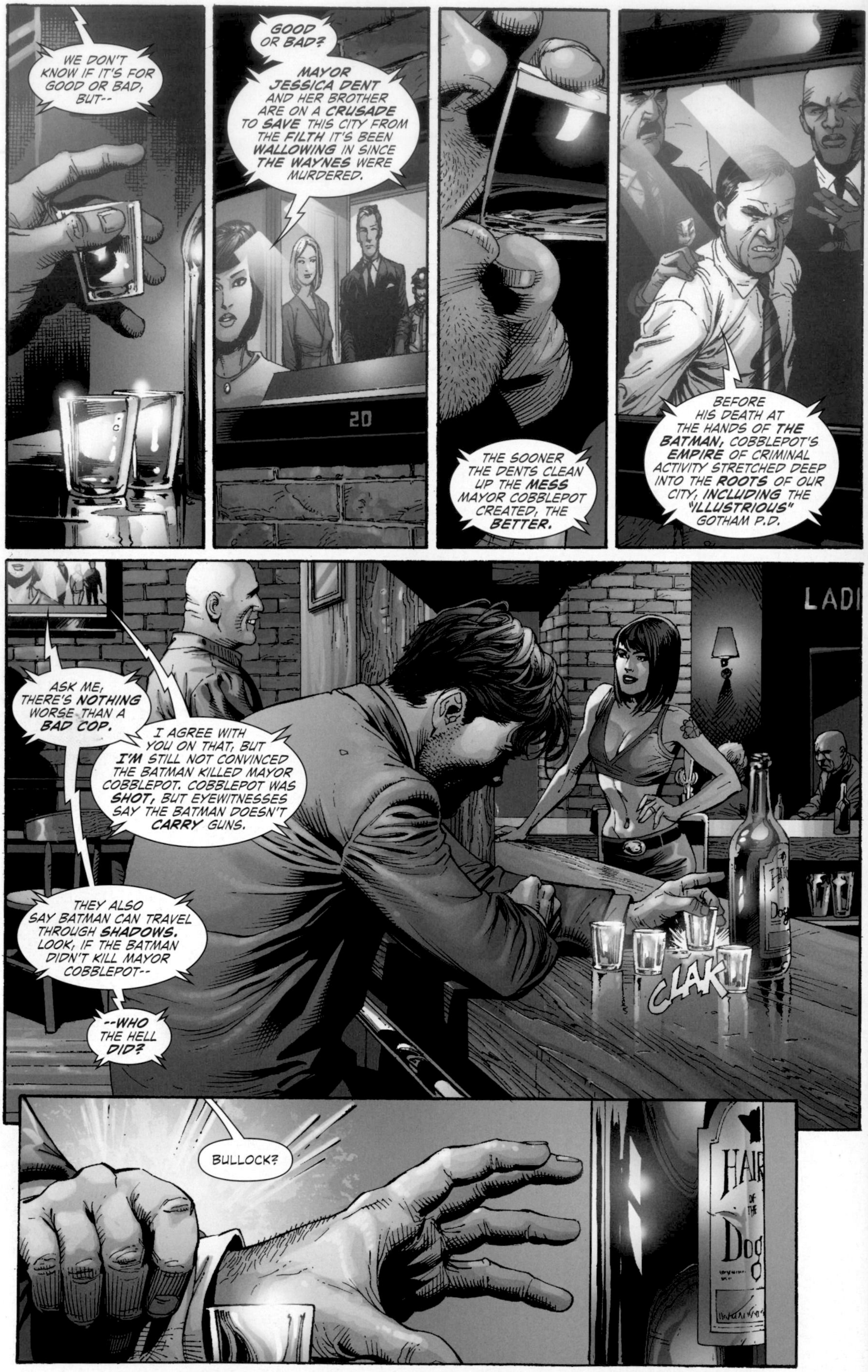

WE DON'T KNOW IF IT'S FOR GOOD OR BAD, BUT--
GOOD OR BAD?
MAYOR JESSICA DENT AND HER BROTHER ARE ON A CRUSADE TO SAVE THIS CITY FROM THE FILTH IT'S BEEN WALLOWING IN SINCE THE WAYNES WERE MURDERED.
20
THE SOONER THE DENTS CLEAN UP THE MESS MAYOR COBBLEPOT CREATED, THE BETTER.
BEFORE HIS DEATH AT THE HANDS OF THE BATMAN, COBBLEPOT'S EMPIRE OF CRIMINAL ACTIVITY STRETCHED DEEP INTO THE ROOTS OF OUR CITY, INCLUDING THE "ILLUSTRIOUS" GOTHAM P.D.
LADI
ASK ME, THERE'S NOTHING WORSE THAN A BAD COP.
I AGREE WITH YOU ON THAT, BUT I'M STILL NOT CONVINCED THE BATMAN KILLED MAYOR COBBLEPOT. COBBLEPOT WAS SHOT, BUT EYEWITNESSES SAY THE BATMAN DOESN'T CARRY GUNS.
THEY ALSO SAY BATMAN CAN TRAVEL THROUGH SHADOWS. LOOK, IF THE BATMAN DIDN'T KILL MAYOR COBBLEPOT--
--WHO THE HELL DID?
CLAK
BULLOCK?
HAIR OF THE DOG

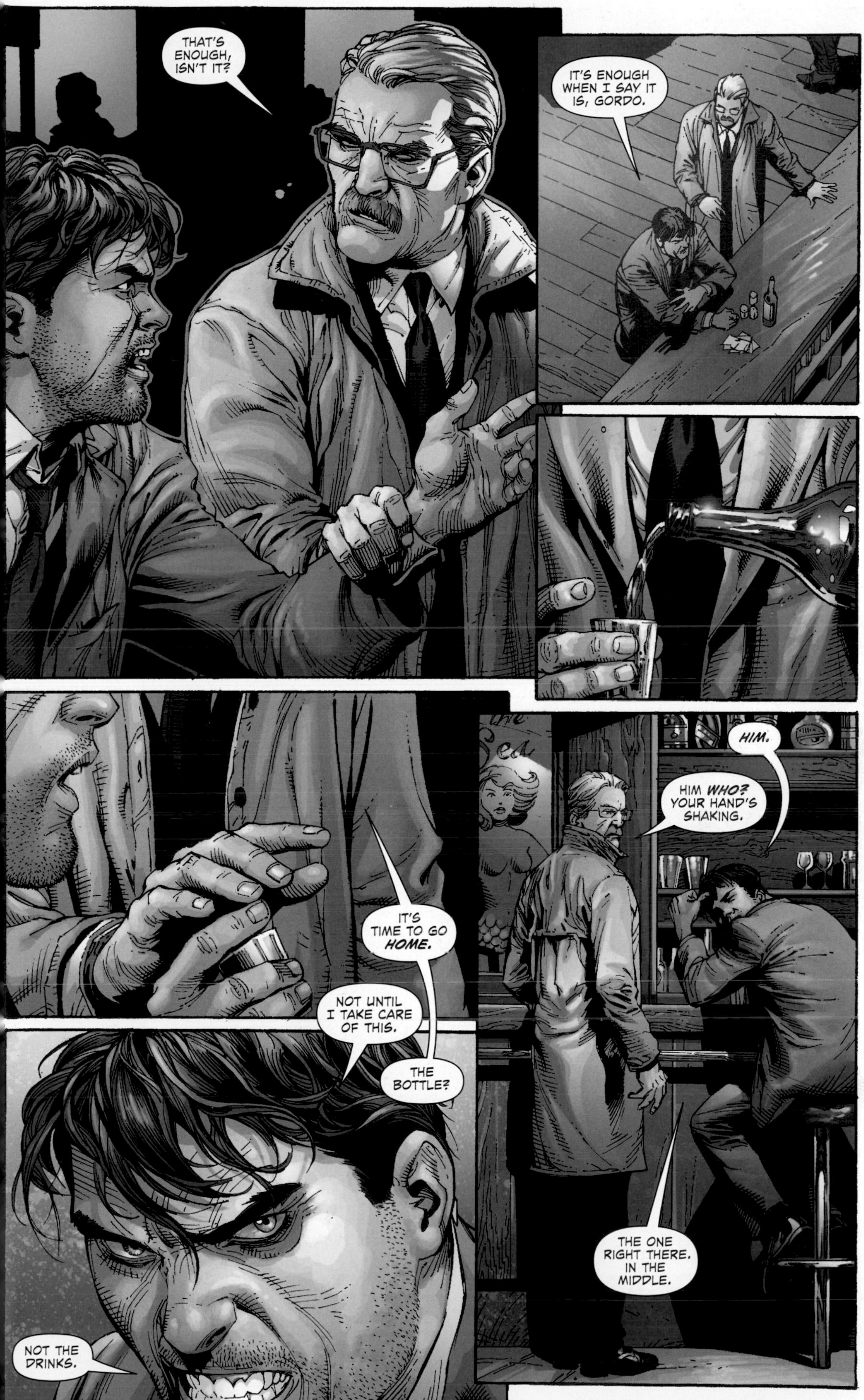
THAT'S ENOUGH, ISN'T IT?
IT'S ENOUGH WHEN I SAY IT IS, GORDO.
HIM.
HIM WHO? YOUR HAND'S SHAKING.
IT'S TIME TO GO HOME.
NOT UNTIL I TAKE CARE OF THIS.
THE BOTTLE?
NOT THE DRINKS.
THE ONE RIGHT THERE. IN THE MIDDLE.

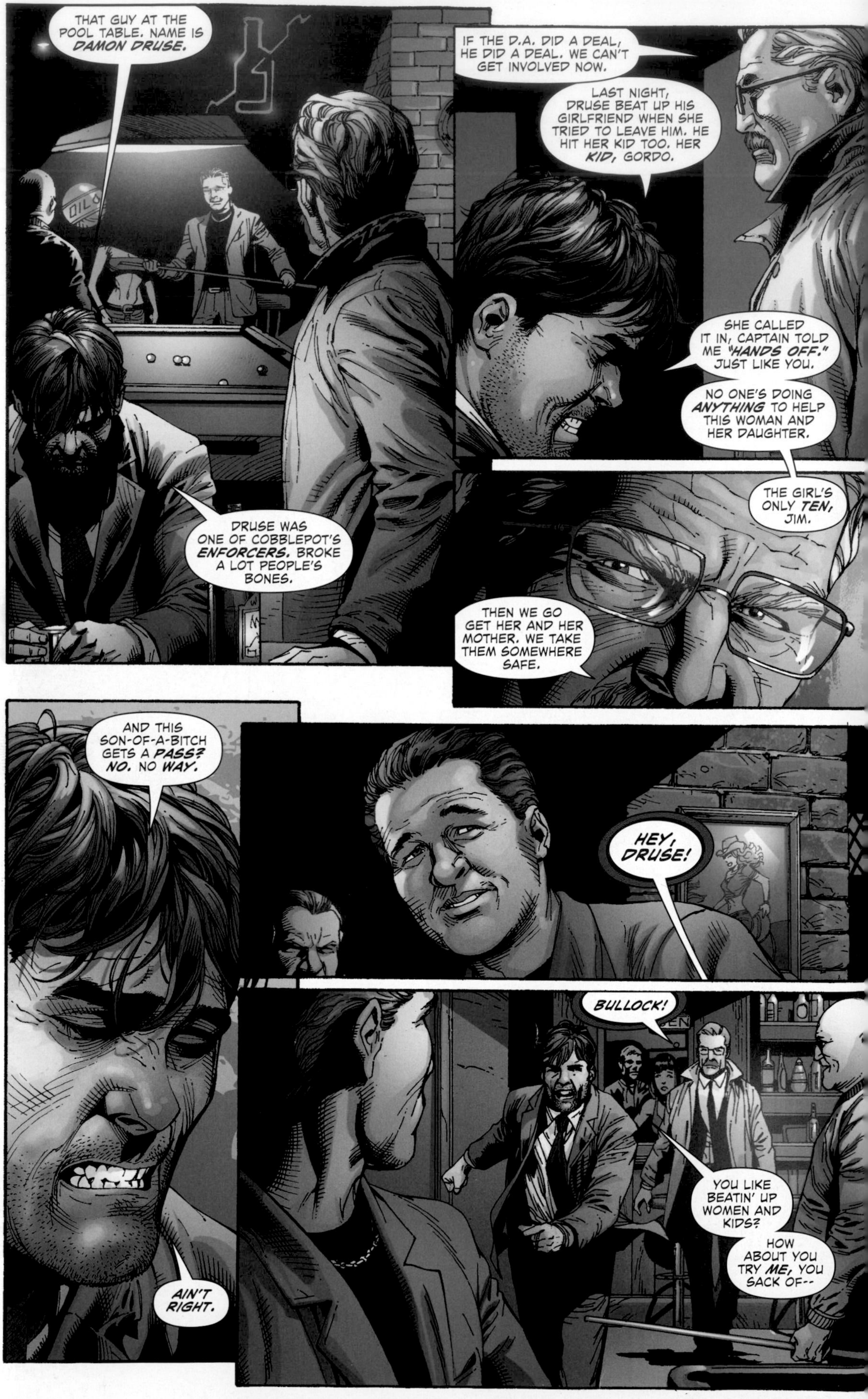
THAT GUY AT THE POOL TABLE. NAME IS DAMON DRUSE.
DRUSE WAS ONE OF COBBLEPOT'S ENFORCERS. BROKE A LOT PEOPLE'S BONES.
IF THE D.A. DID A DEAL, HE DID A DEAL. WE CAN'T GET INVOLVED NOW.
LAST NIGHT, DRUSE BEAT UP HIS GIRLFRIEND WHEN SHE TRIED TO LEAVE HIM. HE HIT HER KID TOO. HER KID, GORDO.
SHE CALLED IT IN, CAPTAIN TOLD ME "HANDS OFF." JUST LIKE YOU.
NO ONE'S DOING ANYTHING TO HELP THIS WOMAN AND HER DAUGHTER.
THE GIRL'S ONLY TEN, JIM.
THEN WE GO GET HER AND HER MOTHER. WE TAKE THEM SOMEWHERE SAFE.
AND THIS SON-OF-A-BITCH GETS A PASS? NO. NO WAY.
AIN'T RIGHT.
HEY, DRUSE!
BULLOCK!
YOU LIKE BEATIN' UP WOMEN AND KIDS?
HOW ABOUT YOU TRY ME, YOU SACK OF--

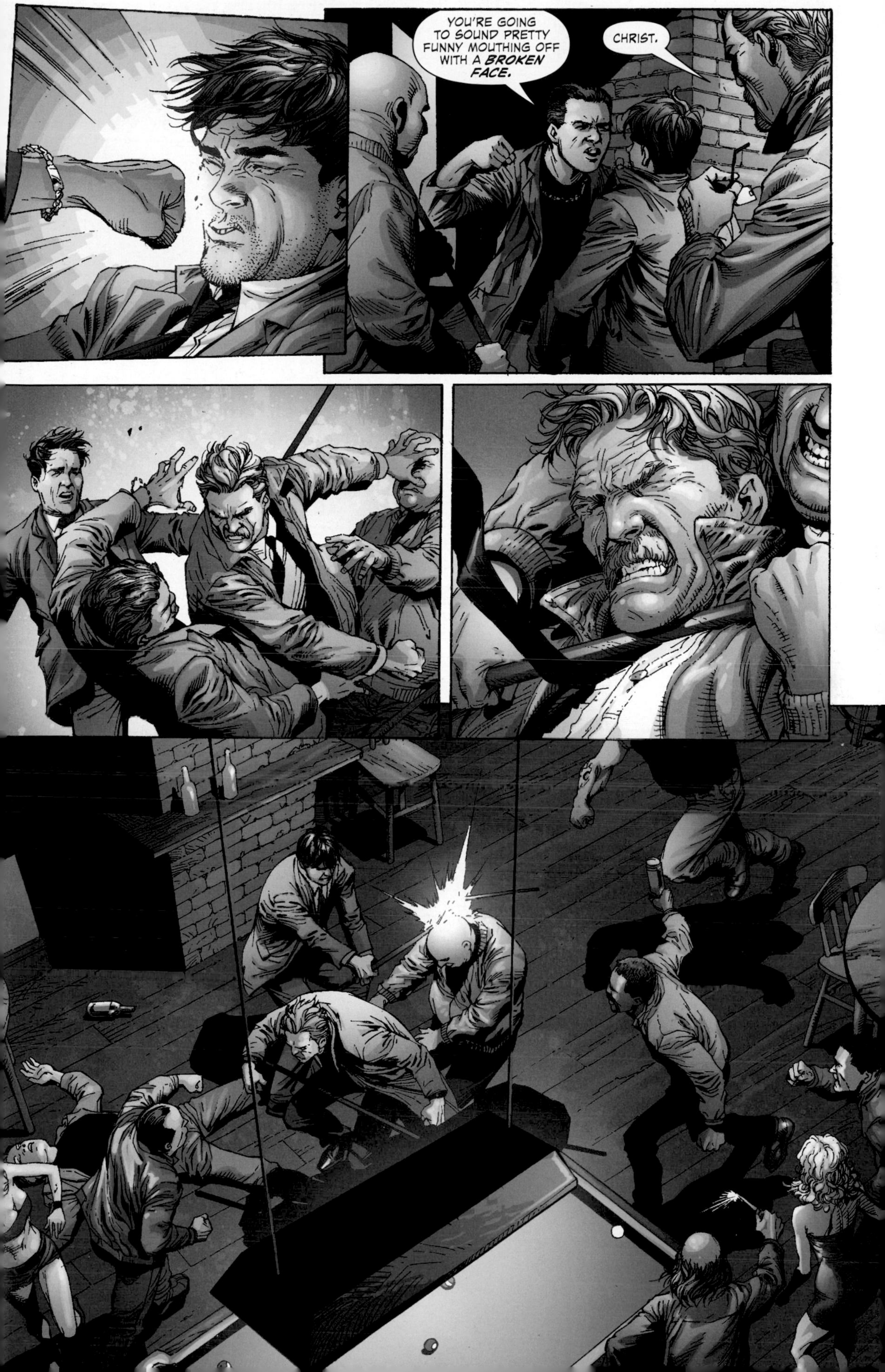
YOU'RE GOING TO SOUND PRETTY FUNNY MOUTHING OFF WITH A BROKEN FACE.
CHRIST.

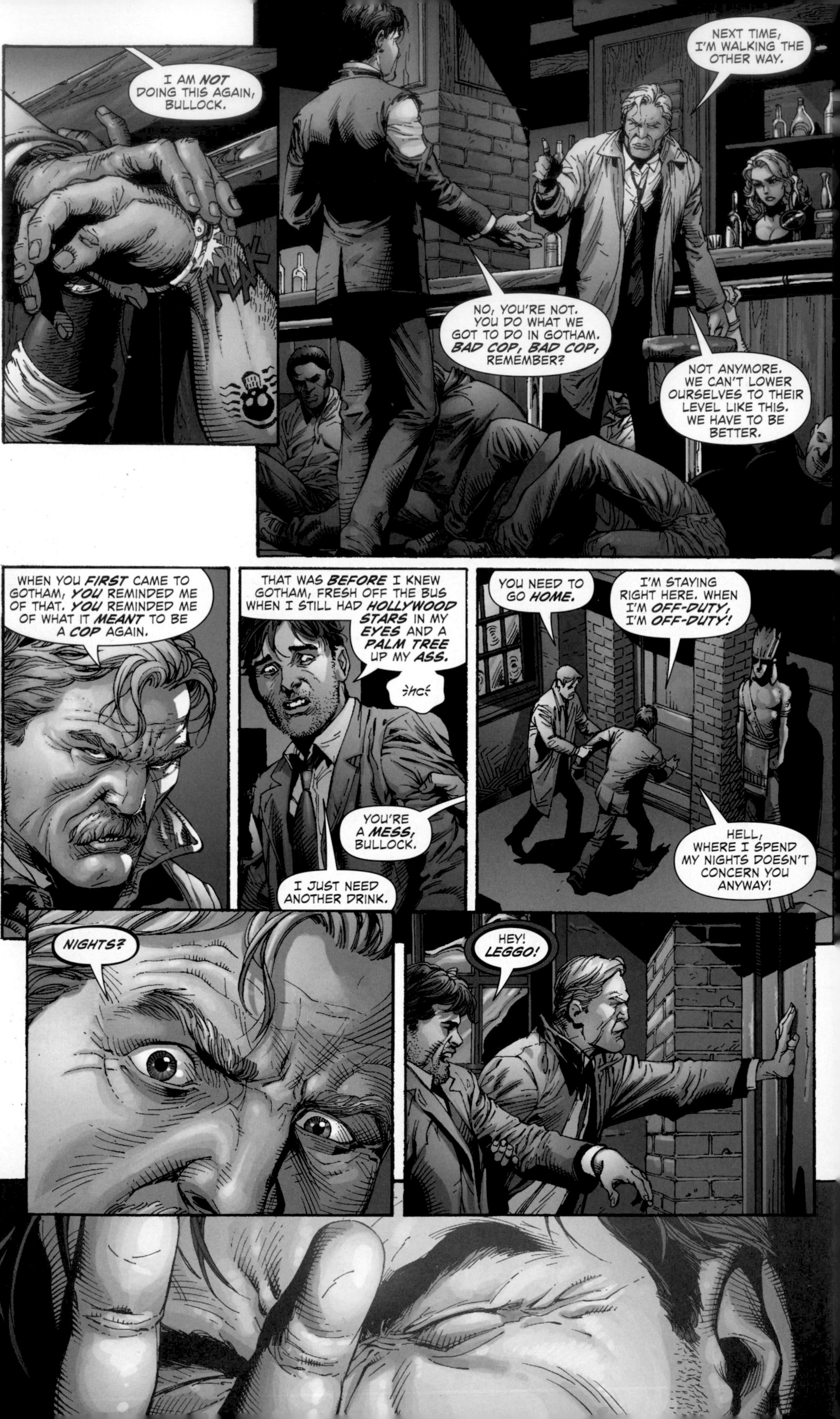
I AM NOT DOING THIS AGAIN, BULLOCK.
NEXT TIME, I'M WALKING THE OTHER WAY.
NO, YOU'RE NOT. YOU DO WHAT WE GOT TO DO IN GOTHAM. BAD COP, BAD COP, REMEMBER?
NOT ANYMORE. WE CAN'T LOWER OURSELVES TO THEIR LEVEL LIKE THIS. WE HAVE TO BE BETTER.
WHEN YOU FIRST CAME TO GOTHAM, YOU REMINDED ME OF THAT. YOU REMINDED ME OF WHAT IT MEANT TO BE A COP AGAIN.
THAT WAS BEFORE I KNEW GOTHAM, FRESH OFF THE BUS WHEN I STILL HAD HOLLYWOOD STARS IN MY EYES AND A PALM TREE UP MY ASS.
hc
YOU'RE A MESS, BULLOCK.
I JUST NEED ANOTHER DRINK.
YOU NEED TO GO HOME.
I'M STAYING RIGHT HERE. WHEN I'M OFF-DUTY, I'M OFF-DUTY!
HELL, WHERE I SPEND MY NIGHTS DOESN'T CONCERN YOU ANYWAY!
NIGHTS?
HEY! LEGGO!

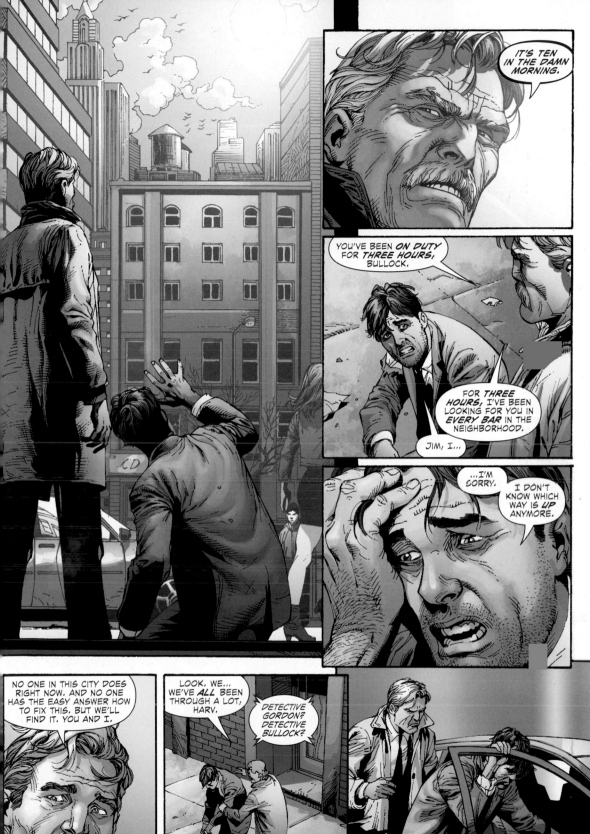

IT'S TEN IN THE DAMN MORNING.

YOU'VE BEEN *ON DUTY* FOR *THREE HOURS,* BULLOCK.

FOR *THREE HOURS,* I'VE BEEN LOOKING FOR YOU IN *EVERY BAR* IN THE NEIGHBORHOOD.

JIM, I...

...I'M SORRY. I DON'T KNOW WHICH WAY IS *UP* ANYMORE.

NO ONE IN THIS CITY DOES RIGHT NOW. AND NO ONE HAS THE EASY ANSWER HOW TO FIX THIS. BUT WE'LL FIND IT. YOU AND I.

LOOK. WE... WE'VE *ALL* BEEN THROUGH A LOT, HARV.

DETECTIVE GORDON? DETECTIVE BULLOCK?

CAPTAIN WANTS YOU TWO OVER AT THE GOTHAM TOWERS.

WE GOT BODIES.

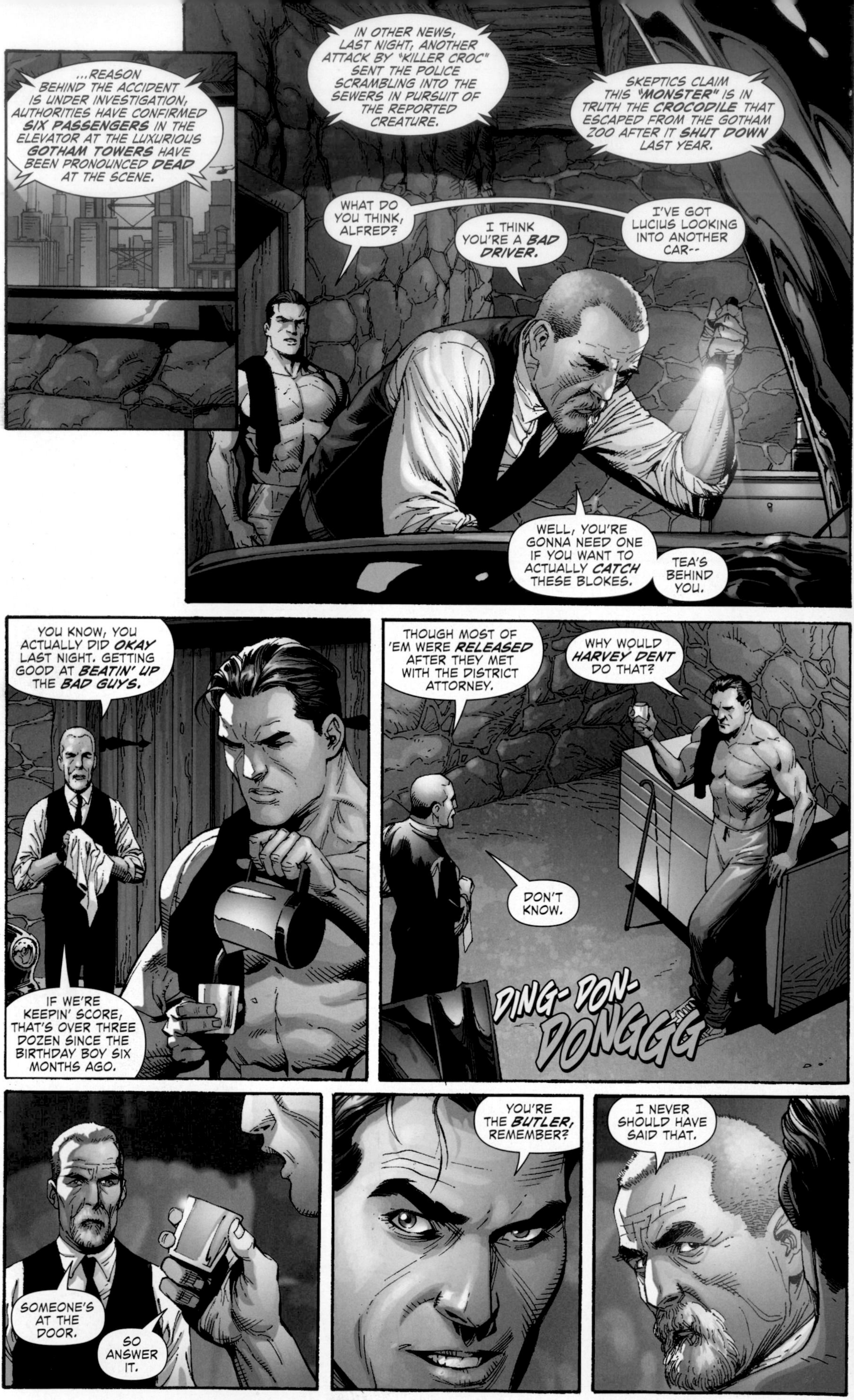
...REASON BEHIND THE ACCIDENT IS UNDER INVESTIGATION, AUTHORITIES HAVE CONFIRMED SIX PASSENGERS IN THE ELEVATOR AT THE LUXURIOUS GOTHAM TOWERS HAVE BEEN PRONOUNCED DEAD AT THE SCENE.
IN OTHER NEWS, LAST NIGHT, ANOTHER ATTACK BY "KILLER CROC" SENT THE POLICE SCRAMBLING INTO THE SEWERS IN PURSUIT OF THE REPORTED CREATURE.
SKEPTICS CLAIM THIS "MONSTER" IS IN TRUTH THE CROCODILE THAT ESCAPED FROM THE GOTHAM ZOO AFTER IT SHUT DOWN LAST YEAR.
WHAT DO YOU THINK, ALFRED?
I THINK YOU'RE A BAD DRIVER.
I'VE GOT LUCIUS LOOKING INTO ANOTHER CAR--
WELL, YOU'RE GONNA NEED ONE IF YOU WANT TO ACTUALLY CATCH THESE BLOKES.
TEA'S BEHIND YOU.
YOU KNOW, YOU ACTUALLY DID OKAY LAST NIGHT. GETTING GOOD AT BEATIN' UP THE BAD GUYS.
IF WE'RE KEEPIN' SCORE, THAT'S OVER THREE DOZEN SINCE THE BIRTHDAY BOY SIX MONTHS AGO.
THOUGH MOST OF 'EM WERE RELEASED AFTER THEY MET WITH THE DISTRICT ATTORNEY.
WHY WOULD HARVEY DENT DO THAT?
DON'T KNOW.
DING-DON-DONGGG
SOMEONE'S AT THE DOOR.
SO ANSWER IT.
YOU'RE THE BUTLER, REMEMBER?
I NEVER SHOULD HAVE SAID THAT.

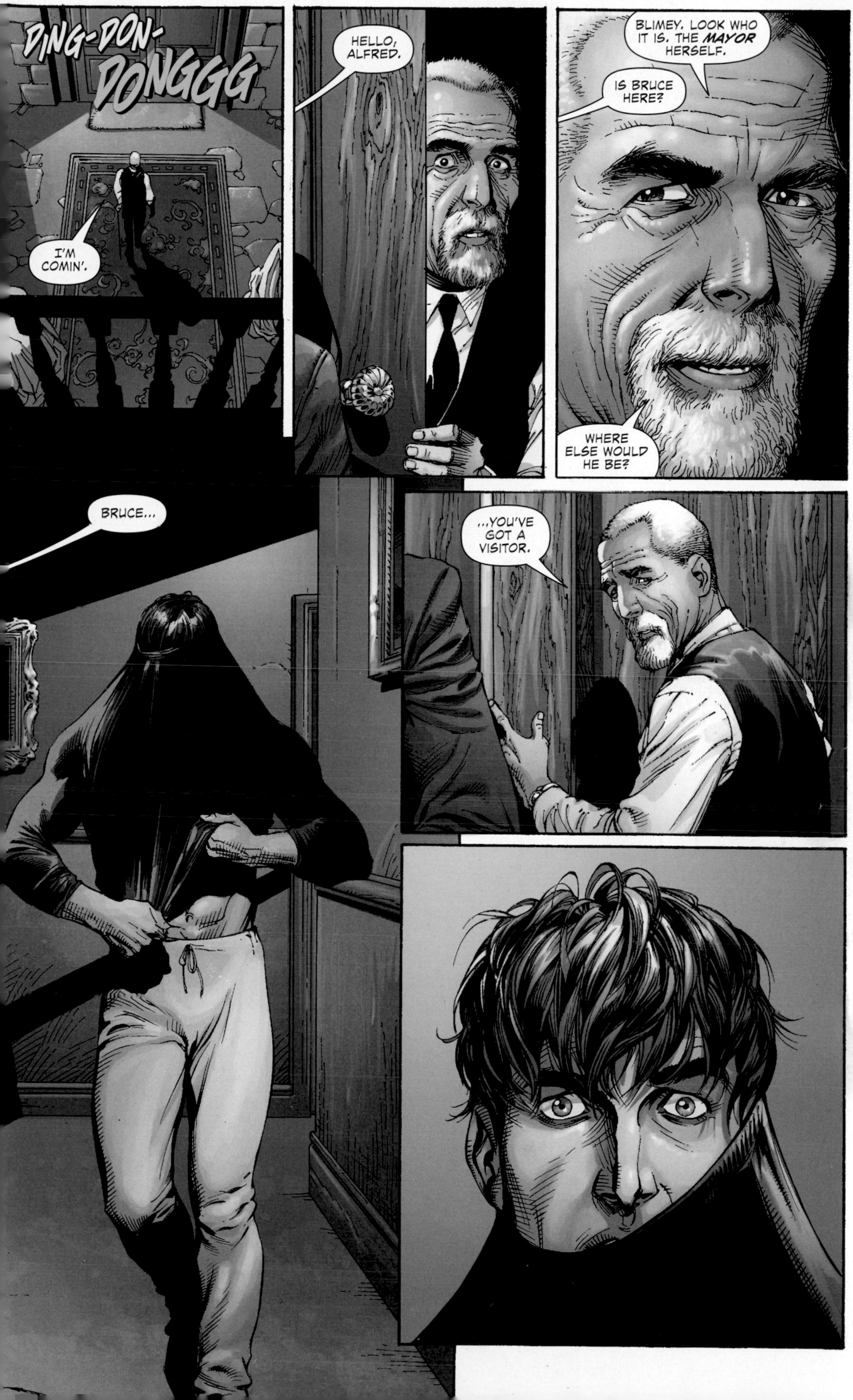
DING-DON-DONGGG
I'M COMIN'.
HELLO, ALFRED.
BLIMEY. LOOK WHO IT IS. THE MAYOR HERSELF.
IS BRUCE HERE?
WHERE ELSE WOULD HE BE?
BRUCE...
...YOU'VE GOT A VISITOR.

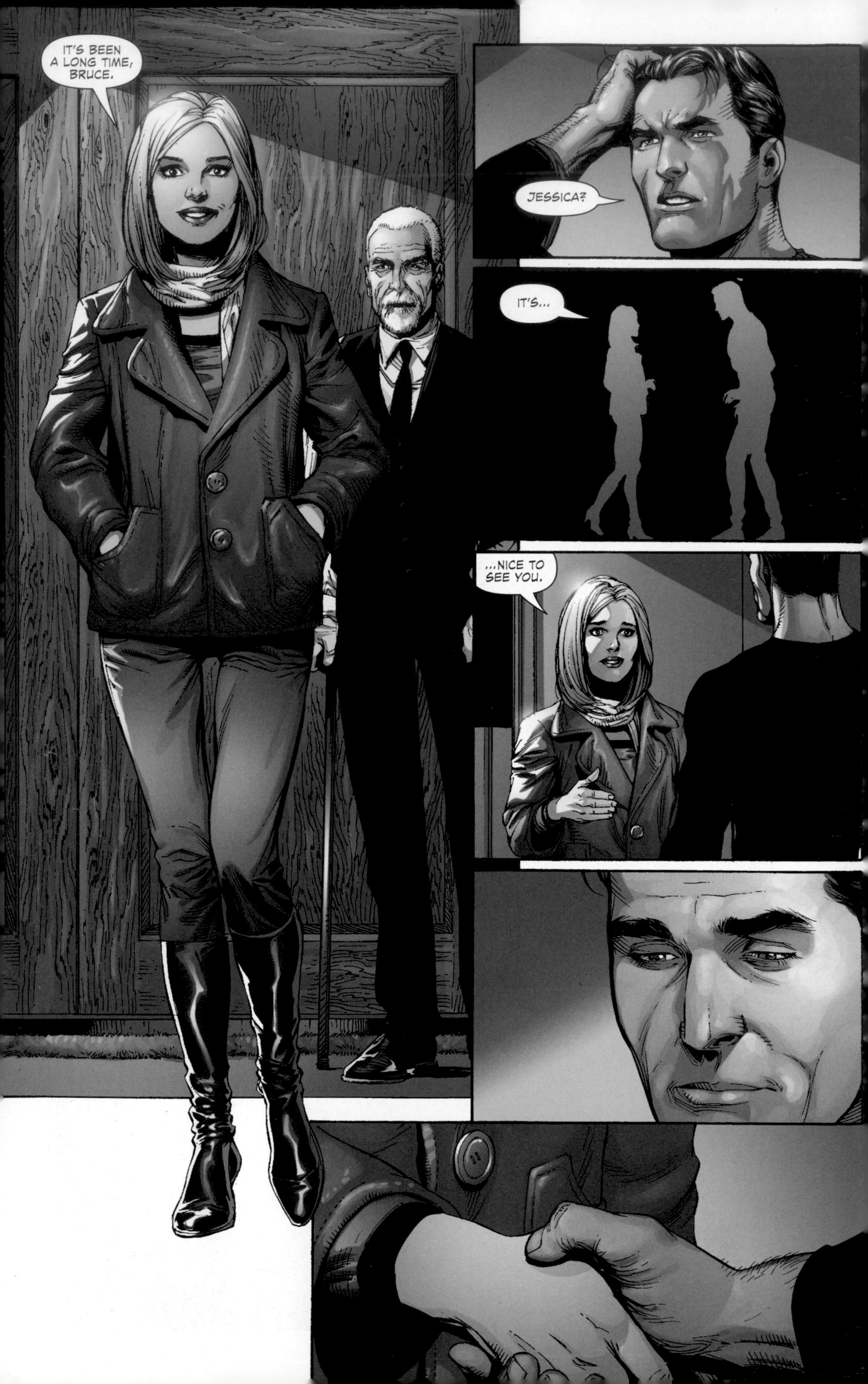
IT'S BEEN A LONG TIME, BRUCE.
JESSICA?
IT'S...
...NICE TO SEE YOU.

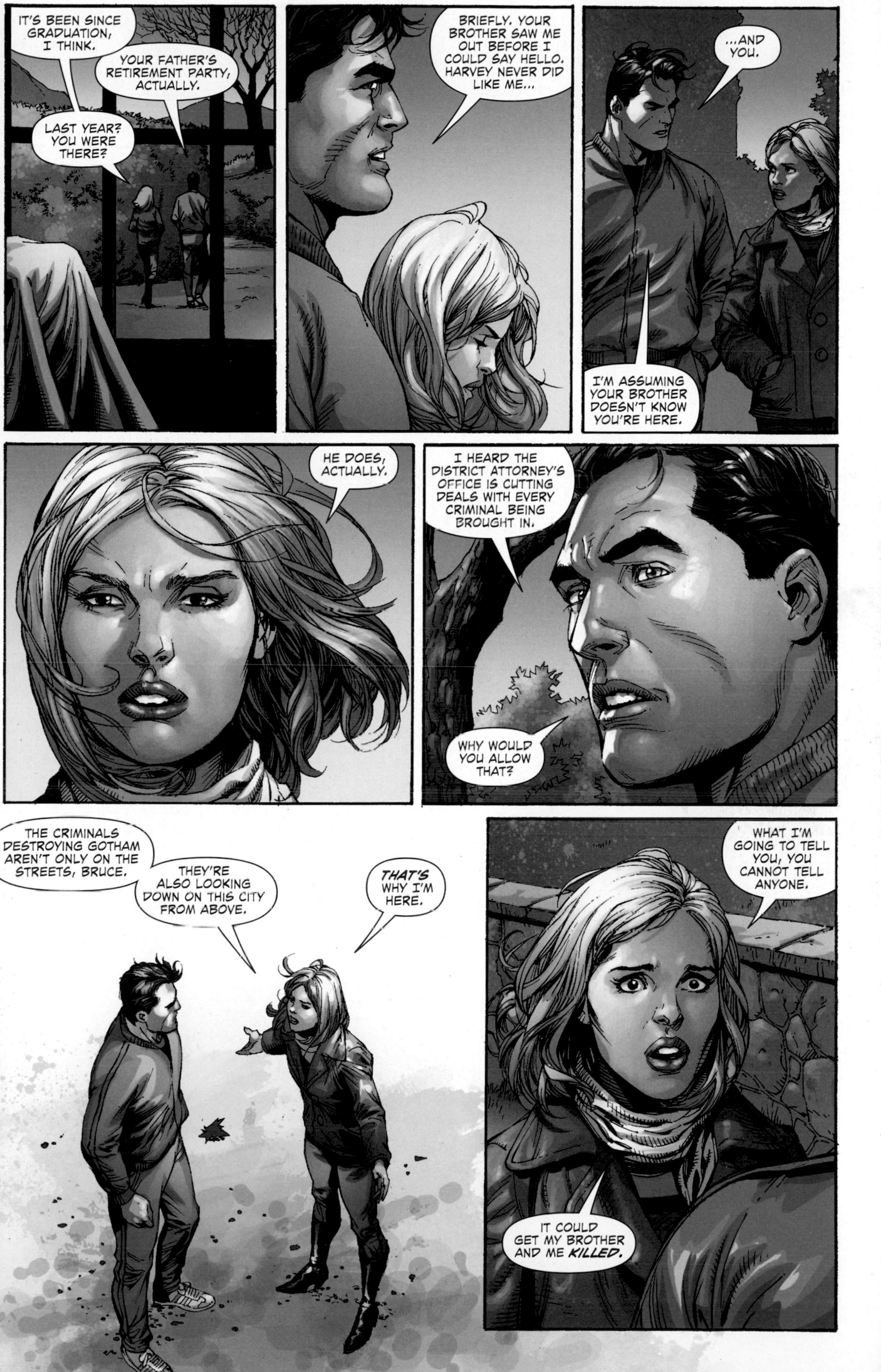
IT'S BEEN SINCE GRADUATION, I THINK.
YOUR FATHER'S RETIREMENT PARTY, ACTUALLY.
LAST YEAR? YOU WERE THERE?
BRIEFLY. YOUR BROTHER SAW ME OUT BEFORE I COULD SAY HELLO. HARVEY NEVER DID LIKE ME...
...AND YOU.
I'M ASSUMING YOUR BROTHER DOESN'T KNOW YOU'RE HERE.
HE DOES, ACTUALLY.
I HEARD THE DISTRICT ATTORNEY'S OFFICE IS CUTTING DEALS WITH EVERY CRIMINAL BEING BROUGHT IN.
WHY WOULD YOU ALLOW THAT?
THE CRIMINALS DESTROYING GOTHAM AREN'T ONLY ON THE STREETS, BRUCE.
THEY'RE ALSO LOOKING DOWN ON THIS CITY FROM ABOVE.
THAT'S WHY I'M HERE.
WHAT I'M GOING TO TELL YOU, YOU CANNOT TELL ANYONE.
IT COULD GET MY BROTHER AND ME KILLED.

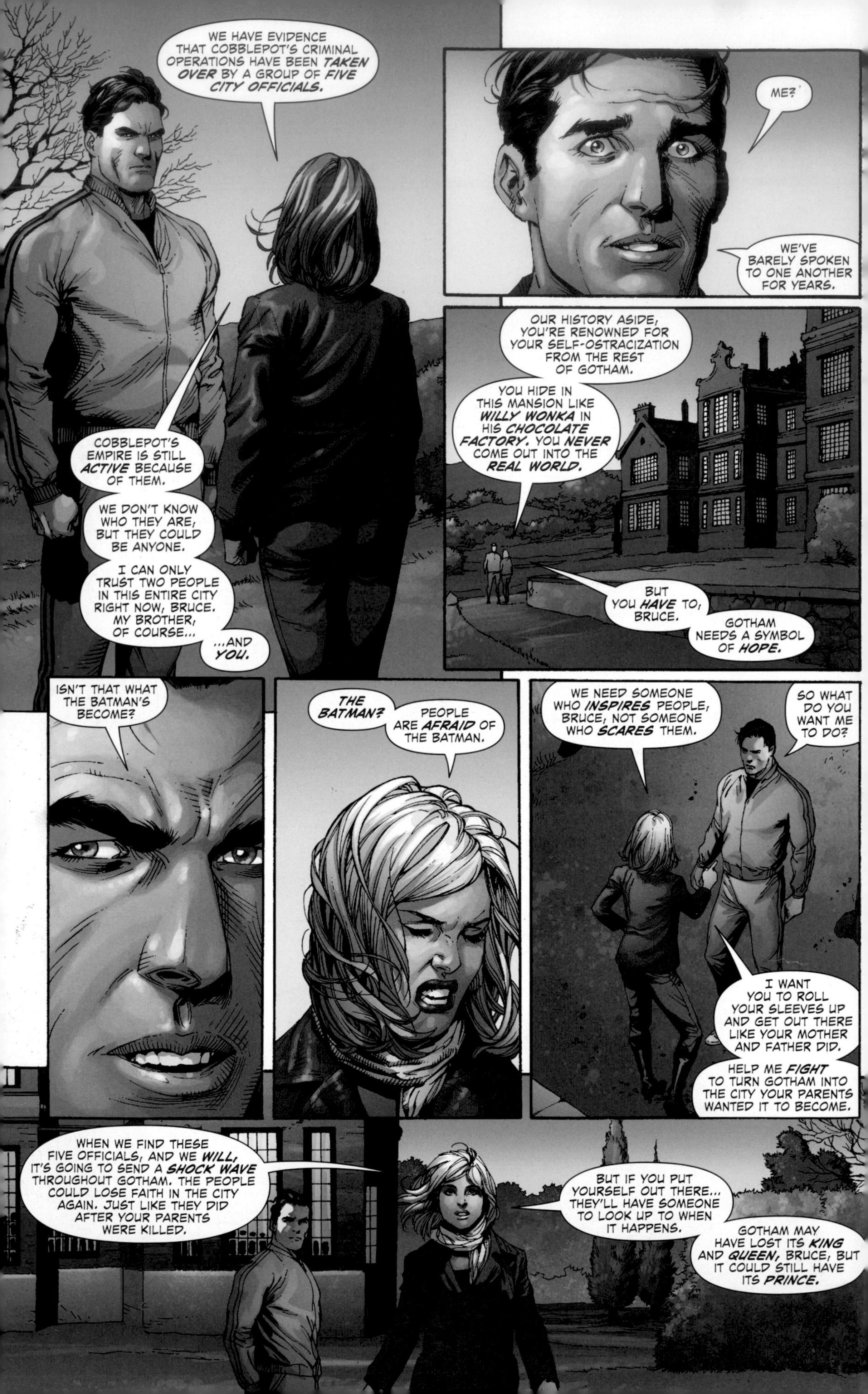
WE HAVE EVIDENCE THAT COBBLEPOT'S CRIMINAL OPERATIONS HAVE BEEN TAKEN OVER BY A GROUP OF FIVE CITY OFFICIALS.
COBBLEPOT'S EMPIRE IS STILL ACTIVE BECAUSE OF THEM.
WE DON'T KNOW WHO THEY ARE, BUT THEY COULD BE ANYONE.
I CAN ONLY TRUST TWO PEOPLE IN THIS ENTIRE CITY RIGHT NOW, BRUCE. MY BROTHER, OF COURSE...
...AND YOU.
ME?
WE'VE BARELY SPOKEN TO ONE ANOTHER FOR YEARS.
OUR HISTORY ASIDE, YOU'RE RENOWNED FOR YOUR SELF-OSTRACIZATION FROM THE REST OF GOTHAM.
YOU HIDE IN THIS MANSION LIKE WILLY WONKA IN HIS CHOCOLATE FACTORY. YOU NEVER COME OUT INTO THE REAL WORLD.
BUT YOU HAVE TO, BRUCE.
GOTHAM NEEDS A SYMBOL OF HOPE.
ISN'T THAT WHAT THE BATMAN'S BECOME?
THE BATMAN?
PEOPLE ARE AFRAID OF THE BATMAN.
WE NEED SOMEONE WHO INSPIRES PEOPLE, BRUCE, NOT SOMEONE WHO SCARES THEM.
SO WHAT DO YOU WANT ME TO DO?
I WANT YOU TO ROLL YOUR SLEEVES UP AND GET OUT THERE LIKE YOUR MOTHER AND FATHER DID.
HELP ME FIGHT TO TURN GOTHAM INTO THE CITY YOUR PARENTS WANTED IT TO BECOME.
WHEN WE FIND THESE FIVE OFFICIALS, AND WE WILL, IT'S GOING TO SEND A SHOCK WAVE THROUGHOUT GOTHAM. THE PEOPLE COULD LOSE FAITH IN THE CITY AGAIN. JUST LIKE THEY DID AFTER YOUR PARENTS WERE KILLED.
BUT IF YOU PUT YOURSELF OUT THERE... THEY'LL HAVE SOMEONE TO LOOK UP TO WHEN IT HAPPENS.
GOTHAM MAY HAVE LOST ITS KING AND QUEEN, BRUCE, BUT IT COULD STILL HAVE ITS PRINCE.

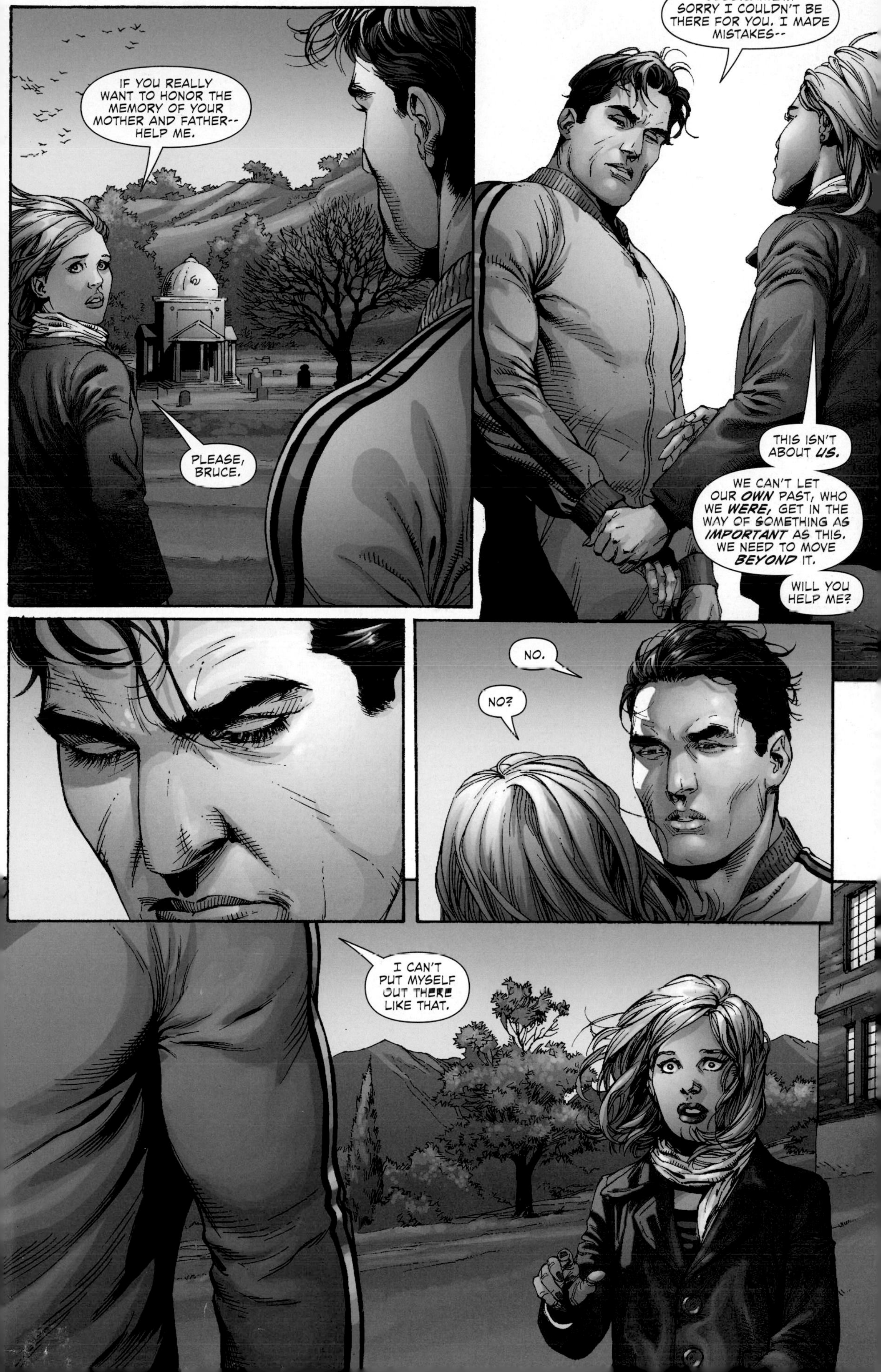
IF YOU REALLY WANT TO HONOR THE MEMORY OF YOUR MOTHER AND FATHER-- HELP ME.
PLEASE, BRUCE.
JESSICA...I'M SORRY I COULDN'T BE THERE FOR YOU. I MADE MISTAKES--
THIS ISN'T ABOUT US.
WE CAN'T LET OUR OWN PAST, WHO WE WERE, GET IN THE WAY OF SOMETHING AS IMPORTANT AS THIS. WE NEED TO MOVE BEYOND IT.
WILL YOU HELP ME?
NO.
NO?
I CAN'T PUT MYSELF OUT THERE LIKE THAT.

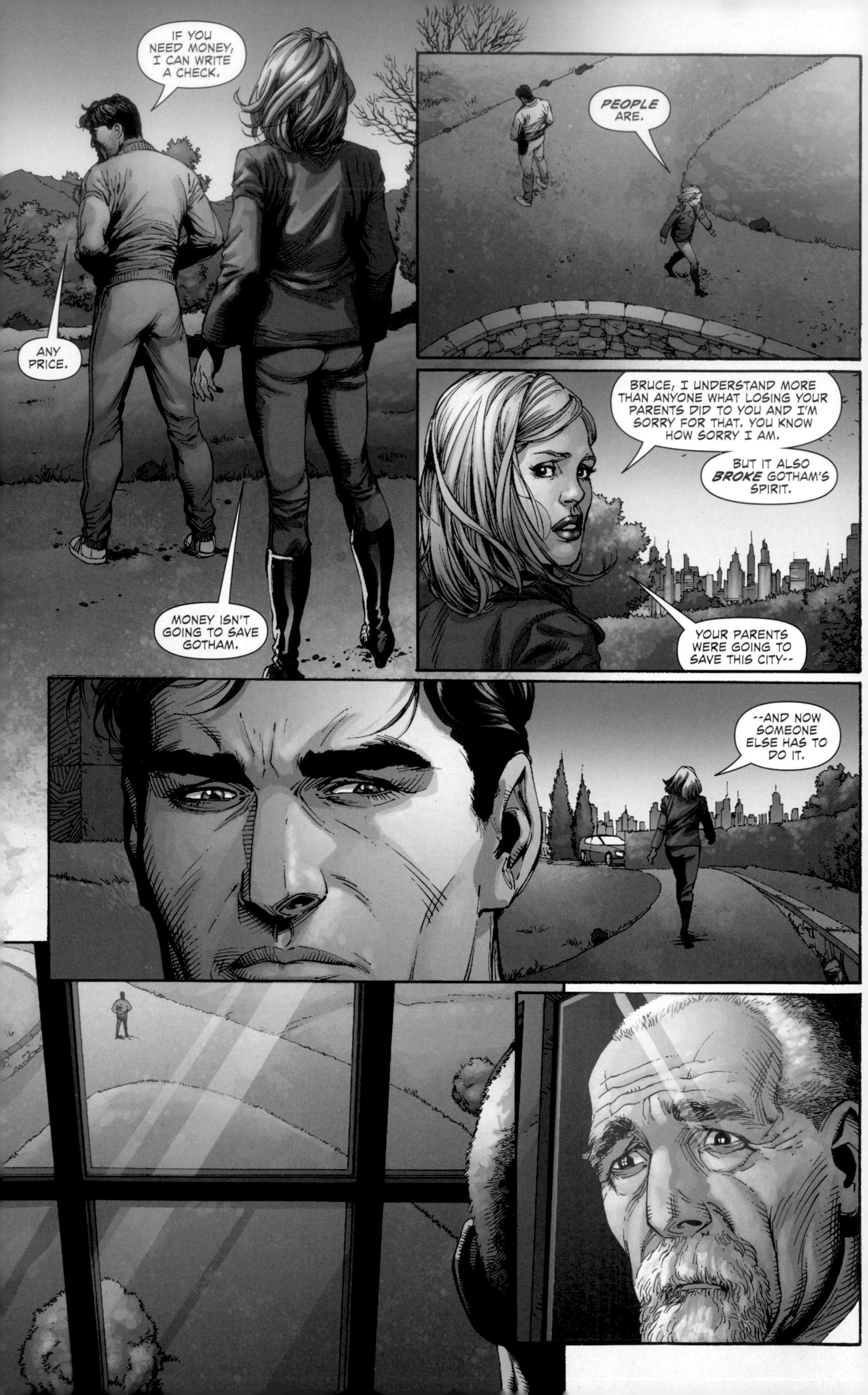
IF YOU NEED MONEY, I CAN WRITE A CHECK.
ANY PRICE.
MONEY ISN'T GOING TO SAVE GOTHAM.
PEOPLE ARE.
BRUCE, I UNDERSTAND MORE THAN ANYONE WHAT LOSING YOUR PARENTS DID TO YOU AND I'M SORRY FOR THAT. YOU KNOW HOW SORRY I AM.
BUT IT ALSO BROKE GOTHAM'S SPIRIT.
YOUR PARENTS WERE GOING TO SAVE THIS CITY--
--AND NOW SOMEONE ELSE HAS TO DO IT.

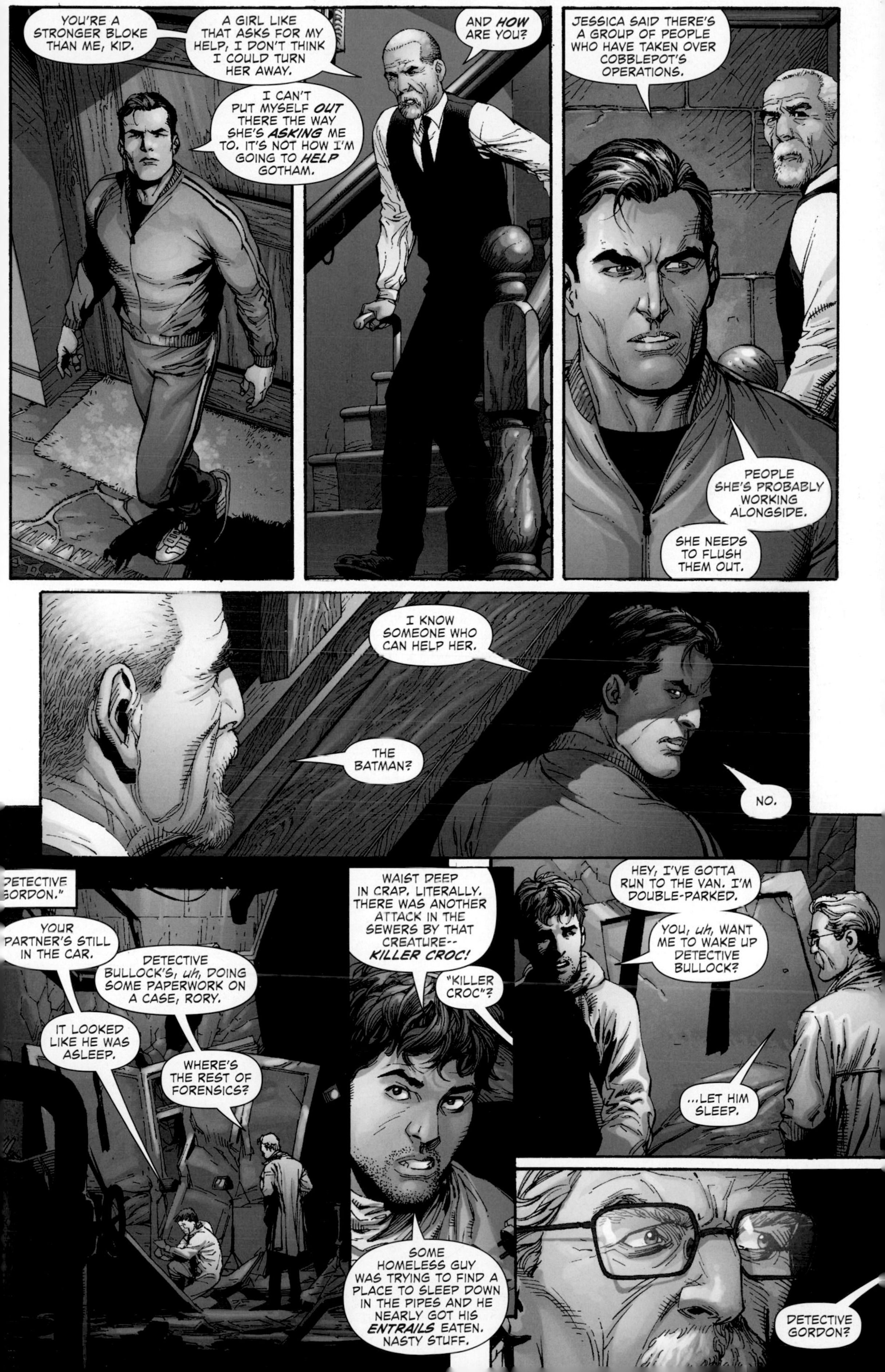
YOU'RE A STRONGER BLOKE THAN ME, KID.
A GIRL LIKE THAT ASKS FOR MY HELP, I DON'T THINK I COULD TURN HER AWAY.
I CAN'T PUT MYSELF OUT THERE THE WAY SHE'S ASKING ME TO. IT'S NOT HOW I'M GOING TO HELP GOTHAM.
AND HOW ARE YOU?
JESSICA SAID THERE'S A GROUP OF PEOPLE WHO HAVE TAKEN OVER COBBLEPOT'S OPERATIONS.
PEOPLE SHE'S PROBABLY WORKING ALONGSIDE.
SHE NEEDS TO FLUSH THEM OUT.
I KNOW SOMEONE WHO CAN HELP HER.
THE BATMAN?
NO.
"DETECTIVE GORDON."
YOUR PARTNER'S STILL IN THE CAR.
DETECTIVE BULLOCK'S, uh, DOING SOME PAPERWORK ON A CASE, RORY.
IT LOOKED LIKE HE WAS ASLEEP.
WHERE'S THE REST OF FORENSICS?
WAIST DEEP IN CRAP. LITERALLY. THERE WAS ANOTHER ATTACK IN THE SEWERS BY THAT CREATURE-- KILLER CROC!
"KILLER CROC"?
SOME HOMELESS GUY WAS TRYING TO FIND A PLACE TO SLEEP DOWN IN THE PIPES AND HE NEARLY GOT HIS ENTRAILS EATEN. NASTY STUFF.
HEY, I'VE GOTTA RUN TO THE VAN. I'M DOUBLE-PARKED.
YOU, uh, WANT ME TO WAKE UP DETECTIVE BULLOCK?
...LET HIM SLEEP.
DETECTIVE GORDON?

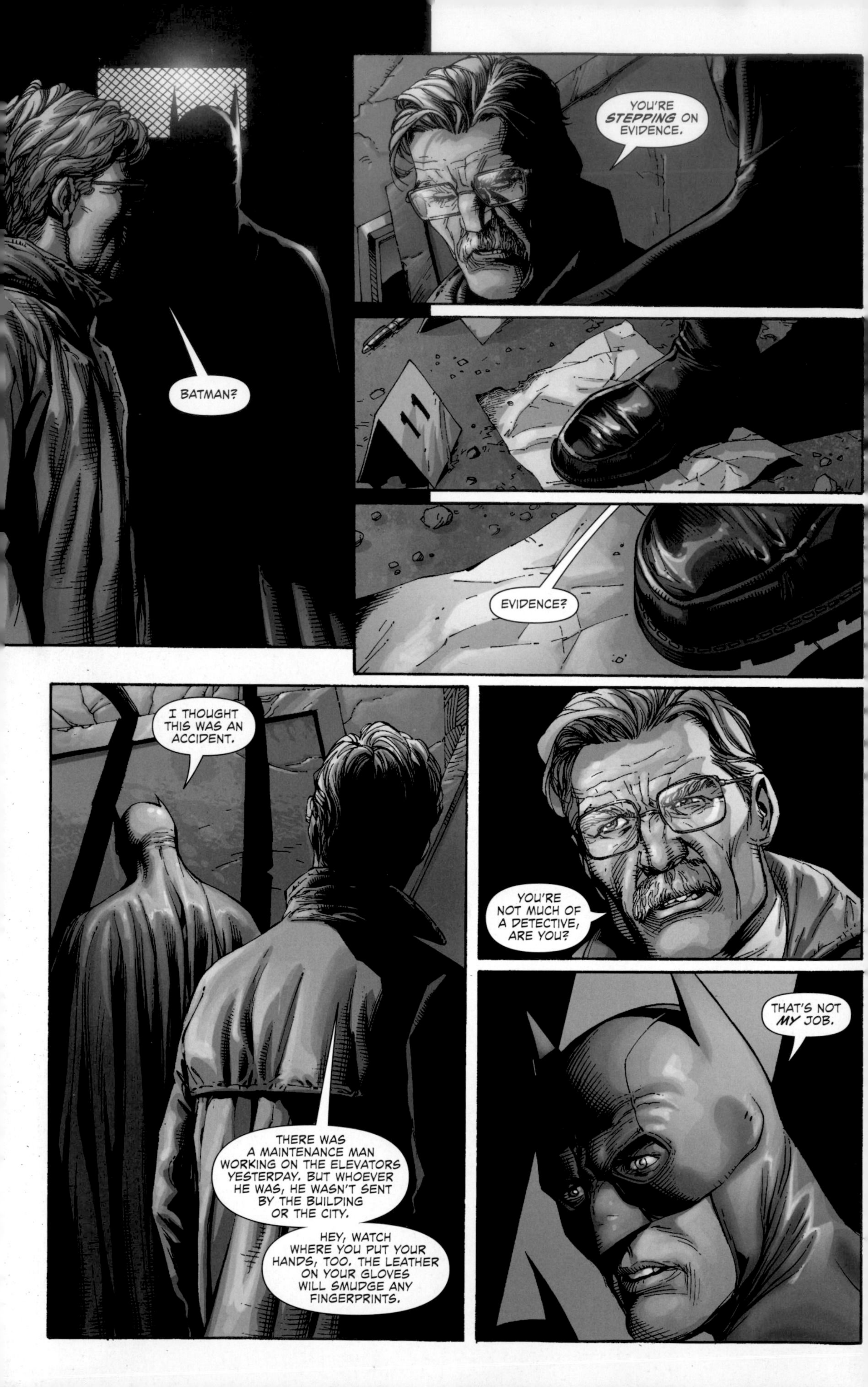
BATMAN?
YOU'RE *STEPPING* ON EVIDENCE.
EVIDENCE?
I THOUGHT THIS WAS AN ACCIDENT.
THERE WAS A MAINTENANCE MAN WORKING ON THE ELEVATORS YESTERDAY. BUT WHOEVER HE WAS, HE WASN'T SENT BY THE BUILDING OR THE CITY.
HEY, WATCH WHERE YOU PUT YOUR HANDS, TOO. THE LEATHER ON YOUR GLOVES WILL SMUDGE ANY FINGERPRINTS.
YOU'RE NOT MUCH OF A DETECTIVE, ARE YOU?
THAT'S NOT *MY* JOB.

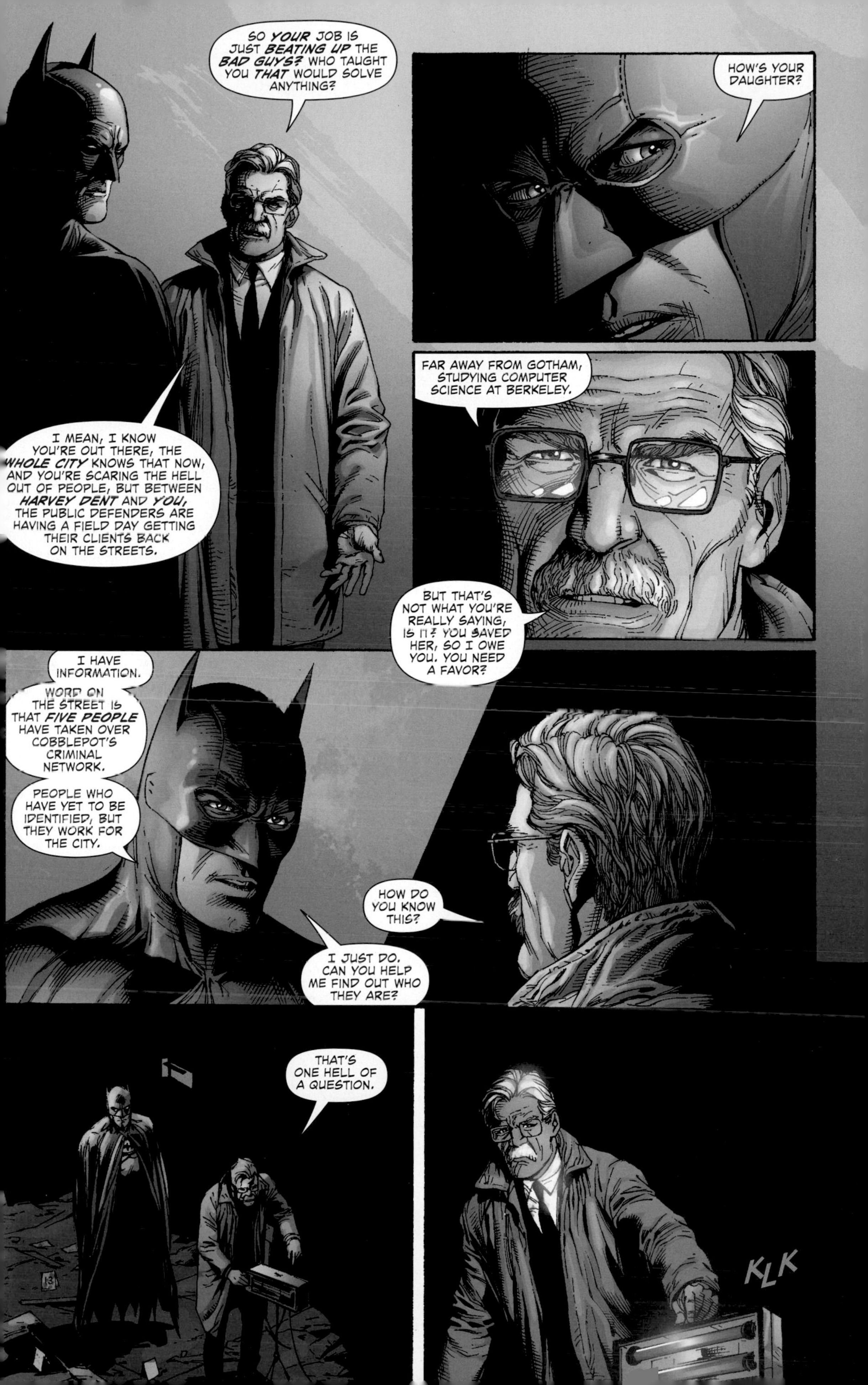
SO YOUR JOB IS JUST BEATING UP THE BAD GUYS? WHO TAUGHT YOU THAT WOULD SOLVE ANYTHING?
I MEAN, I KNOW YOU'RE OUT THERE, THE WHOLE CITY KNOWS THAT NOW, AND YOU'RE SCARING THE HELL OUT OF PEOPLE, BUT BETWEEN HARVEY DENT AND YOU, THE PUBLIC DEFENDERS ARE HAVING A FIELD DAY GETTING THEIR CLIENTS BACK ON THE STREETS.
HOW'S YOUR DAUGHTER?
FAR AWAY FROM GOTHAM, STUDYING COMPUTER SCIENCE AT BERKELEY.
BUT THAT'S NOT WHAT YOU'RE REALLY SAYING, IS IT? YOU SAVED HER, SO I OWE YOU. YOU NEED A FAVOR?
I HAVE INFORMATION.
WORD ON THE STREET IS THAT FIVE PEOPLE HAVE TAKEN OVER COBBLEPOT'S CRIMINAL NETWORK.
PEOPLE WHO HAVE YET TO BE IDENTIFIED, BUT THEY WORK FOR THE CITY.
HOW DO YOU KNOW THIS?
I JUST DO. CAN YOU HELP ME FIND OUT WHO THEY ARE?
THAT'S ONE HELL OF A QUESTION.
KLK

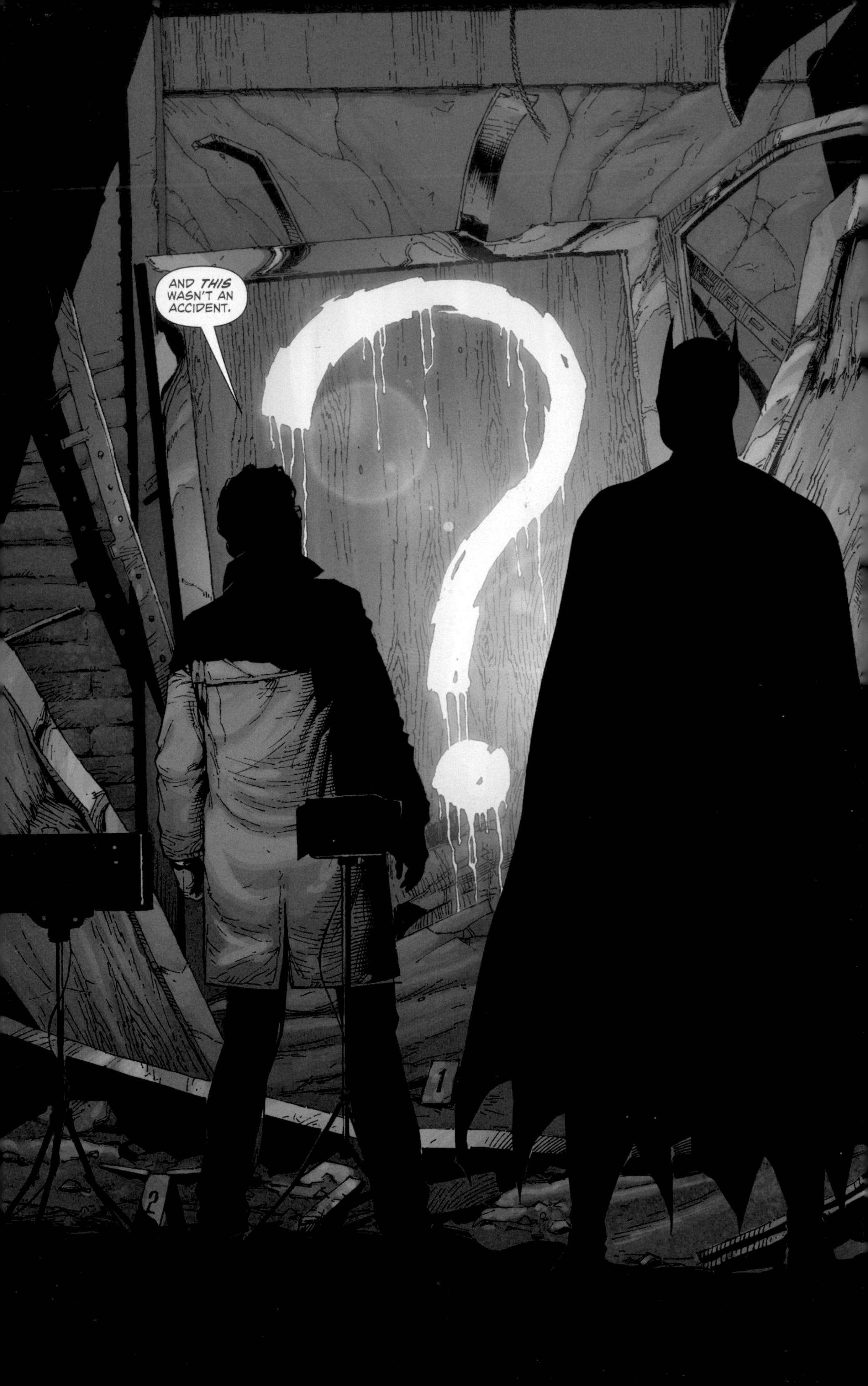
AND *THIS* WASN'T AN ACCIDENT.

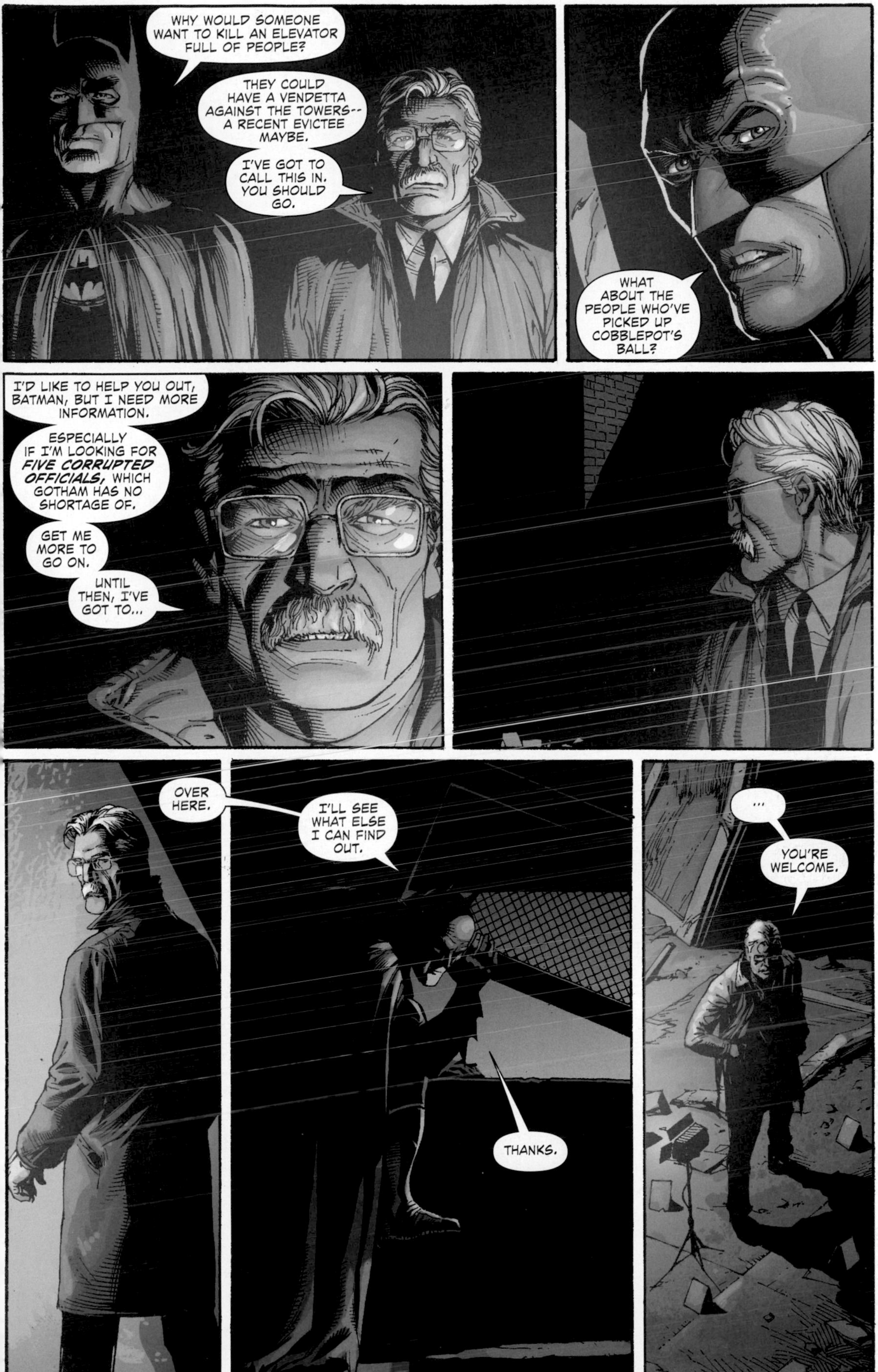
WHY WOULD SOMEONE WANT TO KILL AN ELEVATOR FULL OF PEOPLE?
THEY COULD HAVE A VENDETTA AGAINST THE TOWERS-- A RECENT EVICTEE MAYBE.
I'VE GOT TO CALL THIS IN. YOU SHOULD GO.
WHAT ABOUT THE PEOPLE WHO'VE PICKED UP COBBLEPOT'S BALL?
I'D LIKE TO HELP YOU OUT, BATMAN, BUT I NEED MORE INFORMATION.
ESPECIALLY IF I'M LOOKING FOR FIVE CORRUPTED OFFICIALS, WHICH GOTHAM HAS NO SHORTAGE OF.
GET ME MORE TO GO ON.
UNTIL THEN, I'VE GOT TO...
OVER HERE.
I'LL SEE WHAT ELSE I CAN FIND OUT.
THANKS.
...
YOU'RE WELCOME.

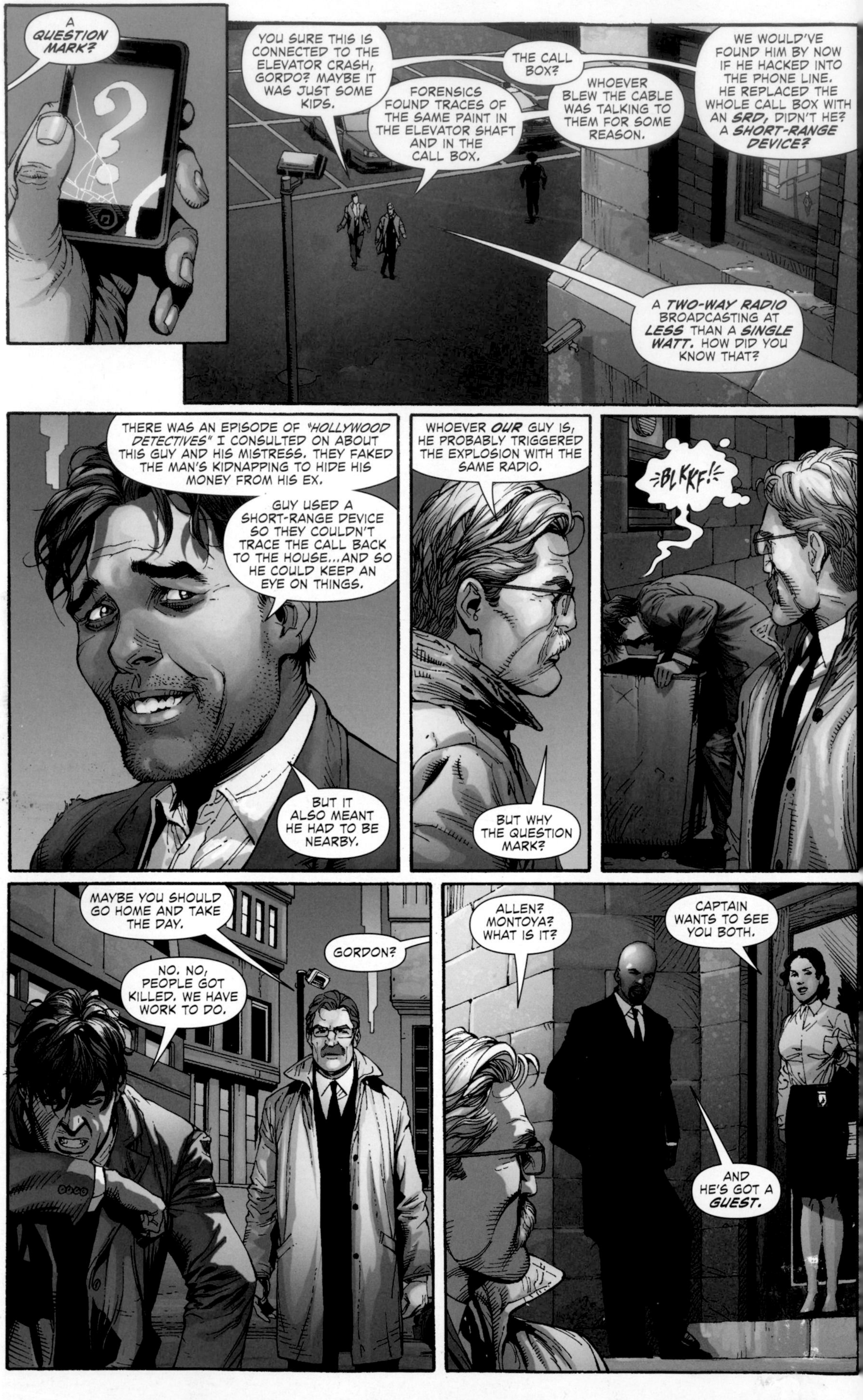
A QUESTION MARK?
YOU SURE THIS IS CONNECTED TO THE ELEVATOR CRASH, GORDO? MAYBE IT WAS JUST SOME KIDS.
FORENSICS FOUND TRACES OF THE SAME PAINT IN THE ELEVATOR SHAFT AND IN THE CALL BOX.
THE CALL BOX?
WHOEVER BLEW THE CABLE WAS TALKING TO THEM FOR SOME REASON.
WE WOULD'VE FOUND HIM BY NOW IF HE HACKED INTO THE PHONE LINE. HE REPLACED THE WHOLE CALL BOX WITH AN SRD, DIDN'T HE? A SHORT-RANGE DEVICE?
A TWO-WAY RADIO BROADCASTING AT LESS THAN A SINGLE WATT. HOW DID YOU KNOW THAT?
THERE WAS AN EPISODE OF "HOLLYWOOD DETECTIVES" I CONSULTED ON ABOUT THIS GUY AND HIS MISTRESS. THEY FAKED THE MAN'S KIDNAPPING TO HIDE HIS MONEY FROM HIS EX.
GUY USED A SHORT-RANGE DEVICE SO THEY COULDN'T TRACE THE CALL BACK TO THE HOUSE...AND SO HE COULD KEEP AN EYE ON THINGS.
BUT IT ALSO MEANT HE HAD TO BE NEARBY.
WHOEVER OUR GUY IS, HE PROBABLY TRIGGERED THE EXPLOSION WITH THE SAME RADIO.
BUT WHY THE QUESTION MARK?
BLKKF!
MAYBE YOU SHOULD GO HOME AND TAKE THE DAY.
NO. NO, PEOPLE GOT KILLED. WE HAVE WORK TO DO.
GORDON?
ALLEN? MONTOYA? WHAT IS IT?
CAPTAIN WANTS TO SEE YOU BOTH.
AND HE'S GOT A GUEST.

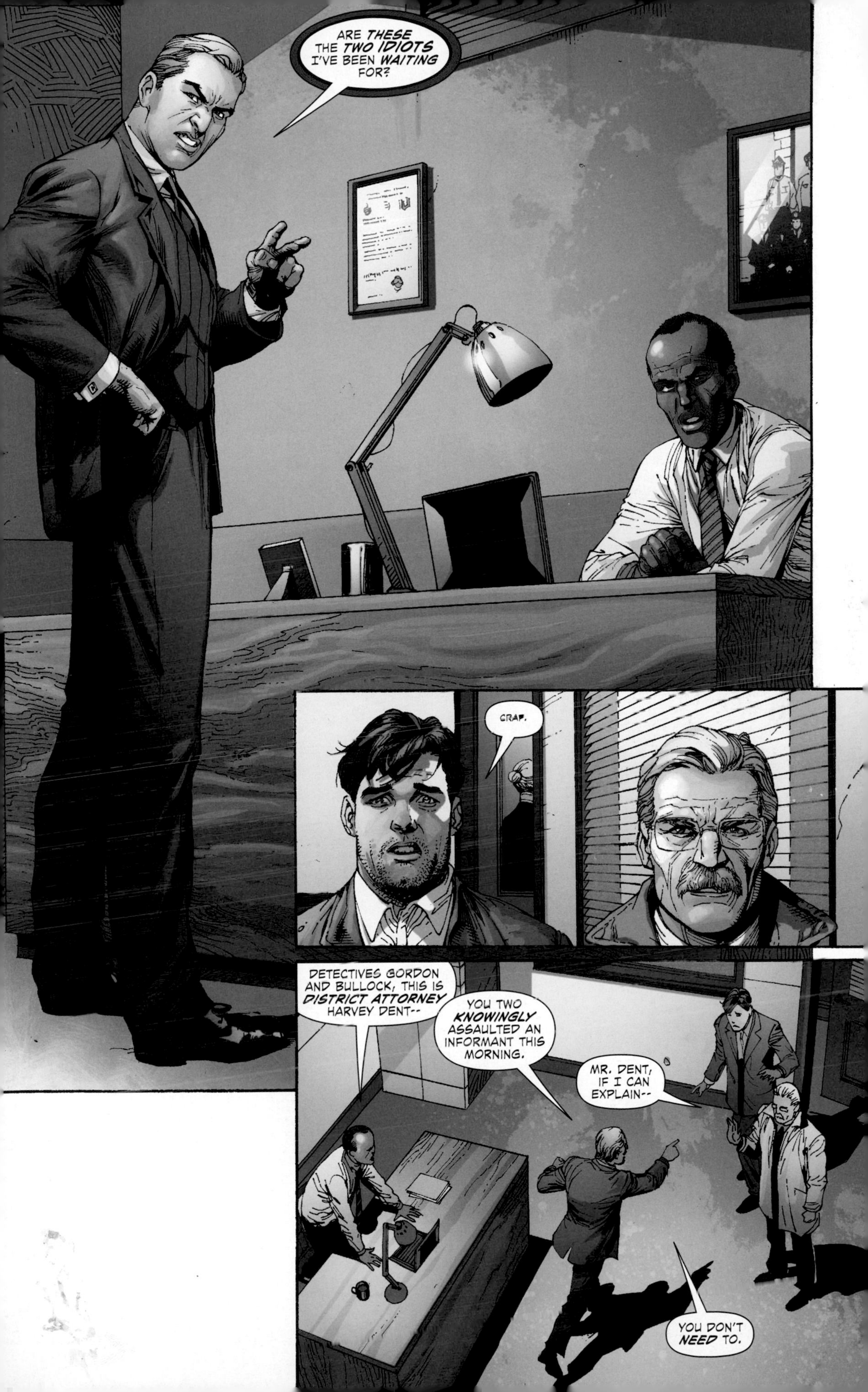

ARE *THESE* THE *TWO IDIOTS* I'VE BEEN *WAITING* FOR?
CRAP.
DETECTIVES GORDON AND BULLOCK, THIS IS *DISTRICT ATTORNEY* HARVEY DENT--
YOU TWO *KNOWINGLY* ASSAULTED AN INFORMANT THIS MORNING.
MR. DENT, IF I CAN EXPLAIN--
YOU DON'T *NEED* TO.

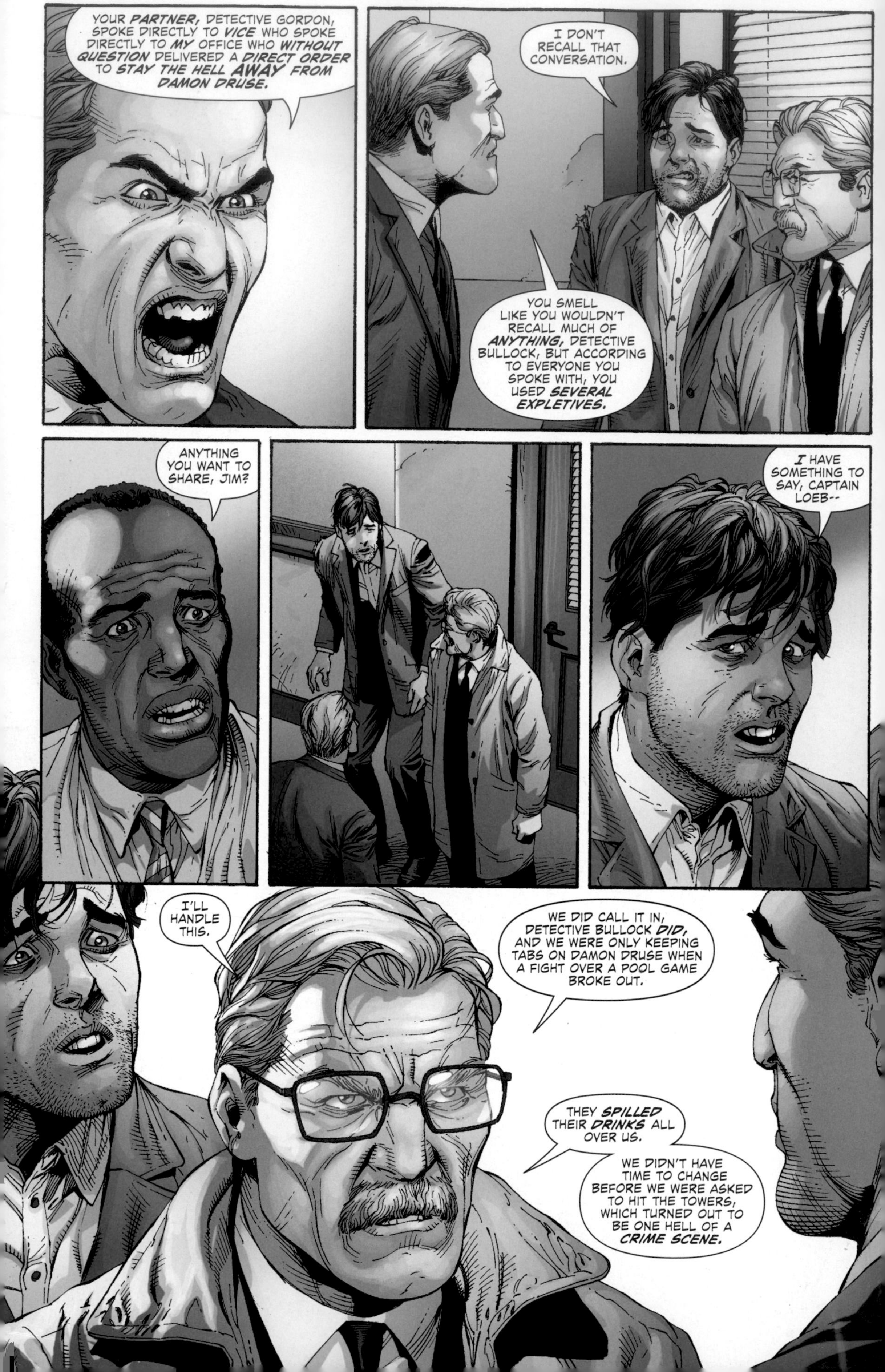
YOUR PARTNER, DETECTIVE GORDON, SPOKE DIRECTLY TO VICE WHO SPOKE DIRECTLY TO MY OFFICE WHO WITHOUT QUESTION DELIVERED A DIRECT ORDER TO STAY THE HELL AWAY FROM DAMON DRUSE.
I DON'T RECALL THAT CONVERSATION.
YOU SMELL LIKE YOU WOULDN'T RECALL MUCH OF ANYTHING, DETECTIVE BULLOCK, BUT ACCORDING TO EVERYONE YOU SPOKE WITH, YOU USED SEVERAL EXPLETIVES.
ANYTHING YOU WANT TO SHARE, JIM?
I HAVE SOMETHING TO SAY, CAPTAIN LOEB--
I'LL HANDLE THIS.
WE DID CALL IT IN, DETECTIVE BULLOCK DID, AND WE WERE ONLY KEEPING TABS ON DAMON DRUSE WHEN A FIGHT OVER A POOL GAME BROKE OUT.
THEY SPILLED THEIR DRINKS ALL OVER US.
WE DIDN'T HAVE TIME TO CHANGE BEFORE WE WERE ASKED TO HIT THE TOWERS, WHICH TURNED OUT TO BE ONE HELL OF A CRIME SCENE.

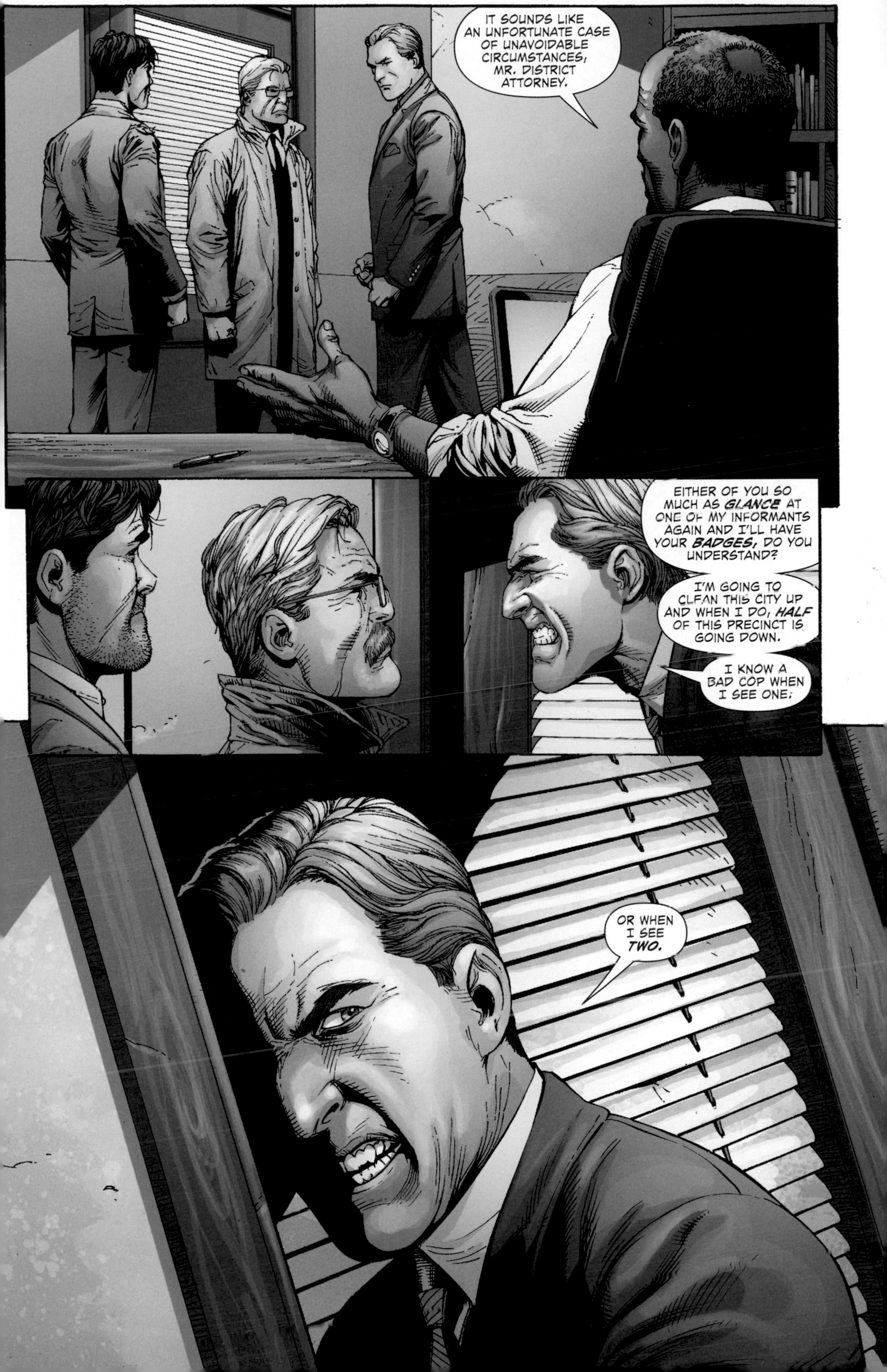
IT SOUNDS LIKE AN UNFORTUNATE CASE OF UNAVOIDABLE CIRCUMSTANCES, MR. DISTRICT ATTORNEY.
EITHER OF YOU SO MUCH AS GLANCE AT ONE OF MY INFORMANTS AGAIN AND I'LL HAVE YOUR BADGES, DO YOU UNDERSTAND?
I'M GOING TO CLEAN THIS CITY UP AND WHEN I DO, HALF OF THIS PRECINCT IS GOING DOWN.
I KNOW A BAD COP WHEN I SEE ONE;
OR WHEN I SEE TWO.

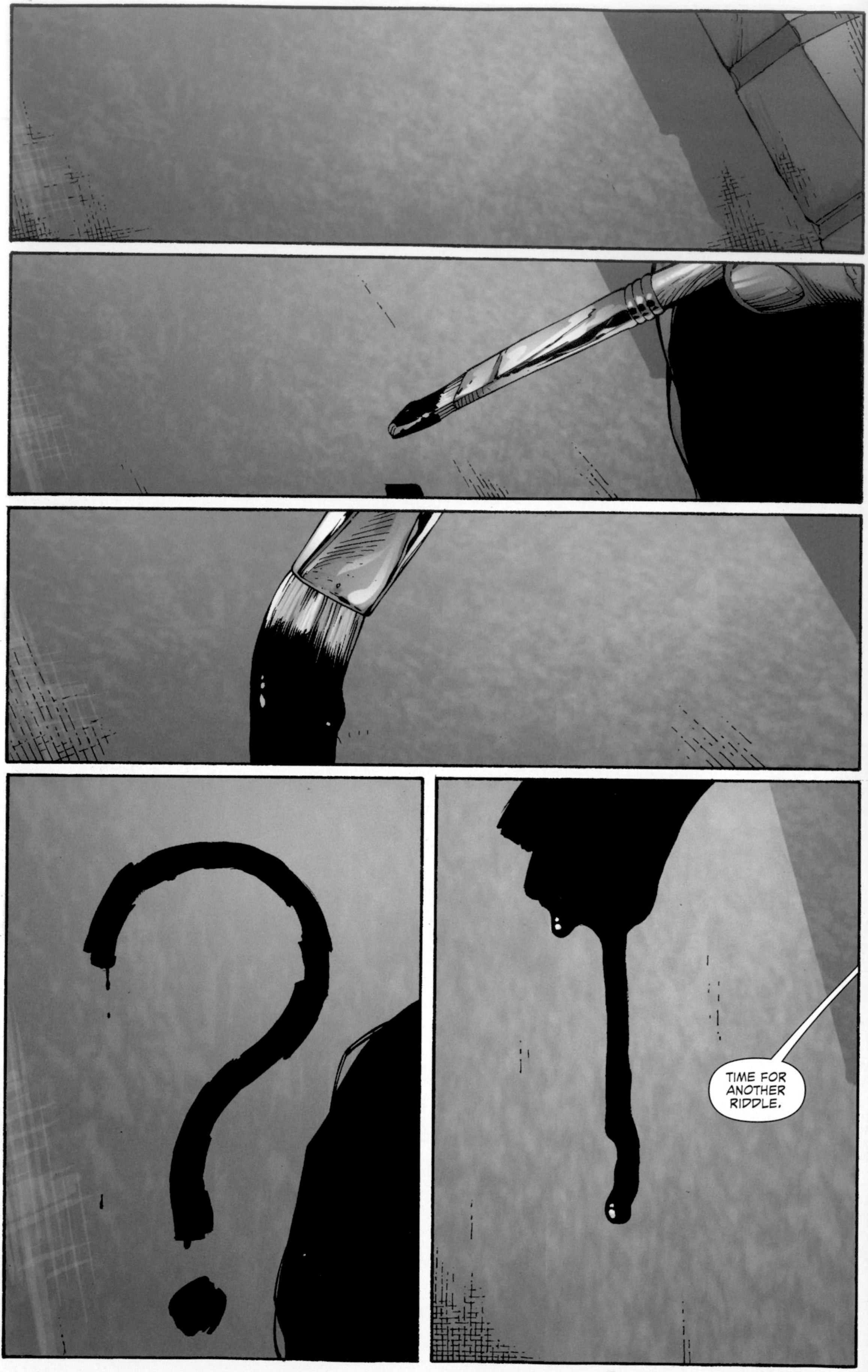
TIME FOR ANOTHER RIDDLE.

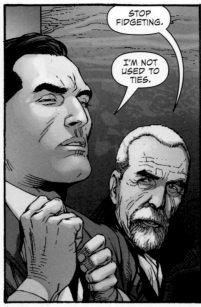

STOP FIDGETING.

I'M NOT USED TO TIES.

YOU'RE WAY OUT OF PRACTICE, BOY.

THIS ISN'T A SOCIAL CALL.

I'M ONLY HERE FOR MORE INFORMATION ON THESE FIVE OFFICIALS. AND ONCE I GET IT, I'LL TALK TO DETECTIVE GORDON--

ENOUGH WITH HIM. DETECTIVE GORDON DOESN'T KNOW YOU OR WHAT YOU'RE DOING OR WHY.

I CAN TRUST HIM.

I WOULDN'T TRUST ANY COP IN GOTHAM.

RIGHT NOW THEY HAVE THEIR HANDS FULL, BUT ONE DAY YOU KEEP THIS UP AND WE DO CLEAN UP GOTHAM...THEY'LL COME AFTER YOU, BRUCE. GORDON WILL.

HE'LL BREAK DOWN THE MANSION DOORS AND COME FOR BOTH OF US.

AND YOU CAN BET I WON'T GO WITHOUT A FIGHT.

28 DING

CAREFUL ABOUT GETTING JESSICA TOO INVOLVED.

I KNOW, ALFRED.

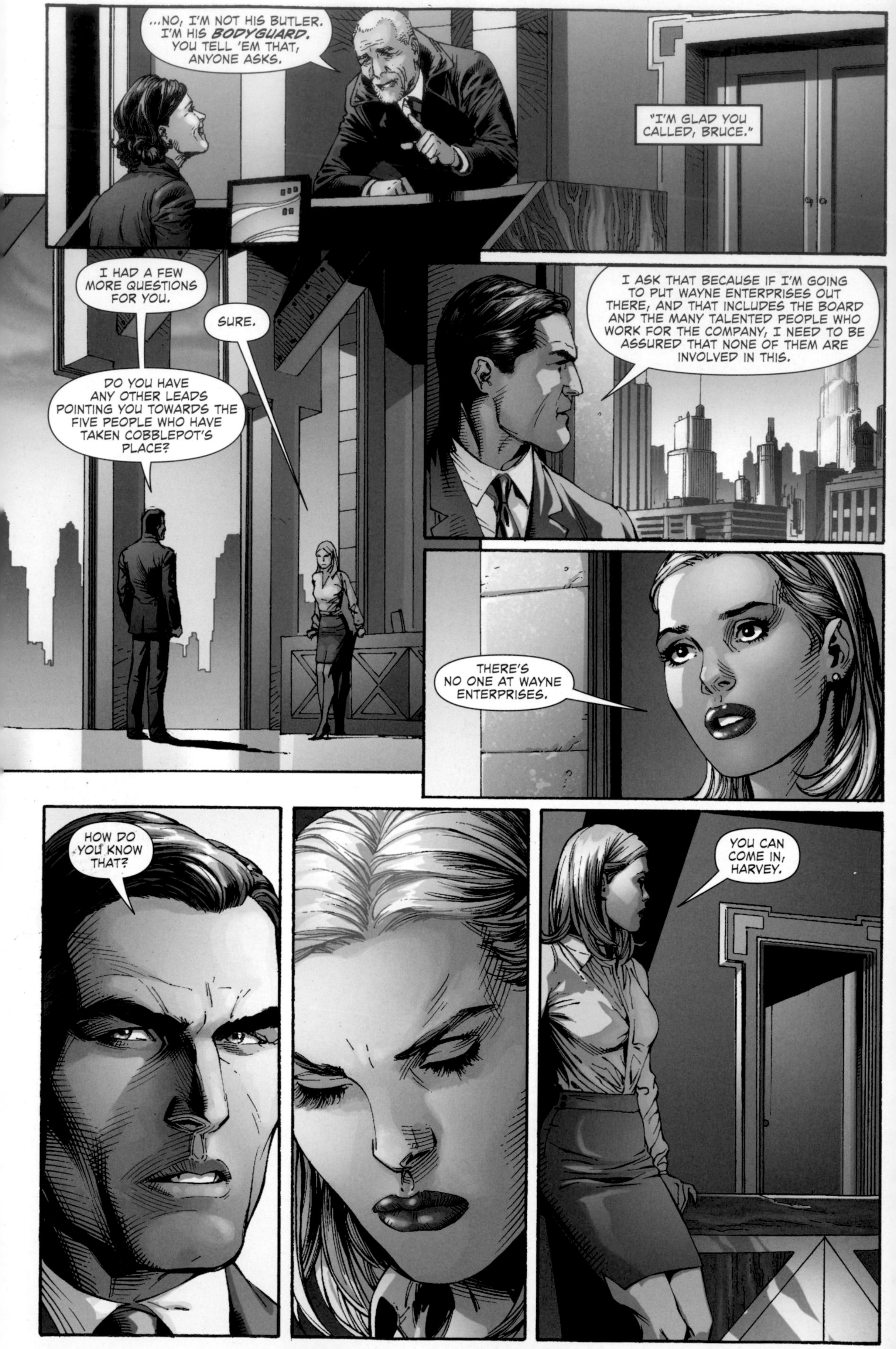
...NO, I'M NOT HIS BUTLER. I'M HIS BODYGUARD. YOU TELL 'EM THAT, ANYONE ASKS.
"I'M GLAD YOU CALLED, BRUCE."
I HAD A FEW MORE QUESTIONS FOR YOU.
SURE.
DO YOU HAVE ANY OTHER LEADS POINTING YOU TOWARDS THE FIVE PEOPLE WHO HAVE TAKEN COBBLEPOT'S PLACE?
I ASK THAT BECAUSE IF I'M GOING TO PUT WAYNE ENTERPRISES OUT THERE, AND THAT INCLUDES THE BOARD AND THE MANY TALENTED PEOPLE WHO WORK FOR THE COMPANY, I NEED TO BE ASSURED THAT NONE OF THEM ARE INVOLVED IN THIS.
THERE'S NO ONE AT WAYNE ENTERPRISES.
HOW DO YOU KNOW THAT?
YOU CAN COME IN, HARVEY.

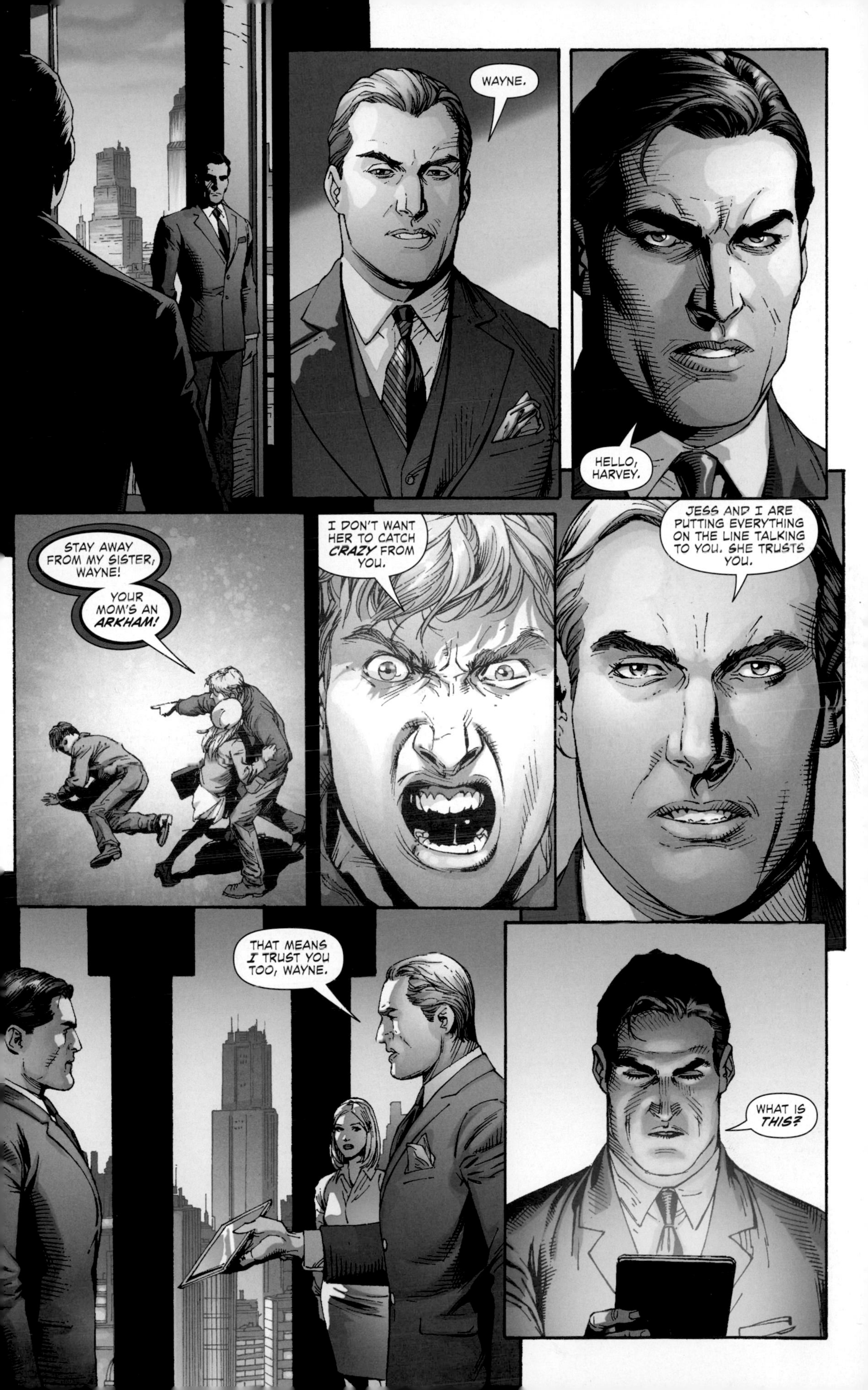
WAYNE.
HELLO, HARVEY.
STAY AWAY FROM MY SISTER, WAYNE!
YOUR MOM'S AN ARKHAM!
I DON'T WANT HER TO CATCH CRAZY FROM YOU.
JESS AND I ARE PUTTING EVERYTHING ON THE LINE TALKING TO YOU. SHE TRUSTS YOU.
THAT MEANS I TRUST YOU TOO, WAYNE.
WHAT IS THIS?

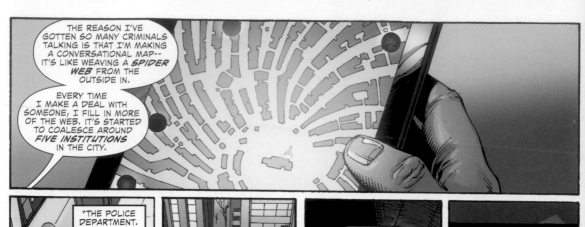

THE REASON I'VE GOTTEN SO MANY CRIMINALS TALKING IS THAT I'M MAKING A CONVERSATIONAL MAP-- IT'S LIKE WEAVING A *SPIDER WEB* FROM THE OUTSIDE IN.

EVERY TIME I MAKE A DEAL WITH SOMEONE, I FILL IN MORE OF THE WEB. IT'S STARTED TO COALESCE AROUND *FIVE INSTITUTIONS* IN THE CITY.

"THE POLICE DEPARTMENT.

"THE HOUSING COMMISSION.

"PUBLIC WORKS.

YOU HEAR THAT? I THINK SOMETHIN'S DOWN HERE.

"THE CITY COUNCIL."

AND THE STATE COURT. SOMEONE I PROBABLY SEE EVERY SINGLE DAY.

THIS IS BAD, WAYNE...

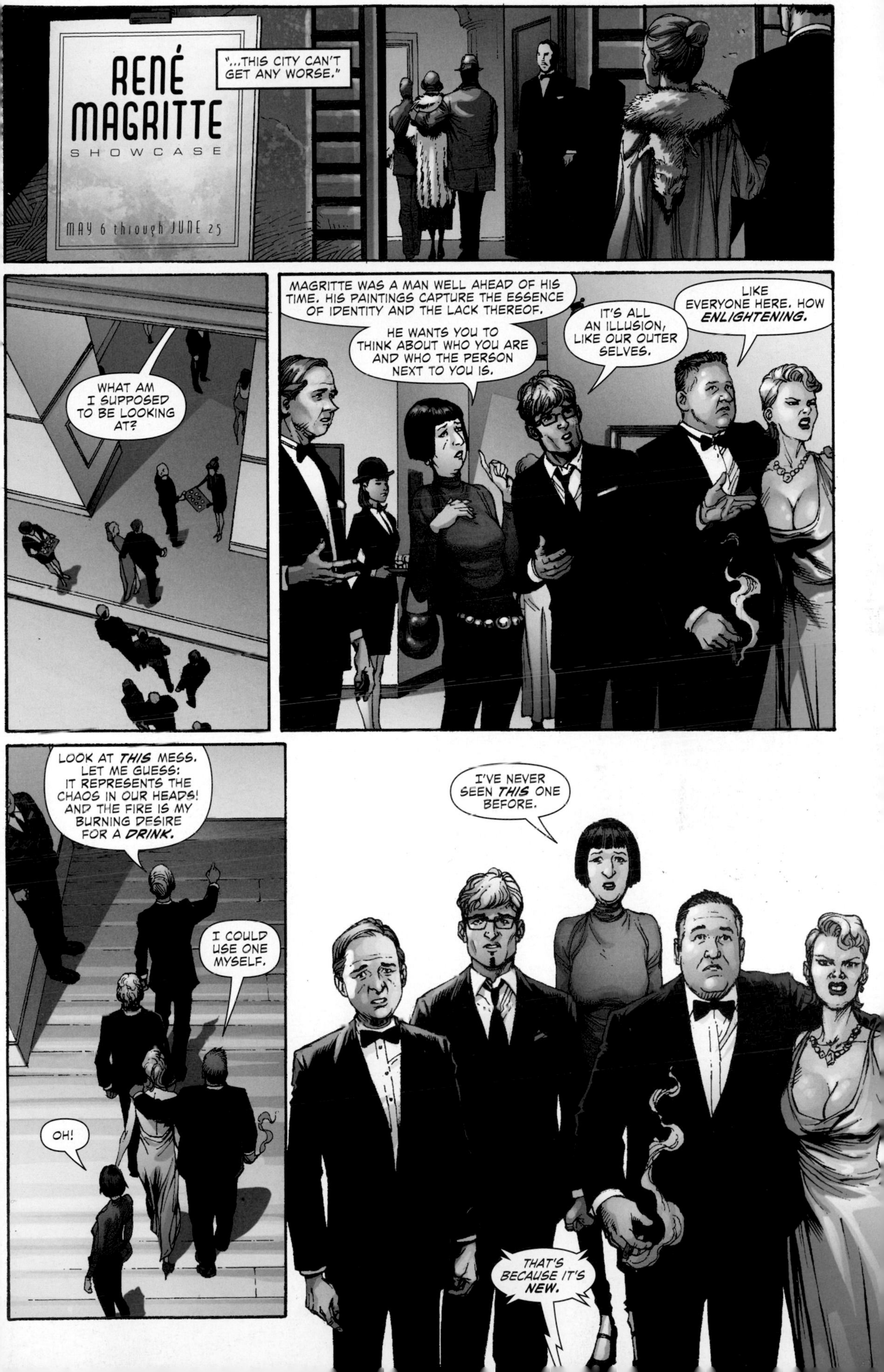
RENÉ MAGRITTE SHOWCASE
MAY 6 through JUNE 25
"...THIS CITY CAN'T GET ANY WORSE."
WHAT AM I SUPPOSED TO BE LOOKING AT?
MAGRITTE WAS A MAN WELL AHEAD OF HIS TIME. HIS PAINTINGS CAPTURE THE ESSENCE OF IDENTITY AND THE LACK THEREOF.
HE WANTS YOU TO THINK ABOUT WHO YOU ARE AND WHO THE PERSON NEXT TO YOU IS.
IT'S ALL AN ILLUSION, LIKE OUR OUTER SELVES.
LIKE EVERYONE HERE. HOW ENLIGHTENING.
LOOK AT THIS MESS. LET ME GUESS: IT REPRESENTS THE CHAOS IN OUR HEADS! AND THE FIRE IS MY BURNING DESIRE FOR A DRINK.
I COULD USE ONE MYSELF.
OH!
I'VE NEVER SEEN THIS ONE BEFORE.
THAT'S BECAUSE IT'S NEW.

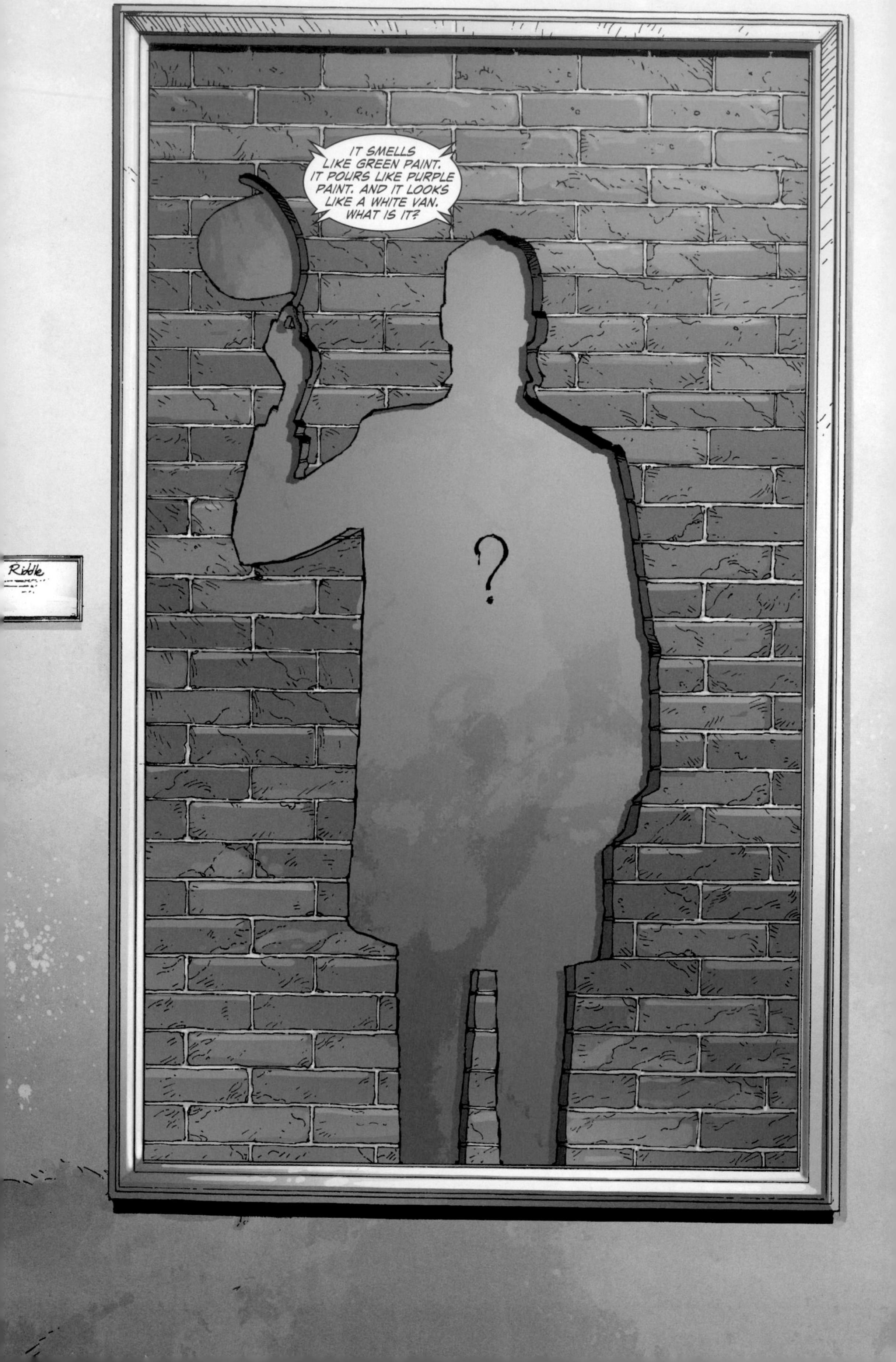
IT SMELLS LIKE GREEN PAINT. IT POURS LIKE PURPLE PAINT. AND IT LOOKS LIKE A WHITE VAN. WHAT IS IT?
Riddle
?

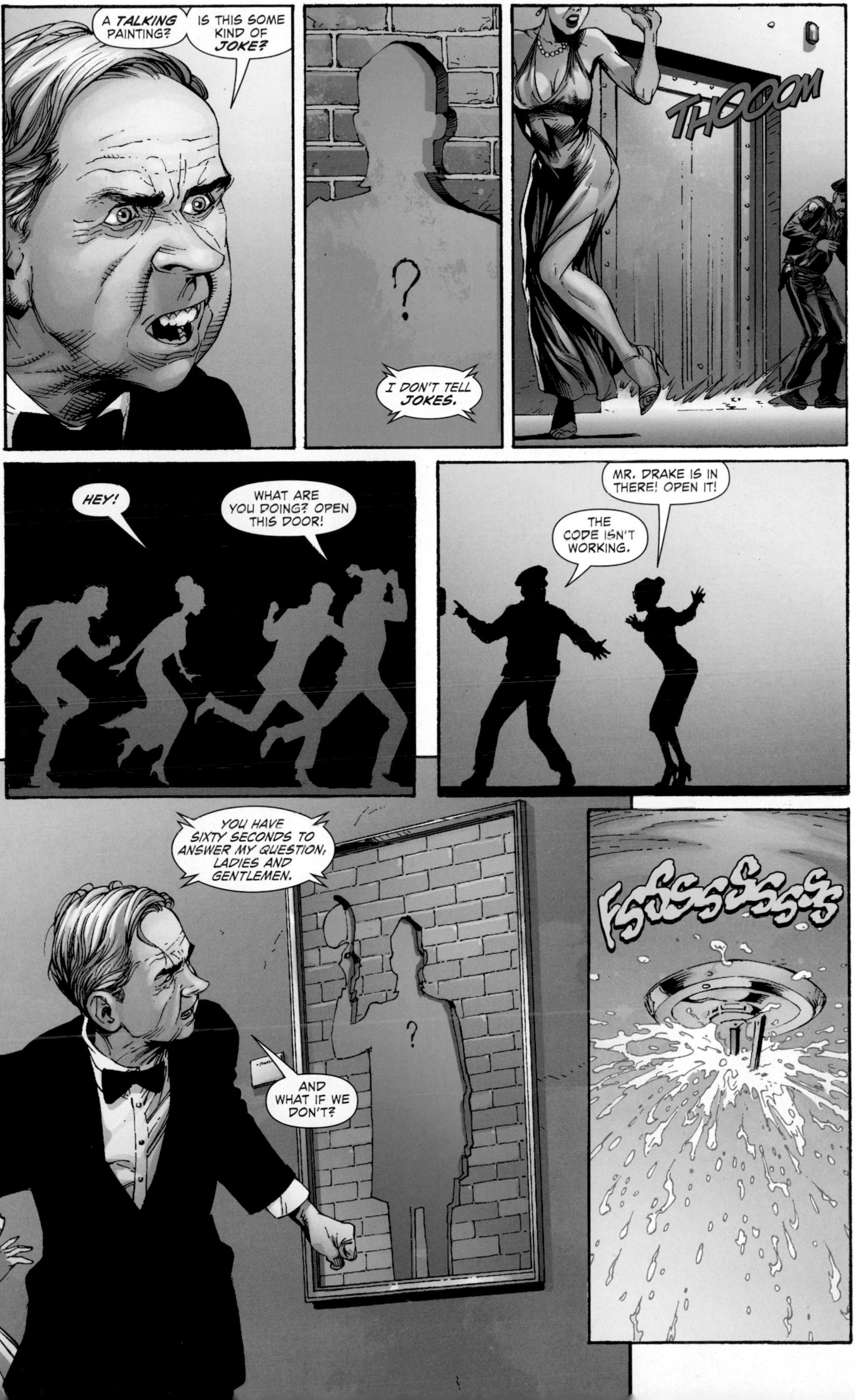
A TALKING PAINTING?
IS THIS SOME KIND OF JOKE?
I DON'T TELL JOKES.
THOOOOM
HEY!
WHAT ARE YOU DOING? OPEN THIS DOOR!
MR. DRAKE IS IN THERE! OPEN IT!
THE CODE ISN'T WORKING.
YOU HAVE SIXTY SECONDS TO ANSWER MY QUESTION, LADIES AND GENTLEMEN.
AND WHAT IF WE DON'T?
FSSSSSSSSS

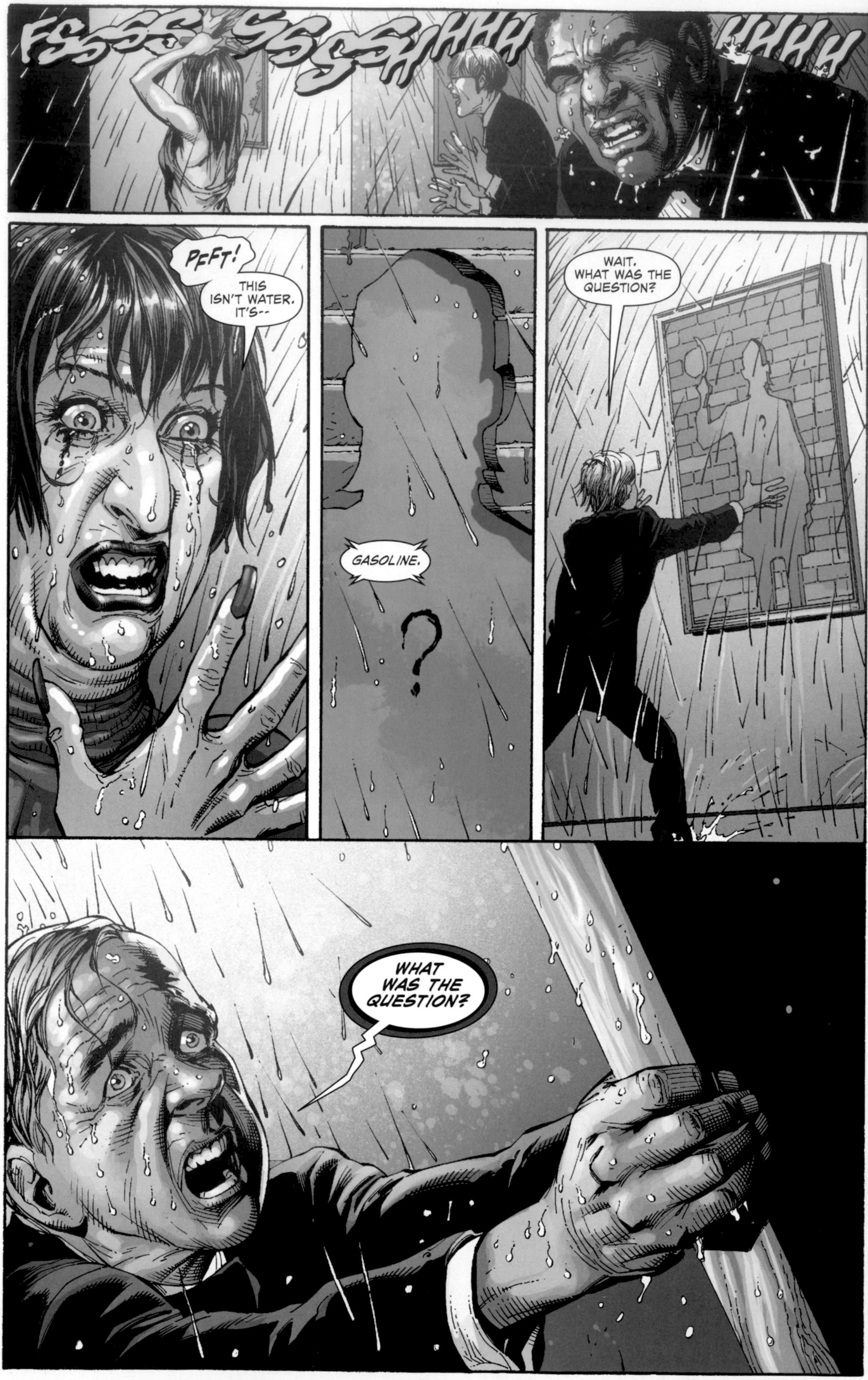
FSSSSSSSSSHHHHHHHH
PFFT!
THIS ISN'T WATER. IT'S--
GASOLINE.
WAIT. WHAT WAS THE QUESTION?
WHAT WAS THE QUESTION?

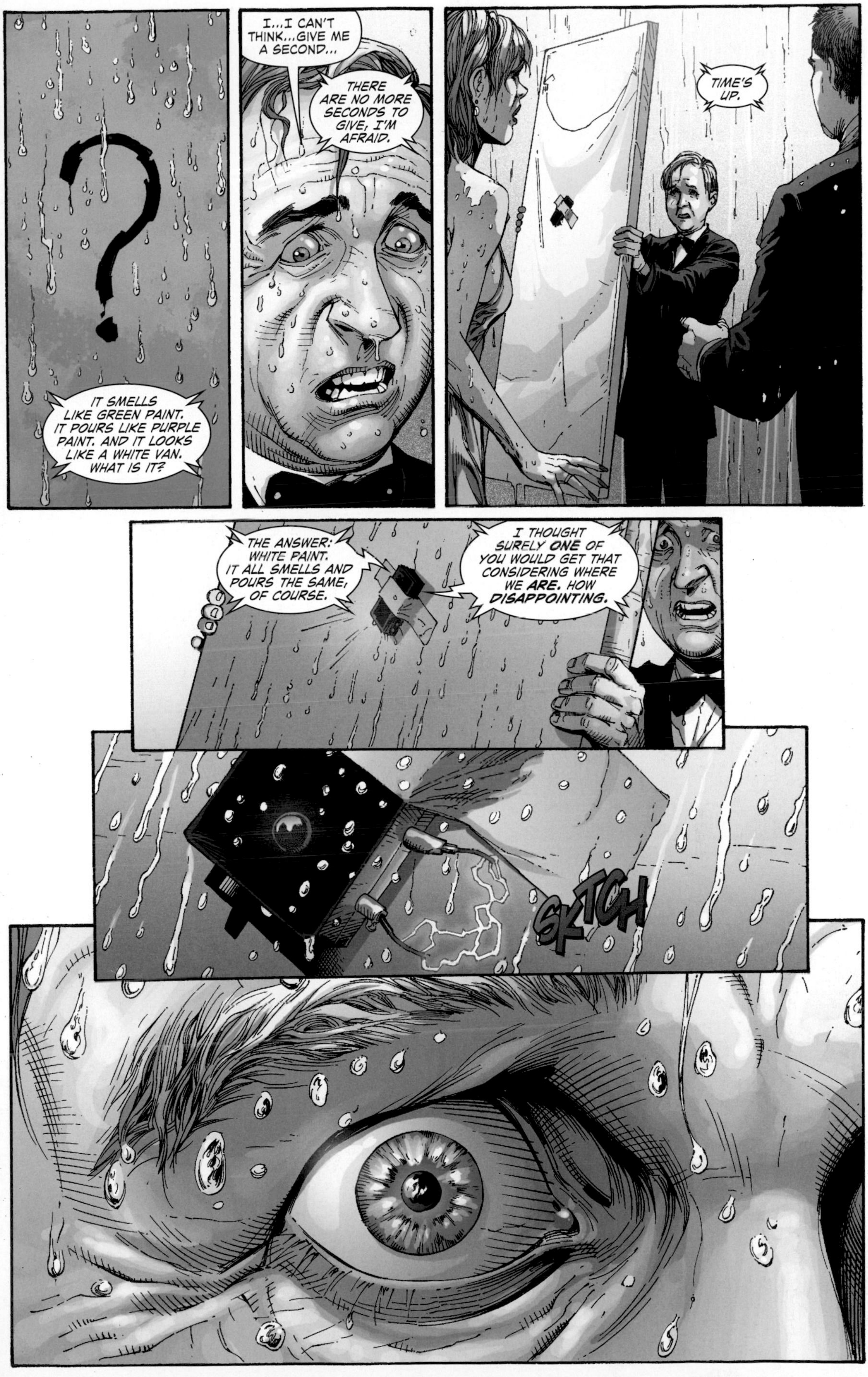
IT SMELLS LIKE GREEN PAINT. IT POURS LIKE PURPLE PAINT. AND IT LOOKS LIKE A WHITE VAN. WHAT IS IT?
I...I CAN'T THINK...GIVE ME A SECOND...
THERE ARE NO MORE SECONDS TO GIVE, I'M AFRAID.
TIME'S UP.
THE ANSWER: WHITE PAINT. IT ALL SMELLS AND POURS THE SAME, OF COURSE.
I THOUGHT SURELY **ONE** OF YOU WOULD GET THAT CONSIDERING WHERE WE **ARE**. HOW **DISAPPOINTING**.
SKTCH

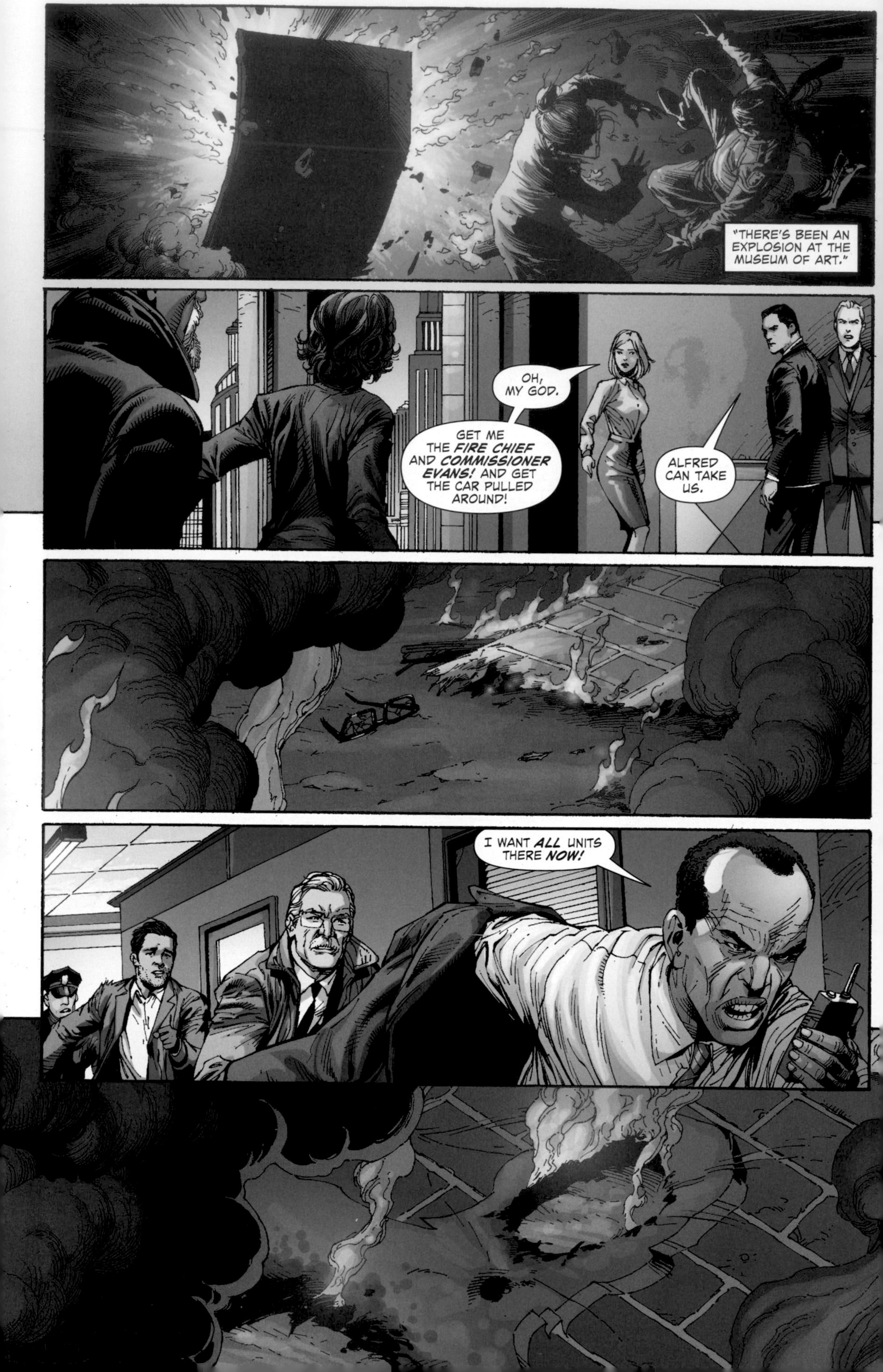
"THERE'S BEEN AN EXPLOSION AT THE MUSEUM OF ART."
OH, MY GOD.
GET ME THE FIRE CHIEF AND COMMISSIONER EVANS! AND GET THE CAR PULLED AROUND!
ALFRED CAN TAKE US.
I WANT ALL UNITS THERE NOW!

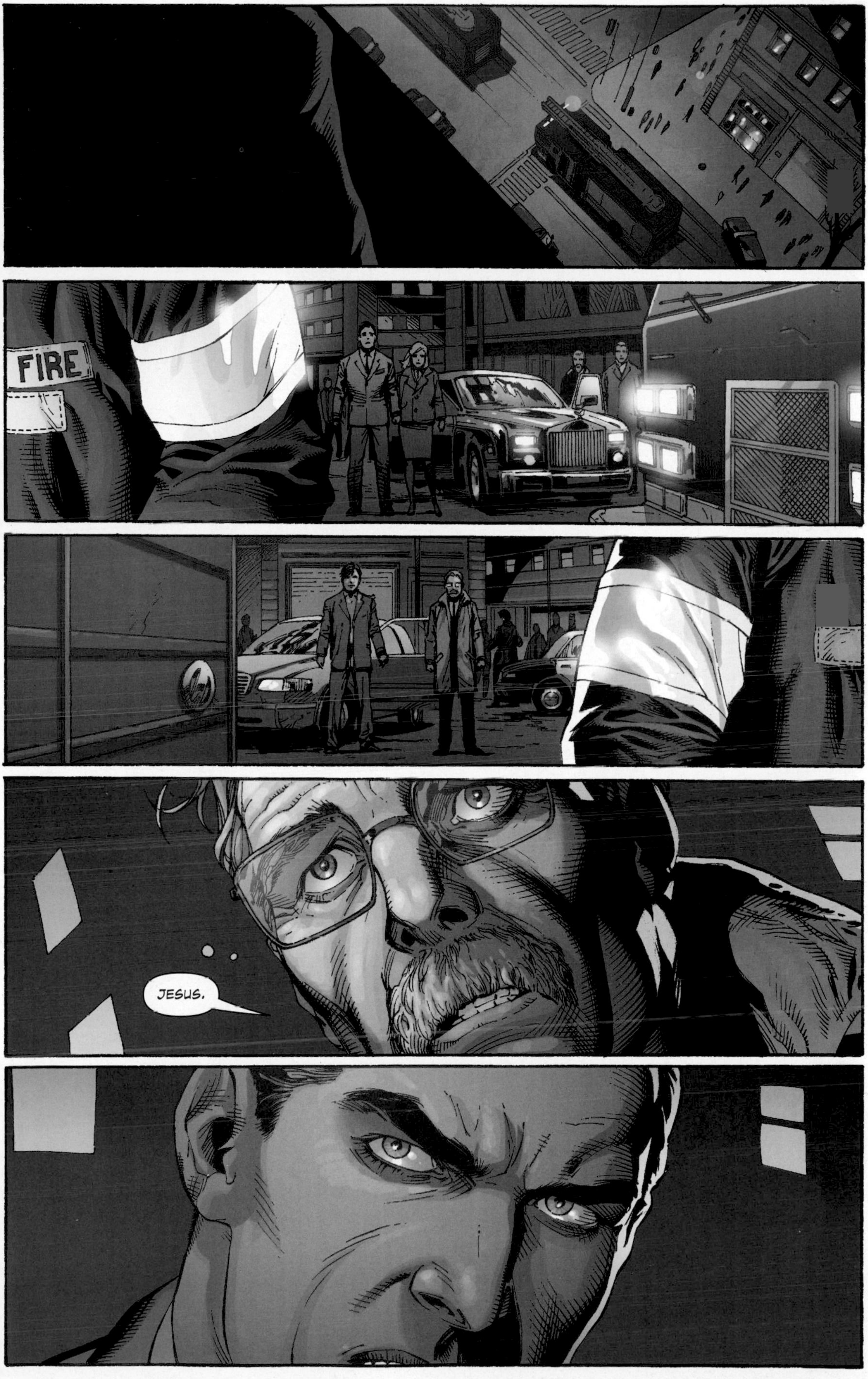
FIRE
JESUS.

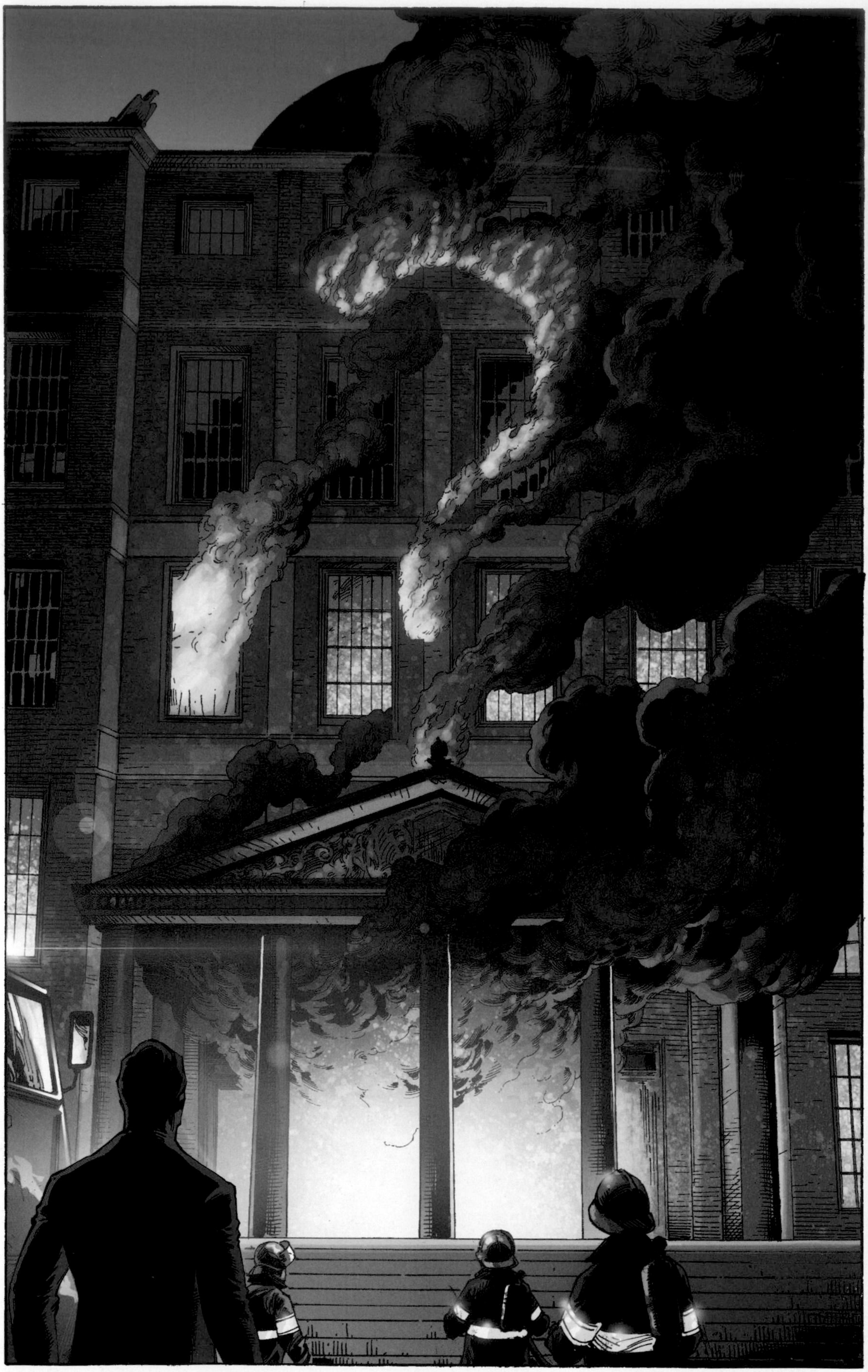

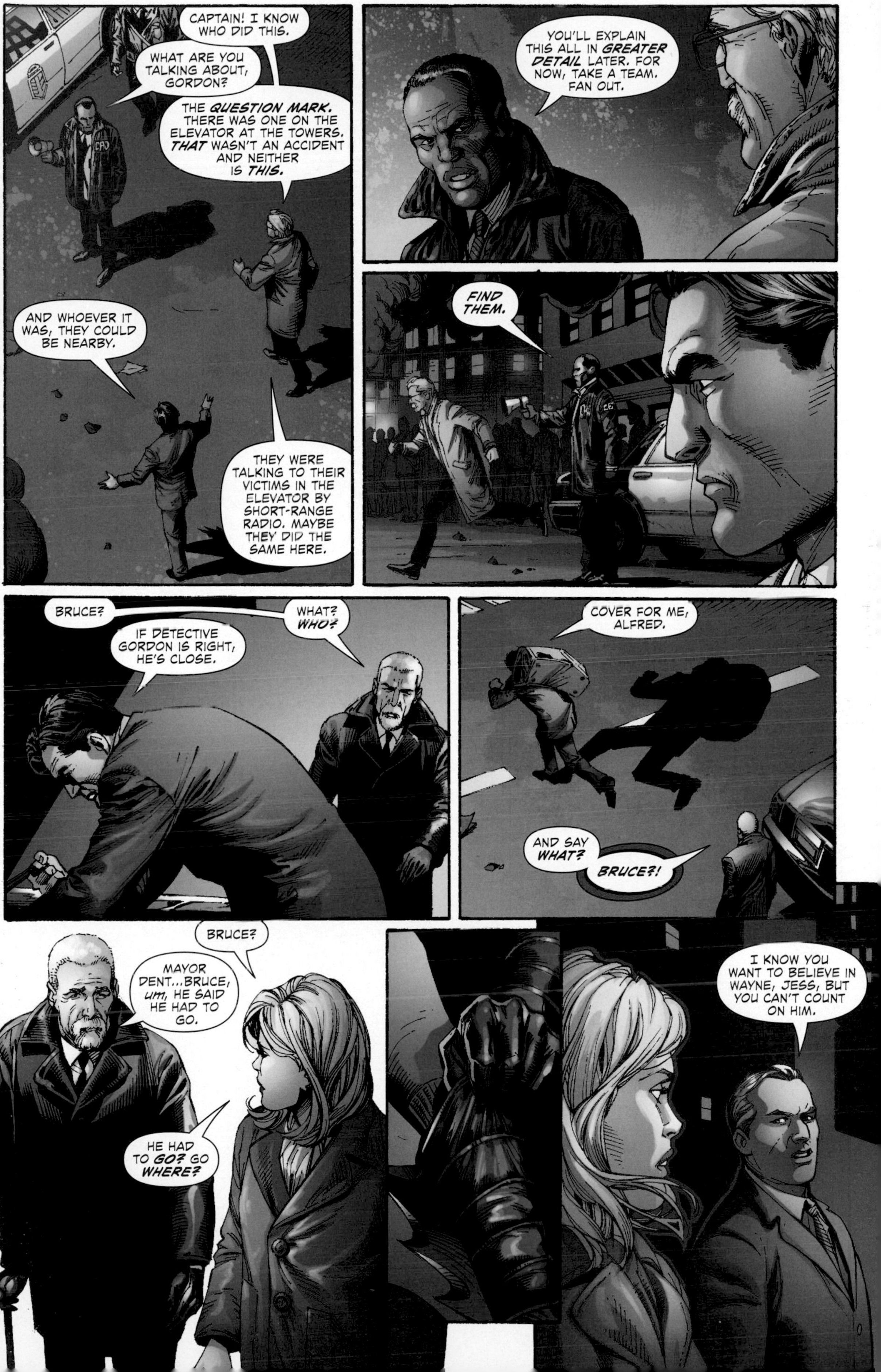

CAPTAIN! I KNOW WHO DID THIS.
WHAT ARE YOU TALKING ABOUT, GORDON?
THE QUESTION MARK. THERE WAS ONE ON THE ELEVATOR AT THE TOWERS. THAT WASN'T AN ACCIDENT AND NEITHER IS THIS.
AND WHOEVER IT WAS, THEY COULD BE NEARBY.
THEY WERE TALKING TO THEIR VICTIMS IN THE ELEVATOR BY SHORT-RANGE RADIO. MAYBE THEY'D DID THE SAME HERE.
YOU'LL EXPLAIN THIS ALL IN GREATER DETAIL LATER. FOR NOW, TAKE A TEAM. FAN OUT.
FIND THEM.
BRUCE?
WHAT? WHO?
IF DETECTIVE GORDON IS RIGHT, HE'S CLOSE.
COVER FOR ME, ALFRED.
AND SAY WHAT?
BRUCE?!
BRUCE?
MAYOR DENT...BRUCE, UM, HE SAID HE HAD TO GO.
HE HAD TO GO? GO WHERE?
I KNOW YOU WANT TO BELIEVE IN WAYNE, JESS, BUT YOU CAN'T COUNT ON HIM.

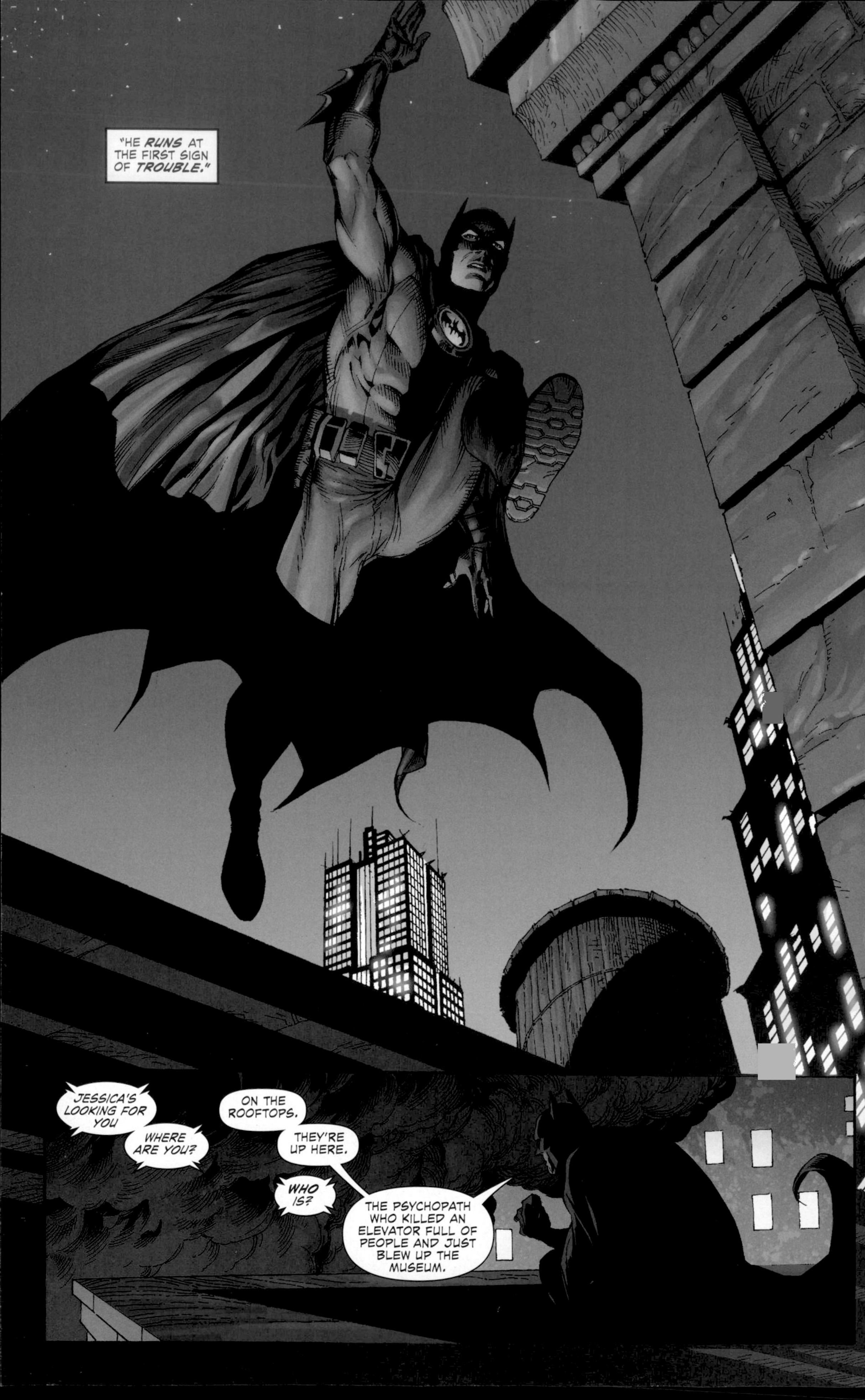
"HE RUNS AT THE FIRST SIGN OF TROUBLE."
JESSICA'S LOOKING FOR YOU
WHERE ARE YOU?
ON THE ROOFTOPS.
THEY'RE UP HERE.
WHO IS?
THE PSYCHOPATH WHO KILLED AN ELEVATOR FULL OF PEOPLE AND JUST BLEW UP THE MUSEUM.

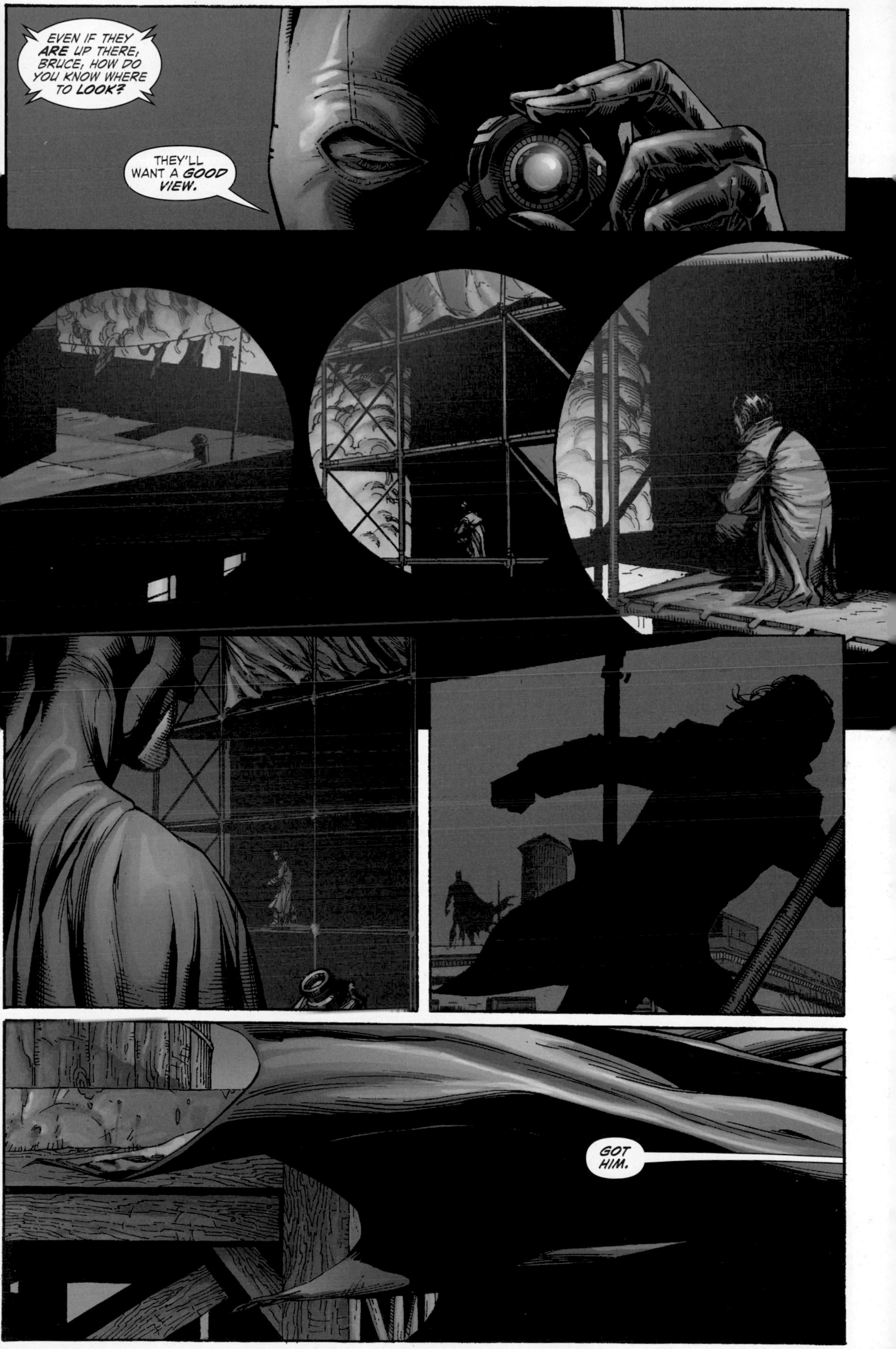
EVEN IF THEY ARE UP THERE, BRUCE, HOW DO YOU KNOW WHERE TO LOOK?
THEY'LL WANT A GOOD VIEW.
GOT HIM.

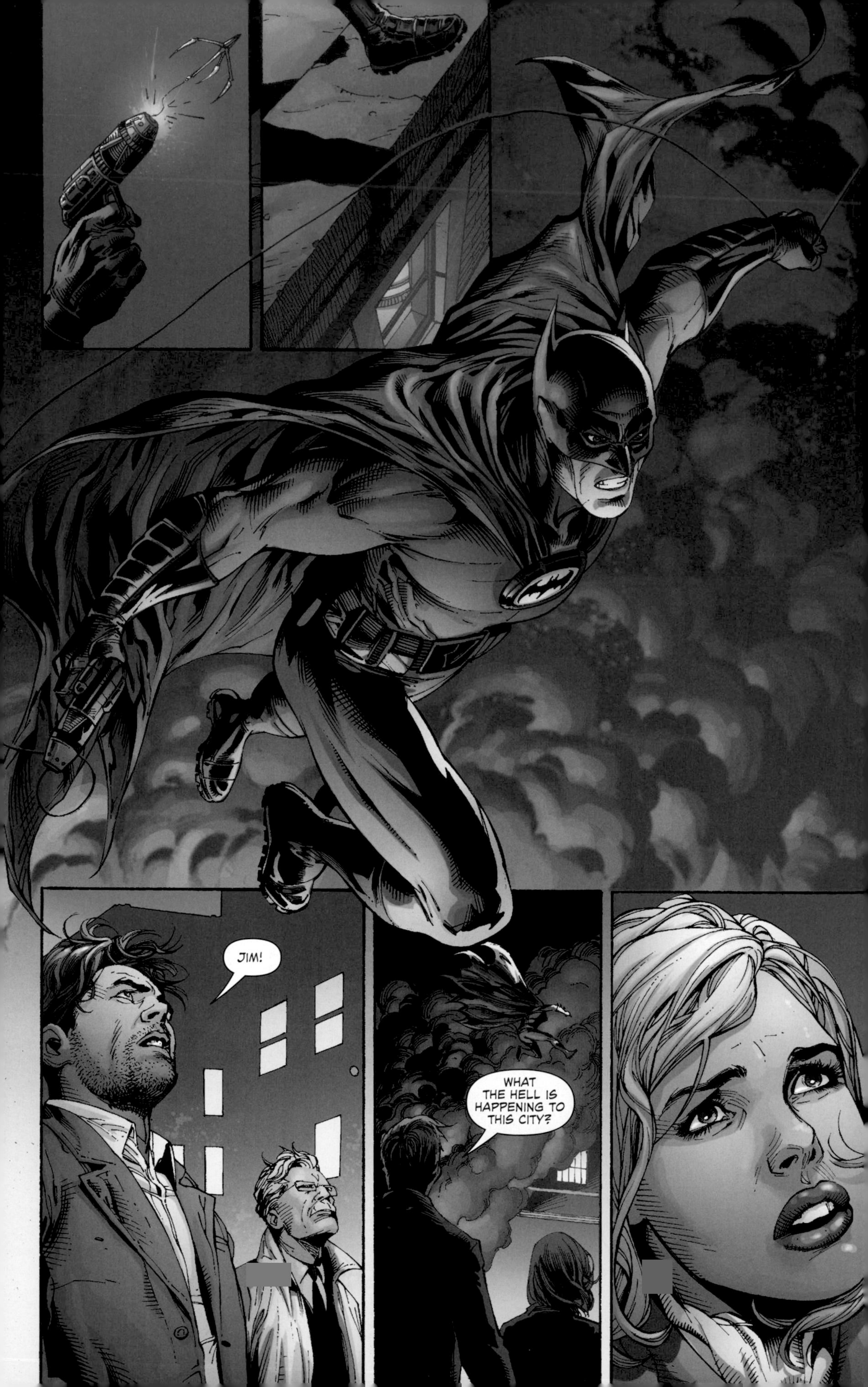
JIM!
WHAT THE HELL IS HAPPENING TO THIS CITY?

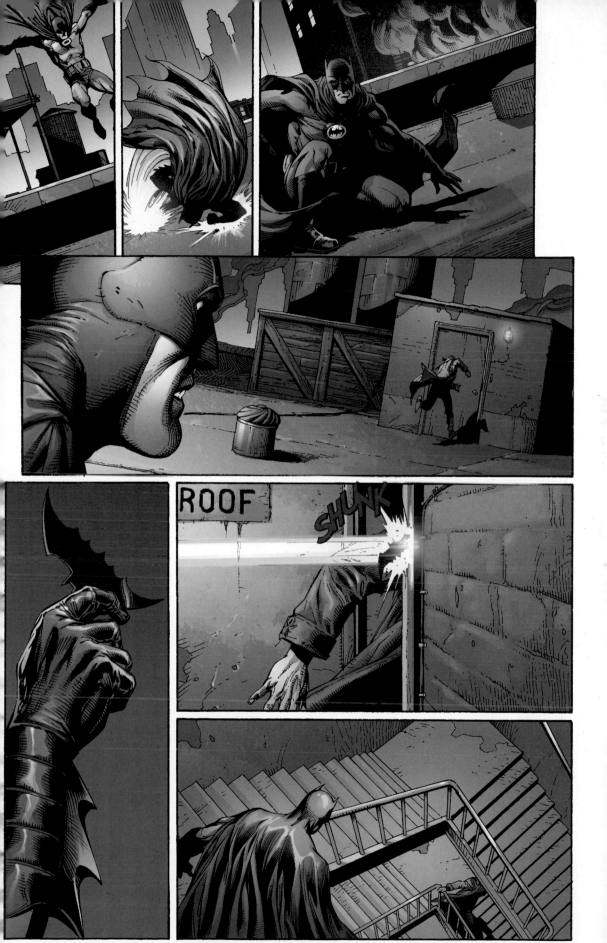

ROOF

SHUNK

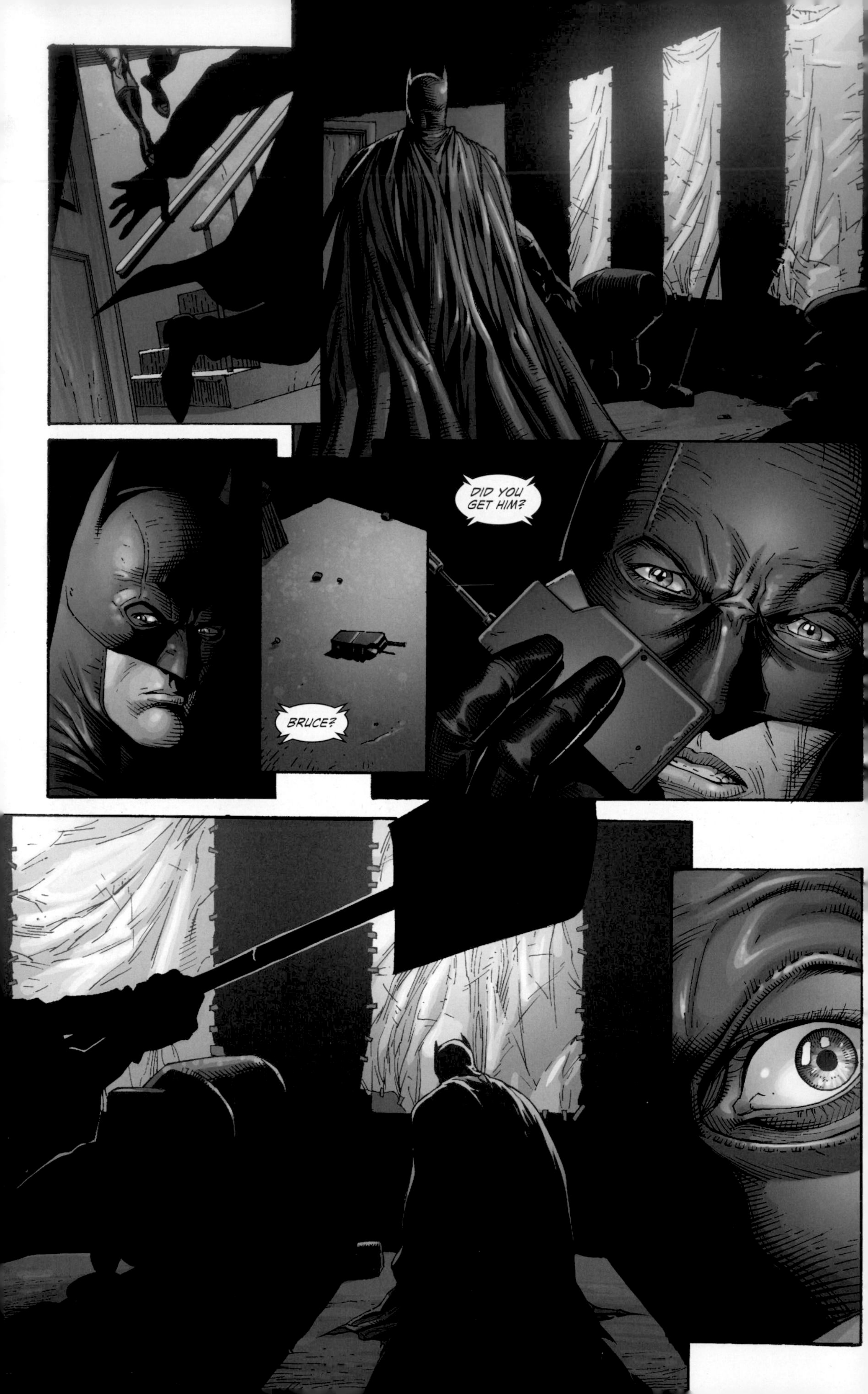
DID YOU GET HIM?
BRUCE?

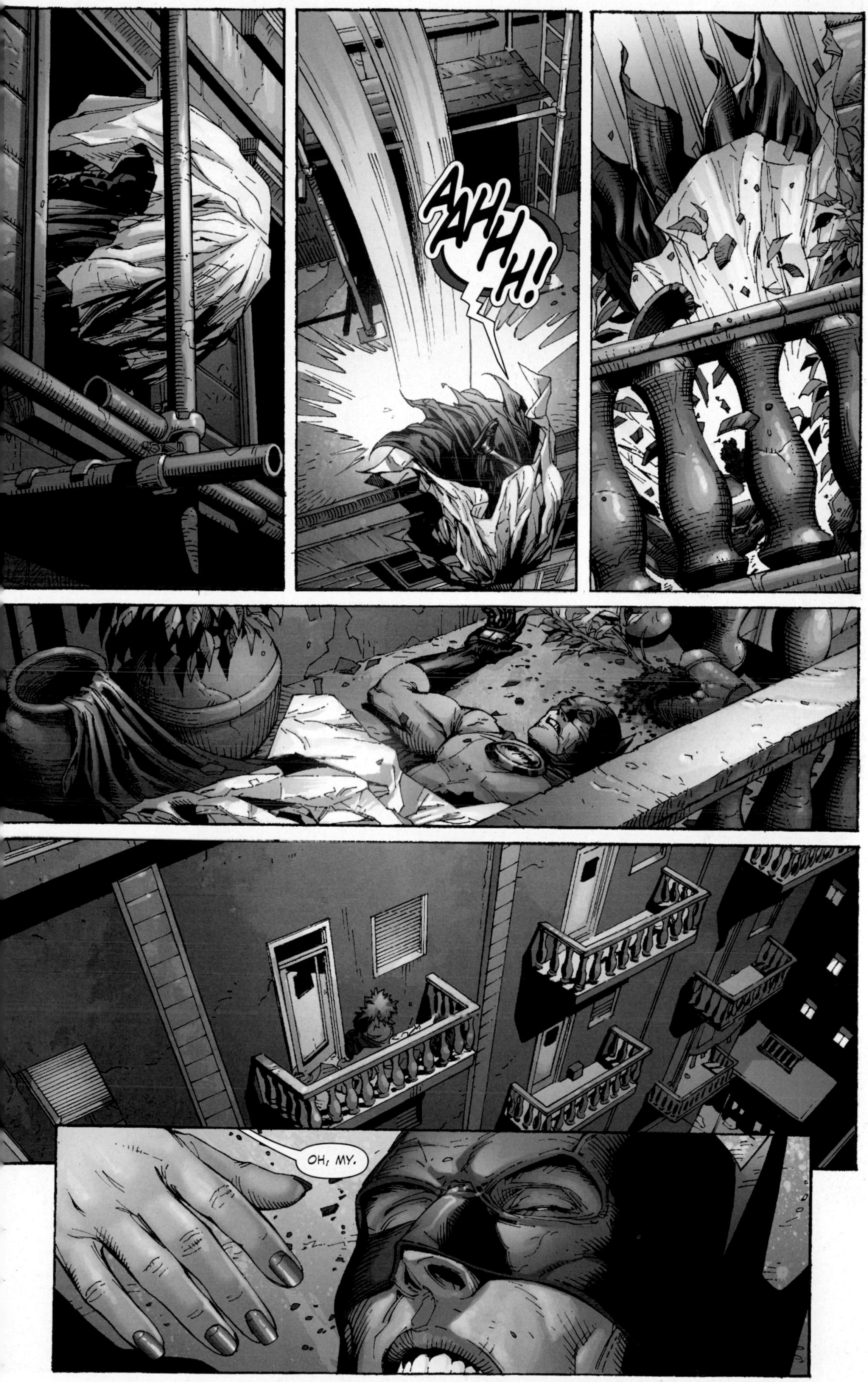
AAHHH!
OH, MY.

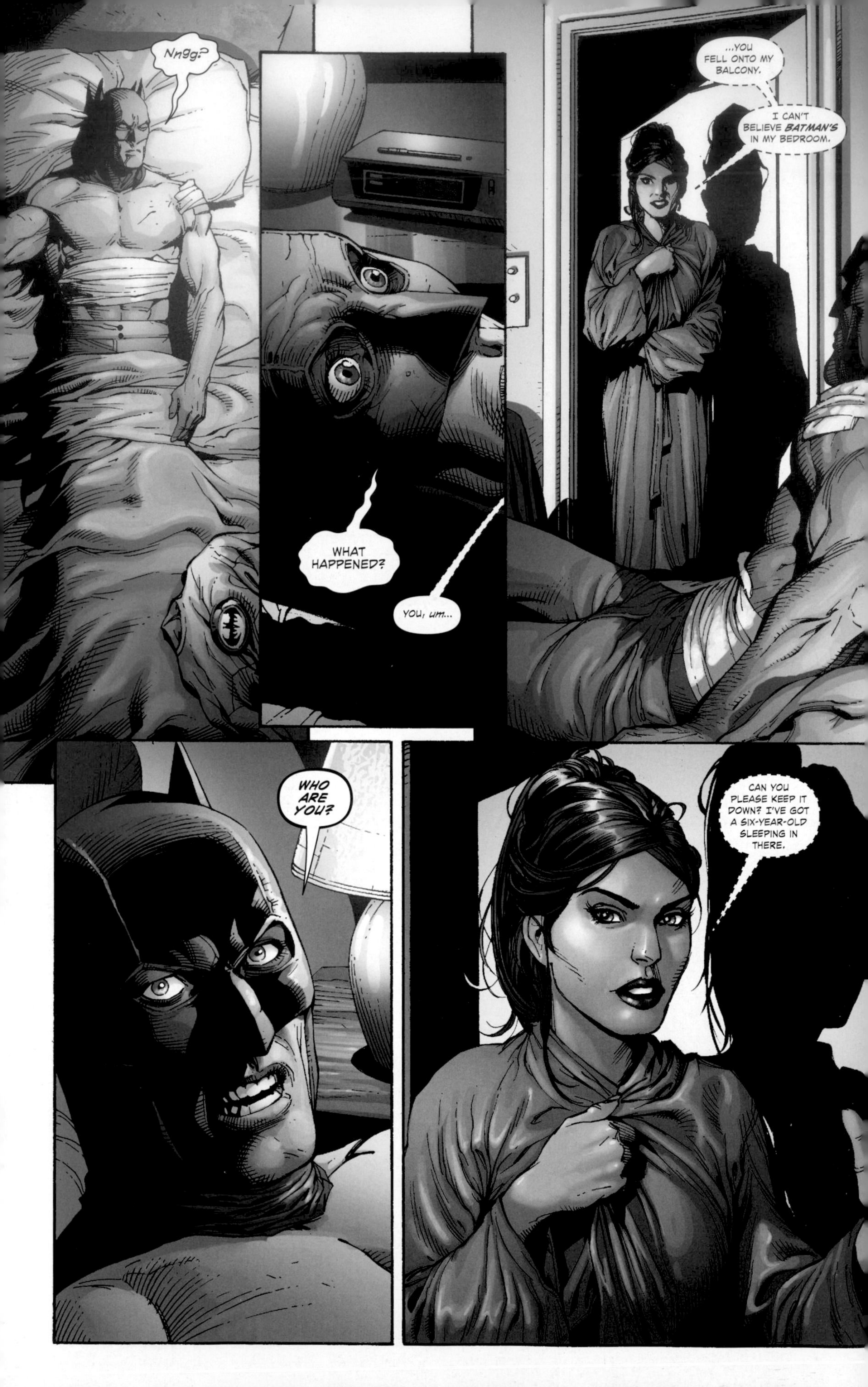
Nngg?
WHAT HAPPENED?
YOU, um...
...YOU FELL ONTO MY BALCONY.
I CAN'T BELIEVE BATMAN'S IN MY BEDROOM.
WHO ARE YOU?
CAN YOU PLEASE KEEP IT DOWN? I'VE GOT A SIX-YEAR-OLD SLEEPING IN THERE.

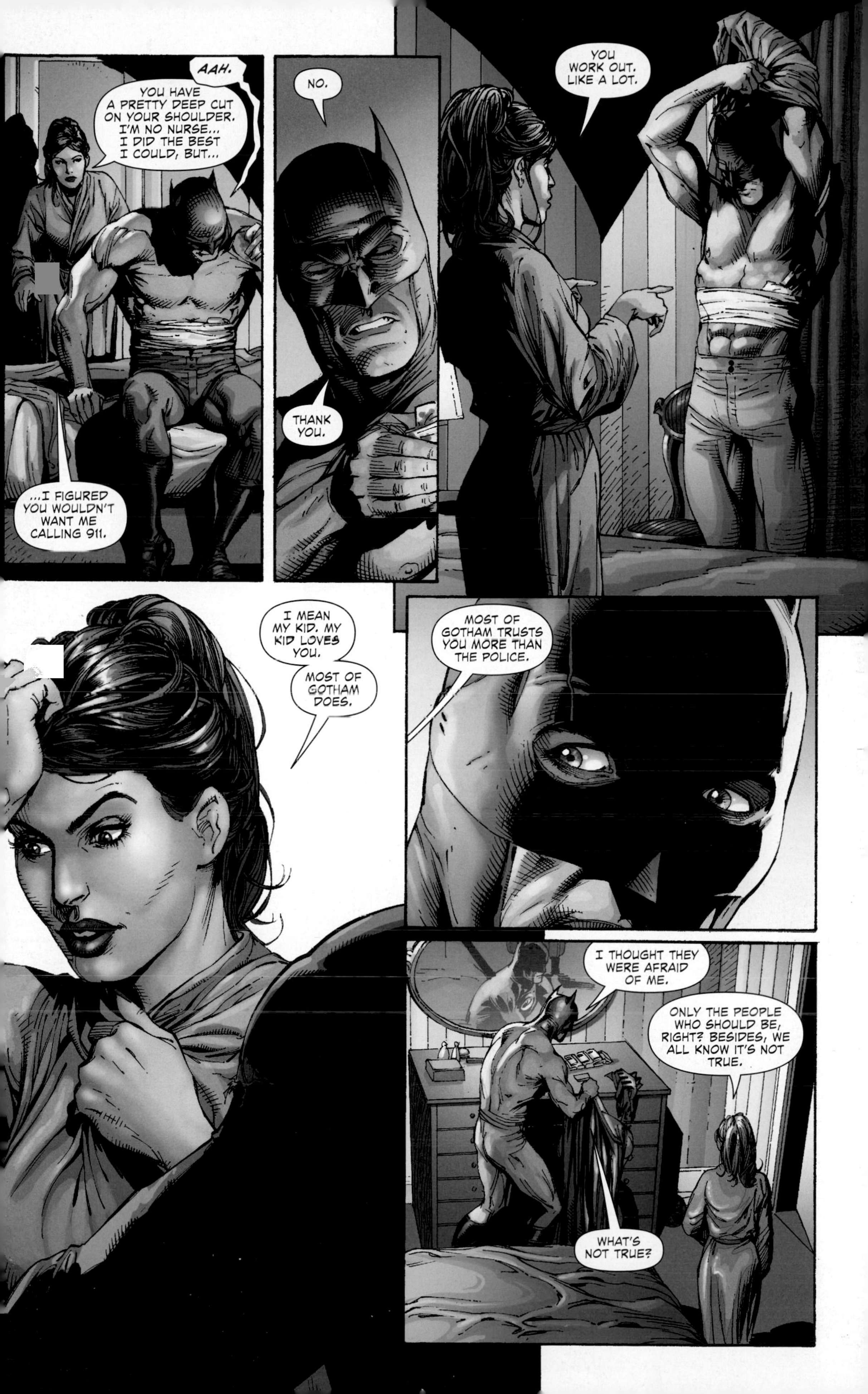
YOU HAVE A PRETTY DEEP CUT ON YOUR SHOULDER. I'M NO NURSE... I DID THE BEST I COULD, BUT...
AAH.
...I FIGURED YOU WOULDN'T WANT ME CALLING 911.
NO.
THANK YOU.
YOU WORK OUT. LIKE A LOT.
I MEAN MY KID. MY KID LOVES YOU.
MOST OF GOTHAM DOES.
MOST OF GOTHAM TRUSTS YOU MORE THAN THE POLICE.
I THOUGHT THEY WERE AFRAID OF ME.
ONLY THE PEOPLE WHO SHOULD BE, RIGHT? BESIDES, WE ALL KNOW IT'S NOT TRUE.
WHAT'S NOT TRUE?

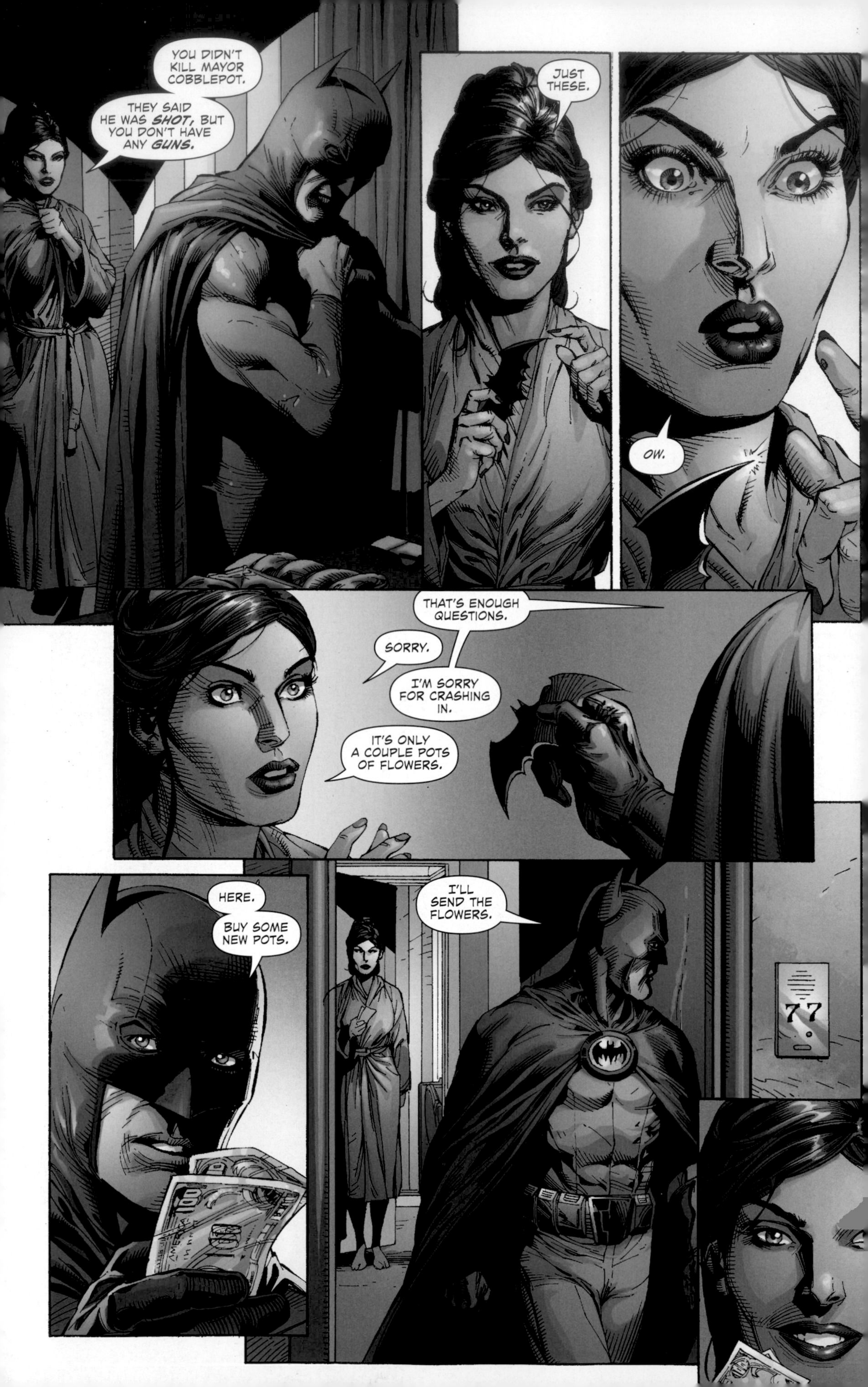
YOU DIDN'T KILL MAYOR COBBLEPOT.
THEY SAID HE WAS SHOT, BUT YOU DON'T HAVE ANY GUNS.
JUST THESE.
OW.
THAT'S ENOUGH QUESTIONS.
SORRY.
I'M SORRY FOR CRASHING IN.
IT'S ONLY A COUPLE POTS OF FLOWERS.
HERE.
BUY SOME NEW POTS.
I'LL SEND THE FLOWERS.
77

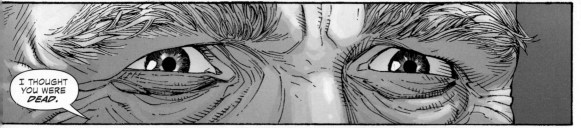

I THOUGHT YOU WERE *DEAD.*

WHO STITCHED YOU UP ANYWAY? DOCTOR FRANKENSTEIN?

SHE DID THE BEST SHE COULD.

SHE?

A WOMAN. I CRASHED INTO HER GARDEN AFTER THE BOMBER PUSHED ME OFF THE BUILDING.

BUT I DID GET SOMETHING FOR MY TROUBLE.

A *SHORT-RANGE RADIO.*

THAT DOESN'T SEEM LIKE A GREAT CONSOLATION PRIZE.

I'M HOPING DETECTIVE GORDON CAN PULL SOME FINGERPRINTS OR TRACE THE SERIAL NUMBER.

DETECTIVE GORDON? YOU'RE GOING TO HIM AGAIN?

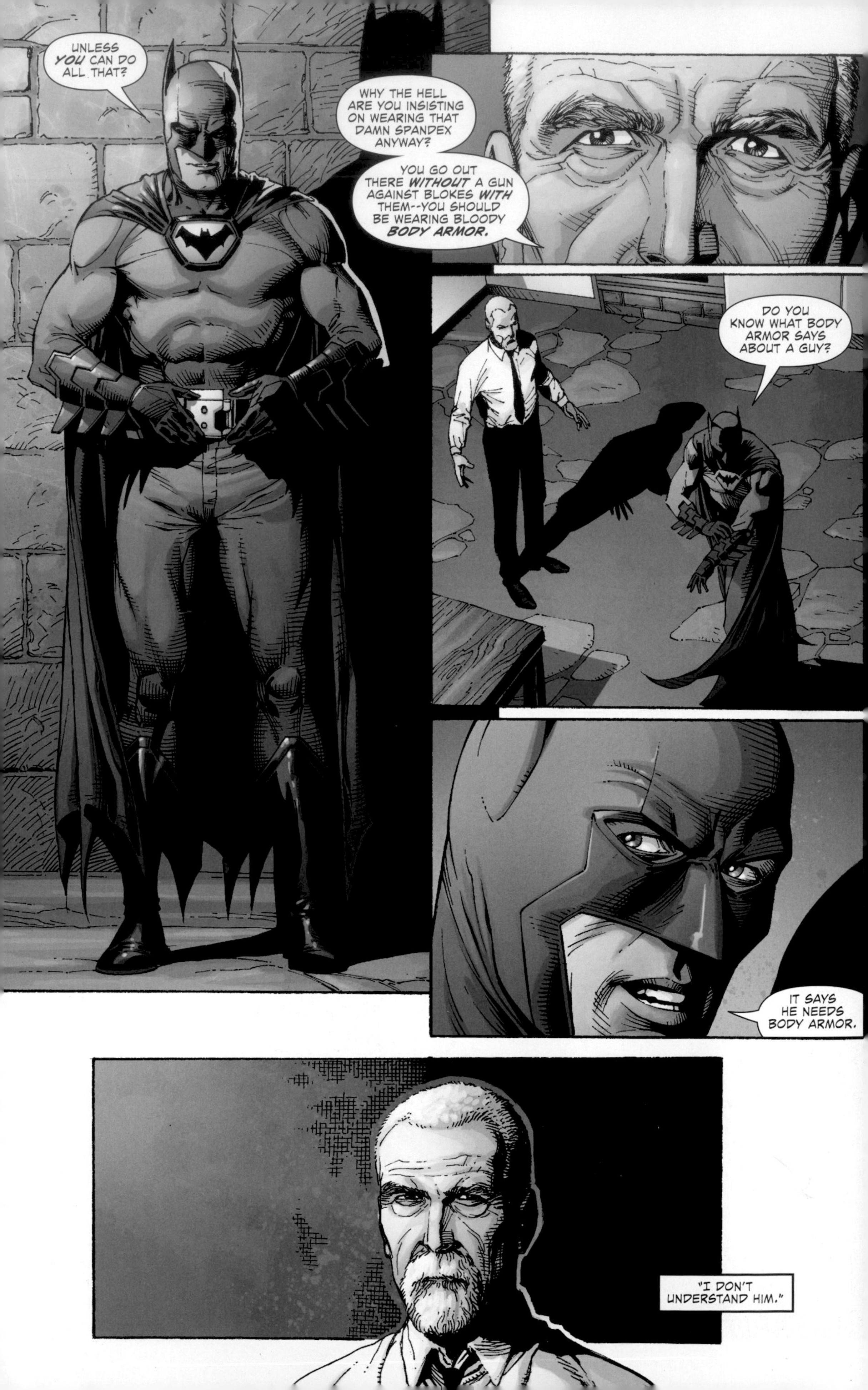
UNLESS YOU CAN DO ALL THAT?
WHY THE HELL ARE YOU INSISTING ON WEARING THAT DAMN SPANDEX ANYWAY?
YOU GO OUT THERE WITHOUT A GUN AGAINST BLOKES WITH THEM--YOU SHOULD BE WEARING BLOODY BODY ARMOR.
DO YOU KNOW WHAT BODY ARMOR SAYS ABOUT A GUY?
IT SAYS HE NEEDS BODY ARMOR.
"I DON'T UNDERSTAND HIM."

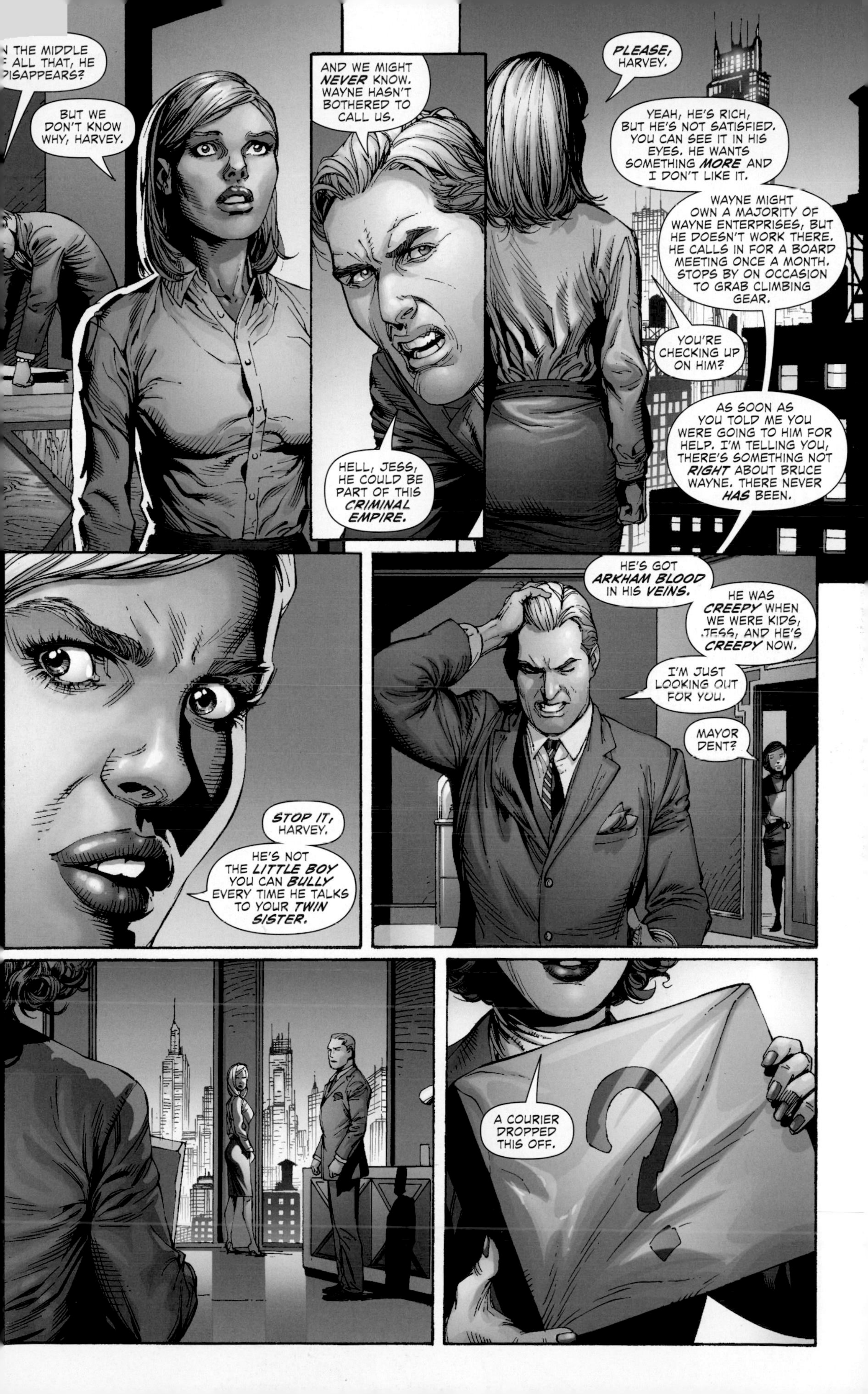
N THE MIDDLE F ALL THAT, HE DISAPPEARS?
BUT WE DON'T KNOW WHY, HARVEY.
AND WE MIGHT NEVER KNOW. WAYNE HASN'T BOTHERED TO CALL US.
HELL, JESS, HE COULD BE PART OF THIS CRIMINAL EMPIRE.
PLEASE, HARVEY.
YEAH, HE'S RICH, BUT HE'S NOT SATISFIED. YOU CAN SEE IT IN HIS EYES. HE WANTS SOMETHING MORE AND I DON'T LIKE IT.
WAYNE MIGHT OWN A MAJORITY OF WAYNE ENTERPRISES, BUT HE DOESN'T WORK THERE. HE CALLS IN FOR A BOARD MEETING ONCE A MONTH. STOPS BY ON OCCASION TO GRAB CLIMBING GEAR.
YOU'RE CHECKING UP ON HIM?
AS SOON AS YOU TOLD ME YOU WERE GOING TO HIM FOR HELP. I'M TELLING YOU, THERE'S SOMETHING NOT RIGHT ABOUT BRUCE WAYNE. THERE NEVER HAS BEEN.
STOP IT, HARVEY.
HE'S NOT THE LITTLE BOY YOU CAN BULLY EVERY TIME HE TALKS TO YOUR TWIN SISTER.
HE'S GOT ARKHAM BLOOD IN HIS VEINS.
HE WAS CREEPY WHEN WE WERE KIDS, JESS, AND HE'S CREEPY NOW.
I'M JUST LOOKING OUT FOR YOU.
MAYOR DENT?
A COURIER DROPPED THIS OFF.

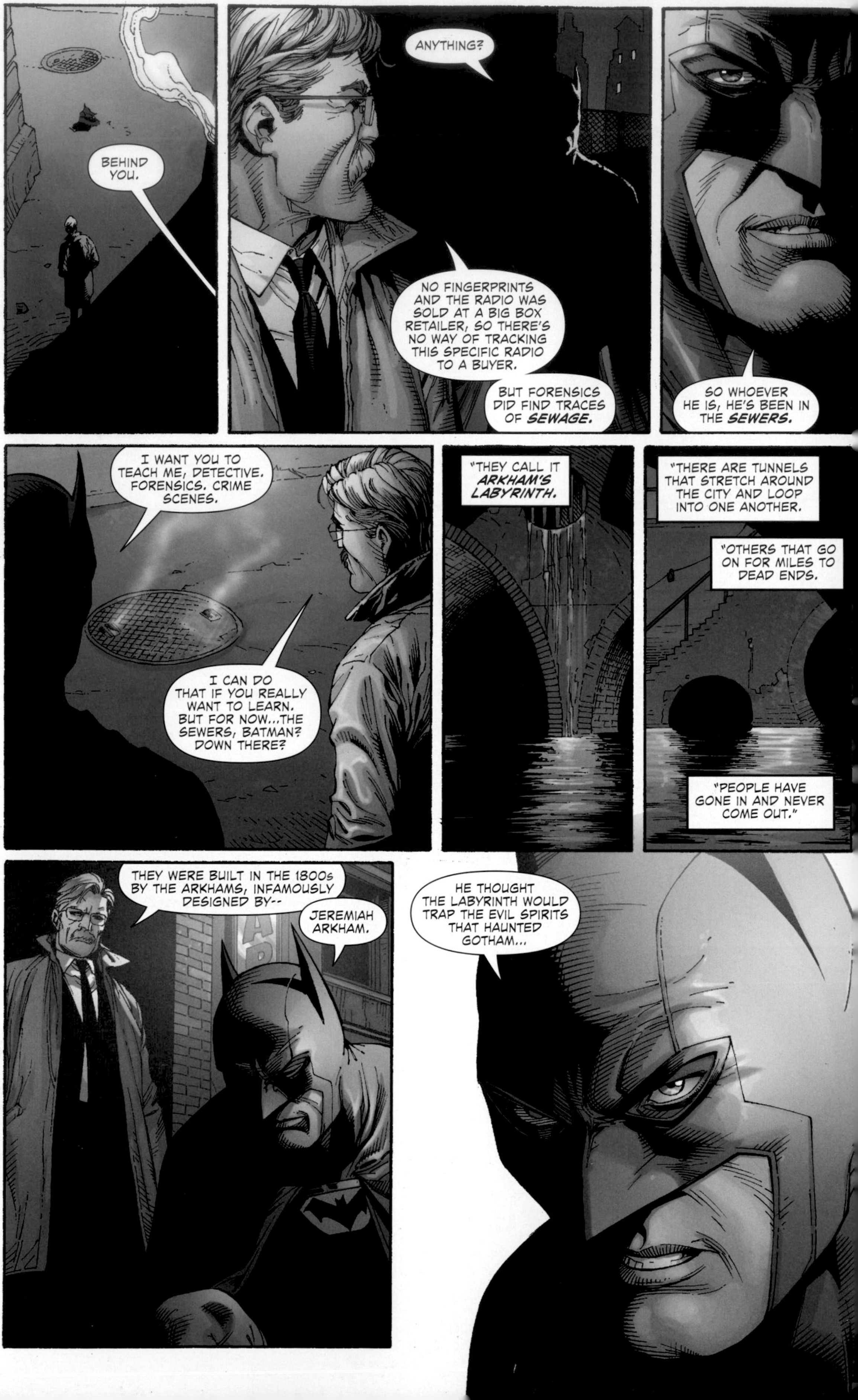
BEHIND YOU.
ANYTHING?
NO FINGERPRINTS AND THE RADIO WAS SOLD AT A BIG BOX RETAILER, SO THERE'S NO WAY OF TRACKING THIS SPECIFIC RADIO TO A BUYER.
BUT FORENSICS DID FIND TRACES OF *SEWAGE.*
SO WHOEVER HE IS, HE'S BEEN IN THE *SEWERS.*
I WANT YOU TO TEACH ME, DETECTIVE. FORENSICS. CRIME SCENES.
I CAN DO THAT IF YOU REALLY WANT TO LEARN. BUT FOR NOW...THE SEWERS, BATMAN? DOWN THERE?
"THEY CALL IT *ARKHAM'S LABYRINTH.*
"THERE ARE TUNNELS THAT STRETCH AROUND THE CITY AND LOOP INTO ONE ANOTHER.
"OTHERS THAT GO ON FOR MILES TO DEAD ENDS.
"PEOPLE HAVE GONE IN AND NEVER COME OUT."
THEY WERE BUILT IN THE 1800s BY THE ARKHAMS, INFAMOUSLY DESIGNED BY--
JEREMIAH ARKHAM.
HE THOUGHT THE LABYRINTH WOULD TRAP THE EVIL SPIRITS THAT HAUNTED GOTHAM...

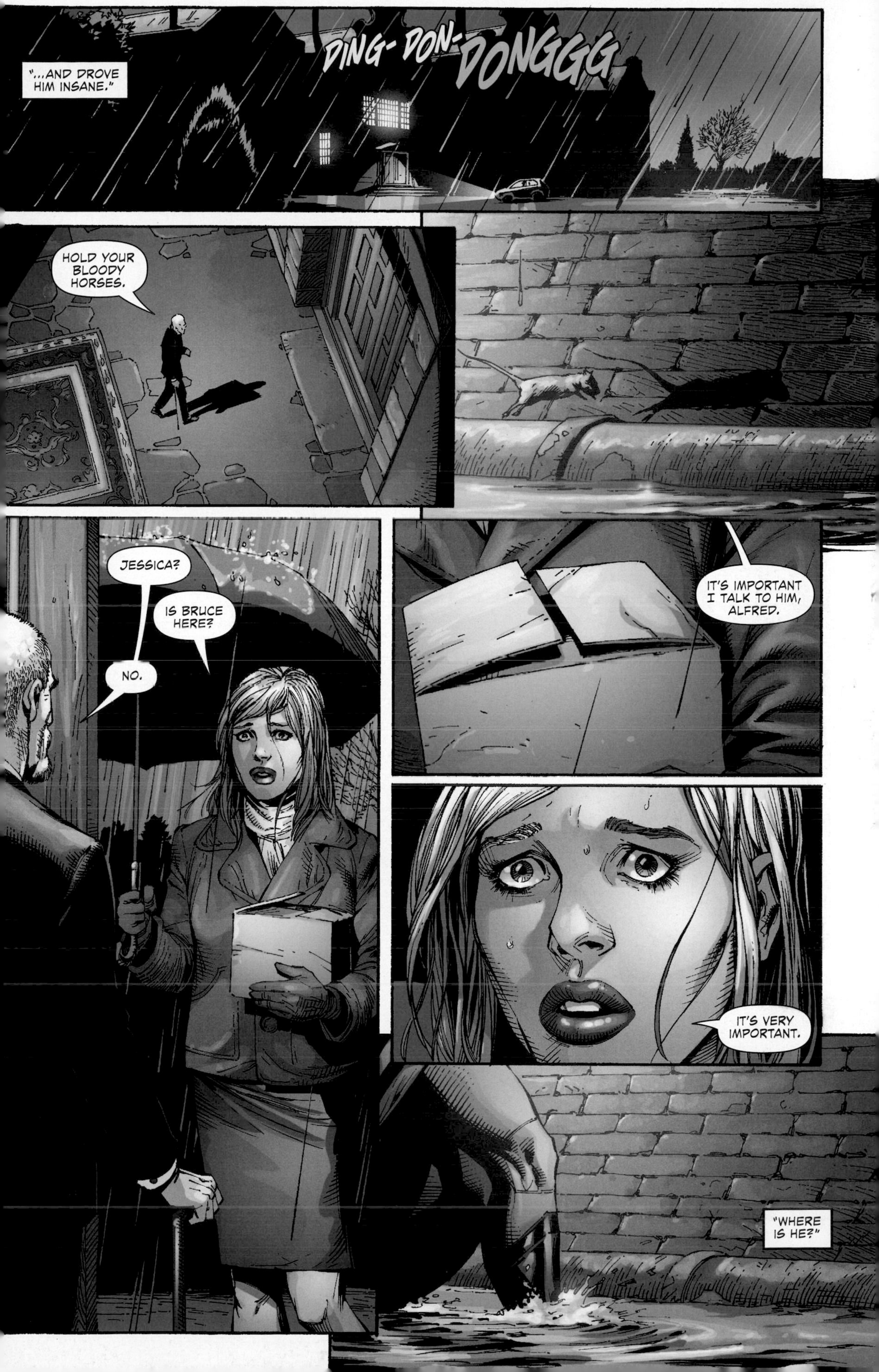
"...AND DROVE HIM INSANE."
DING- DON- DONGGG
HOLD YOUR BLOODY HORSES.
JESSICA?
IS BRUCE HERE?
NO.
IT'S IMPORTANT I TALK TO HIM, ALFRED.
IT'S VERY IMPORTANT.
"WHERE IS HE?"

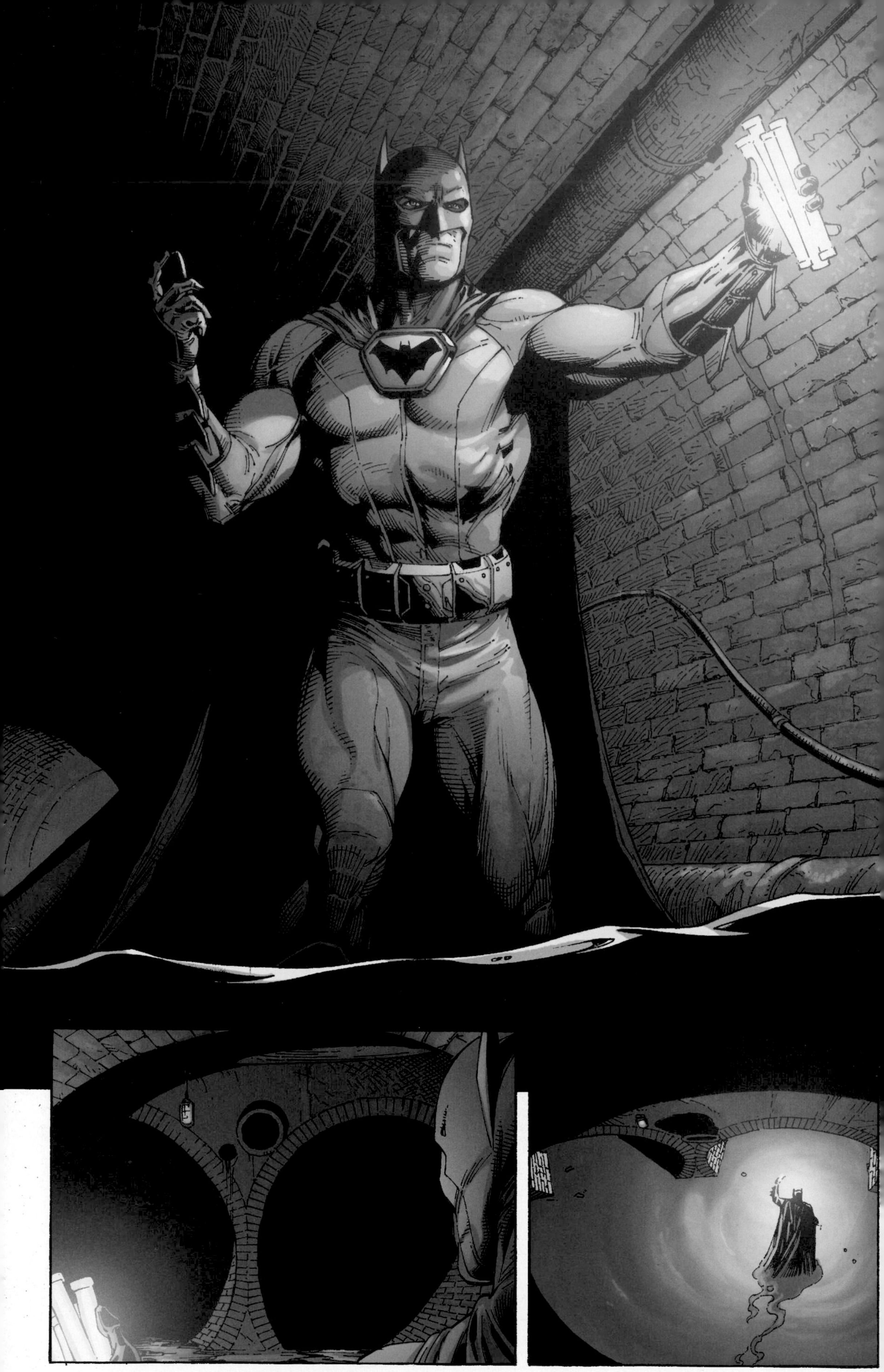

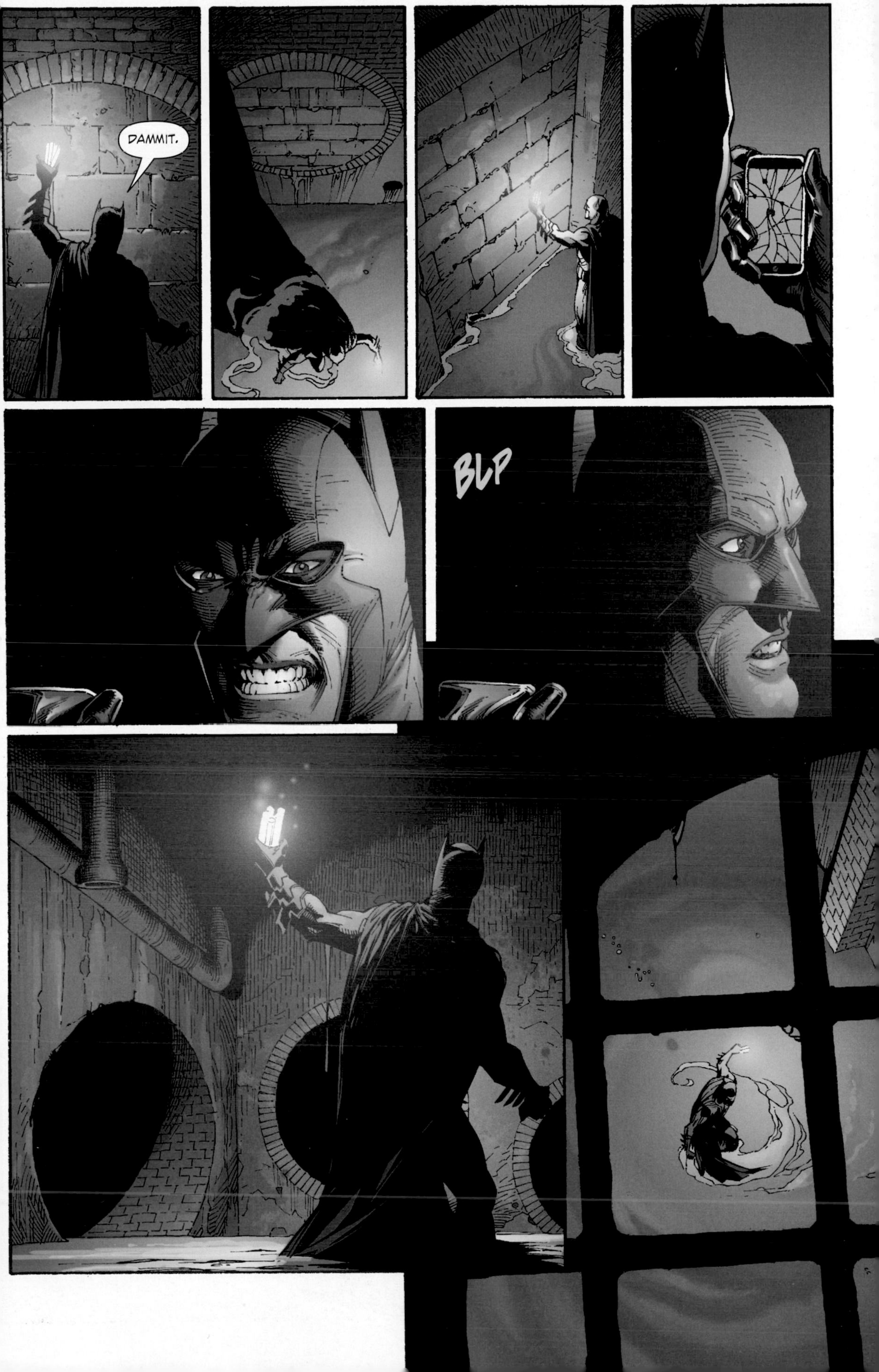
DAMMIT.
BLP

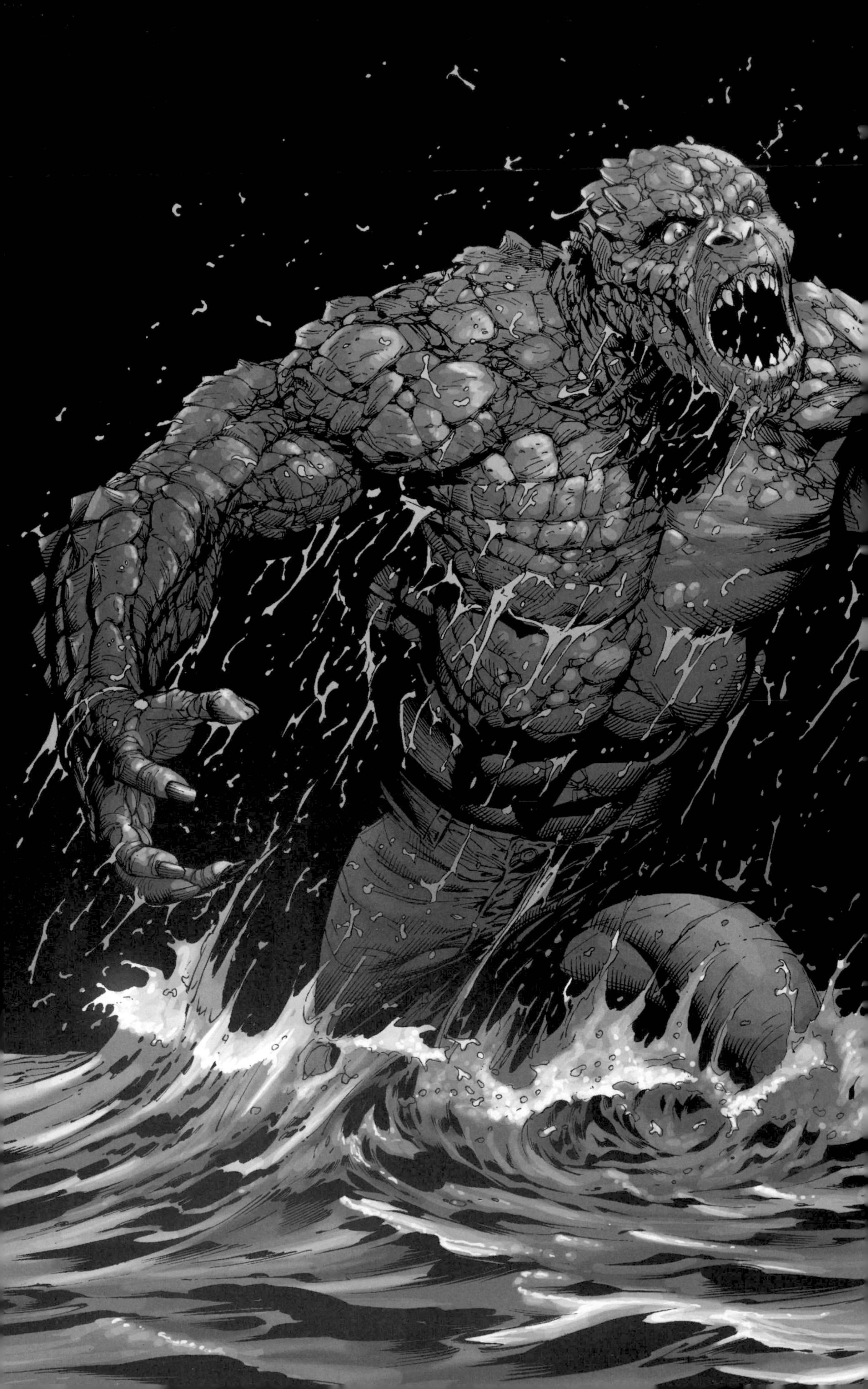

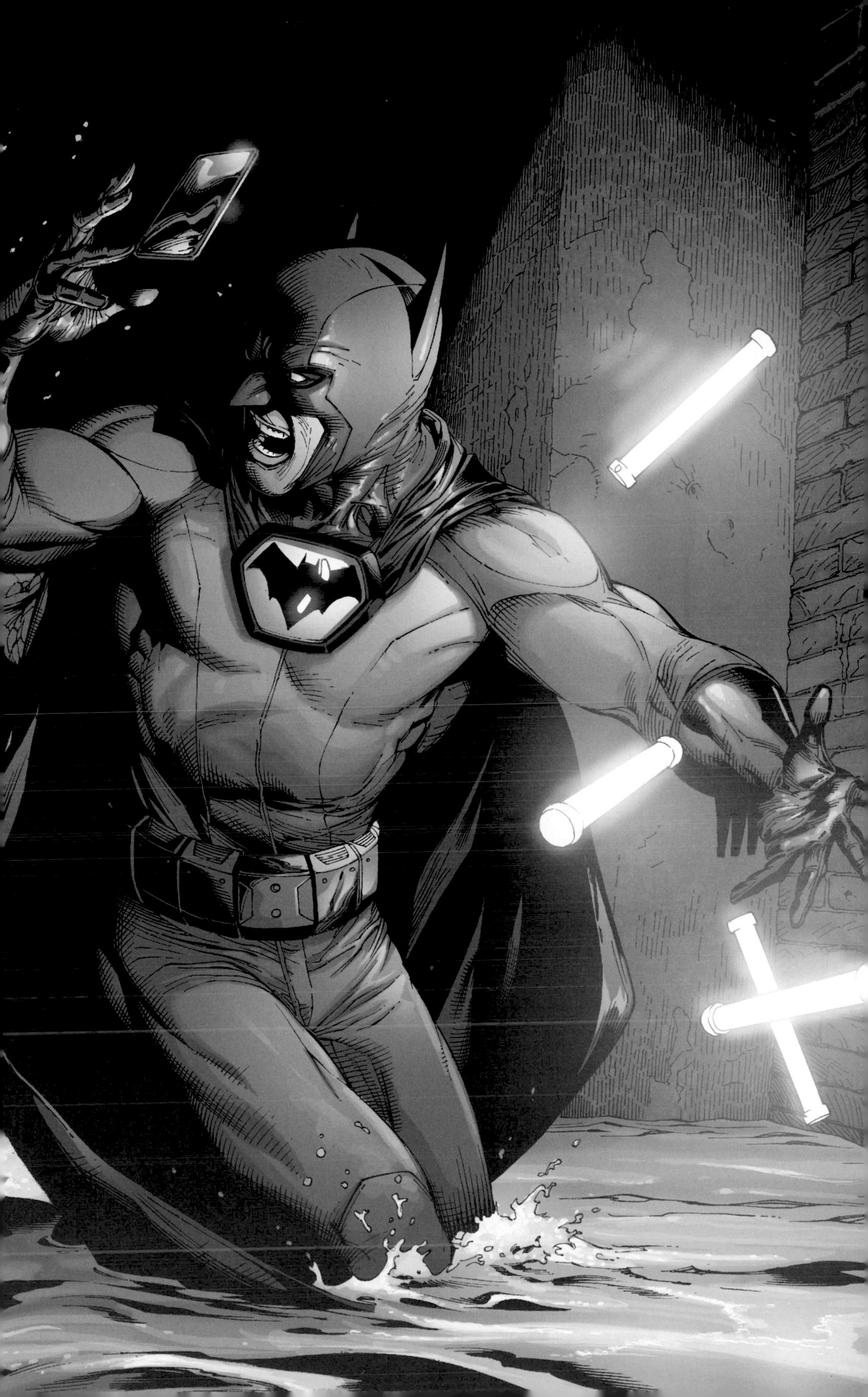

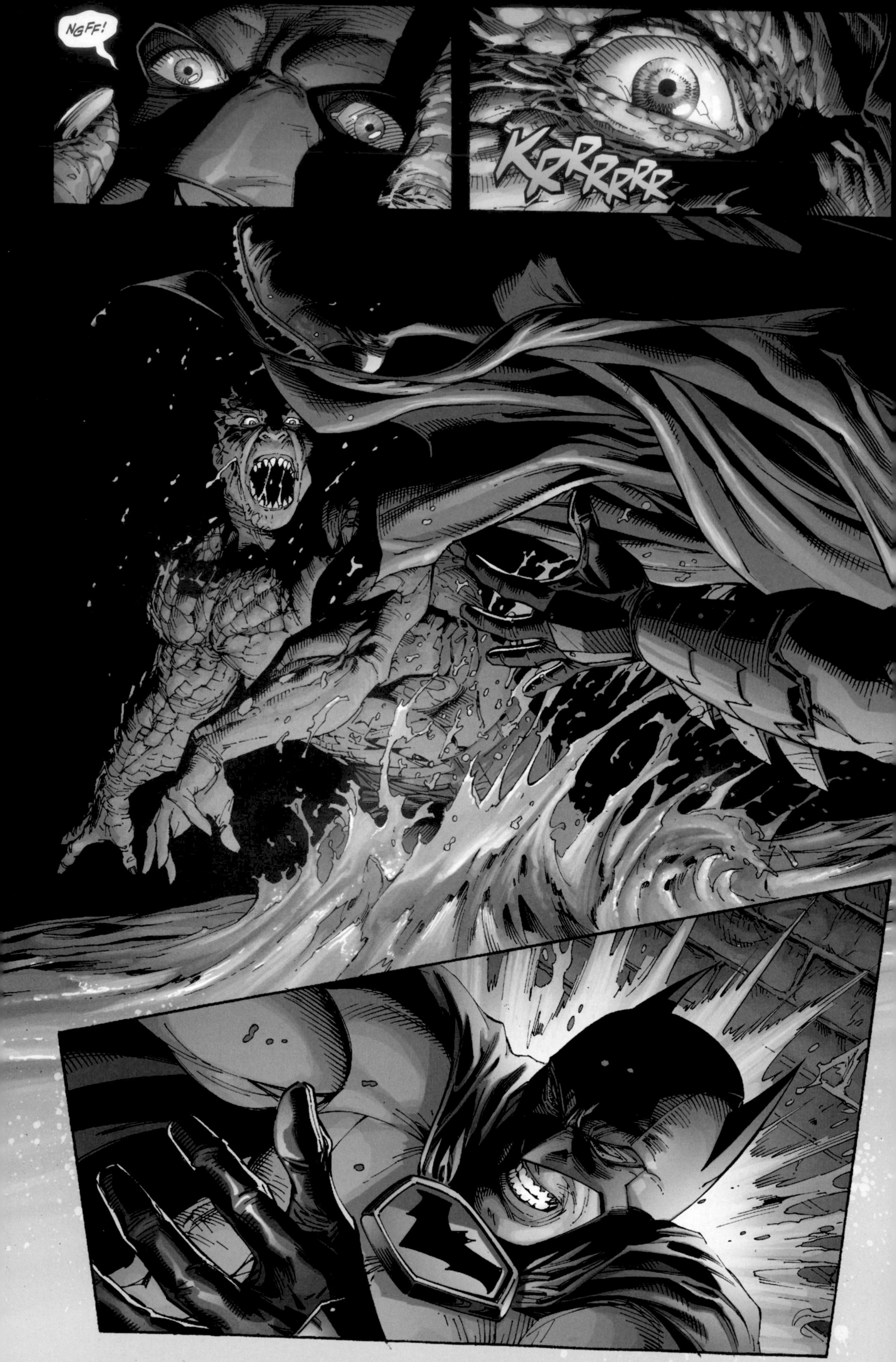
NGFF!
KRRRRRR

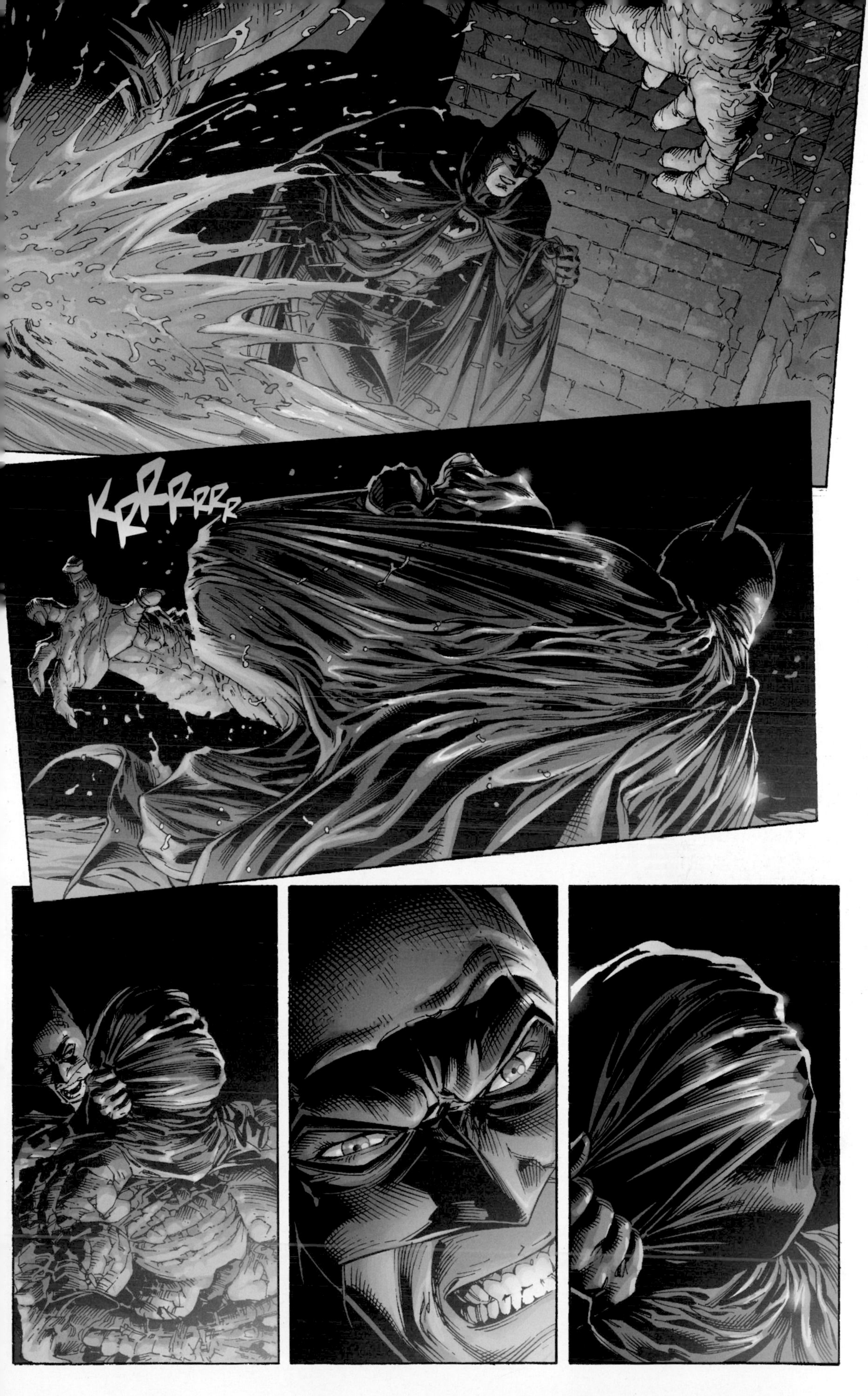
KRRRrrr

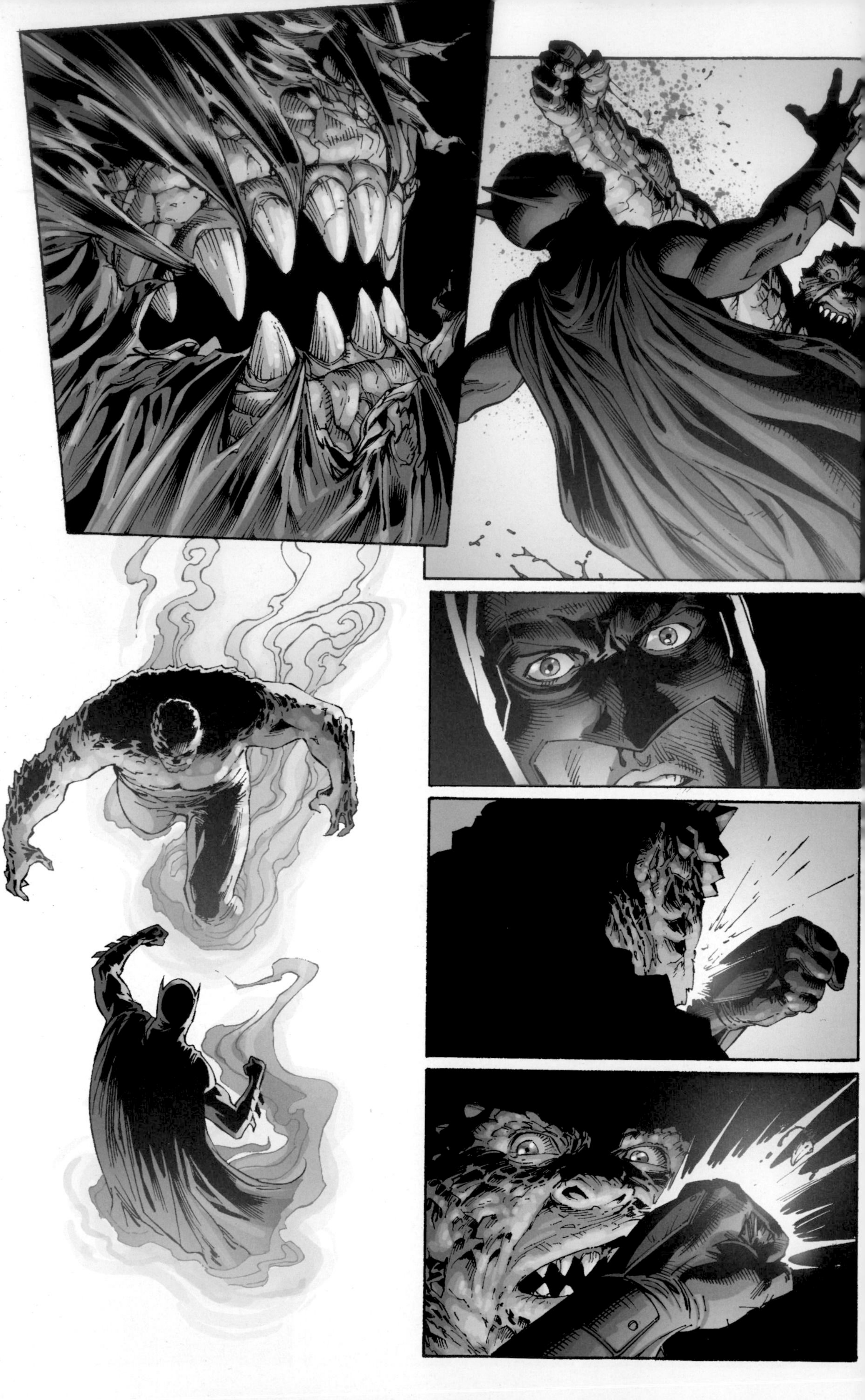

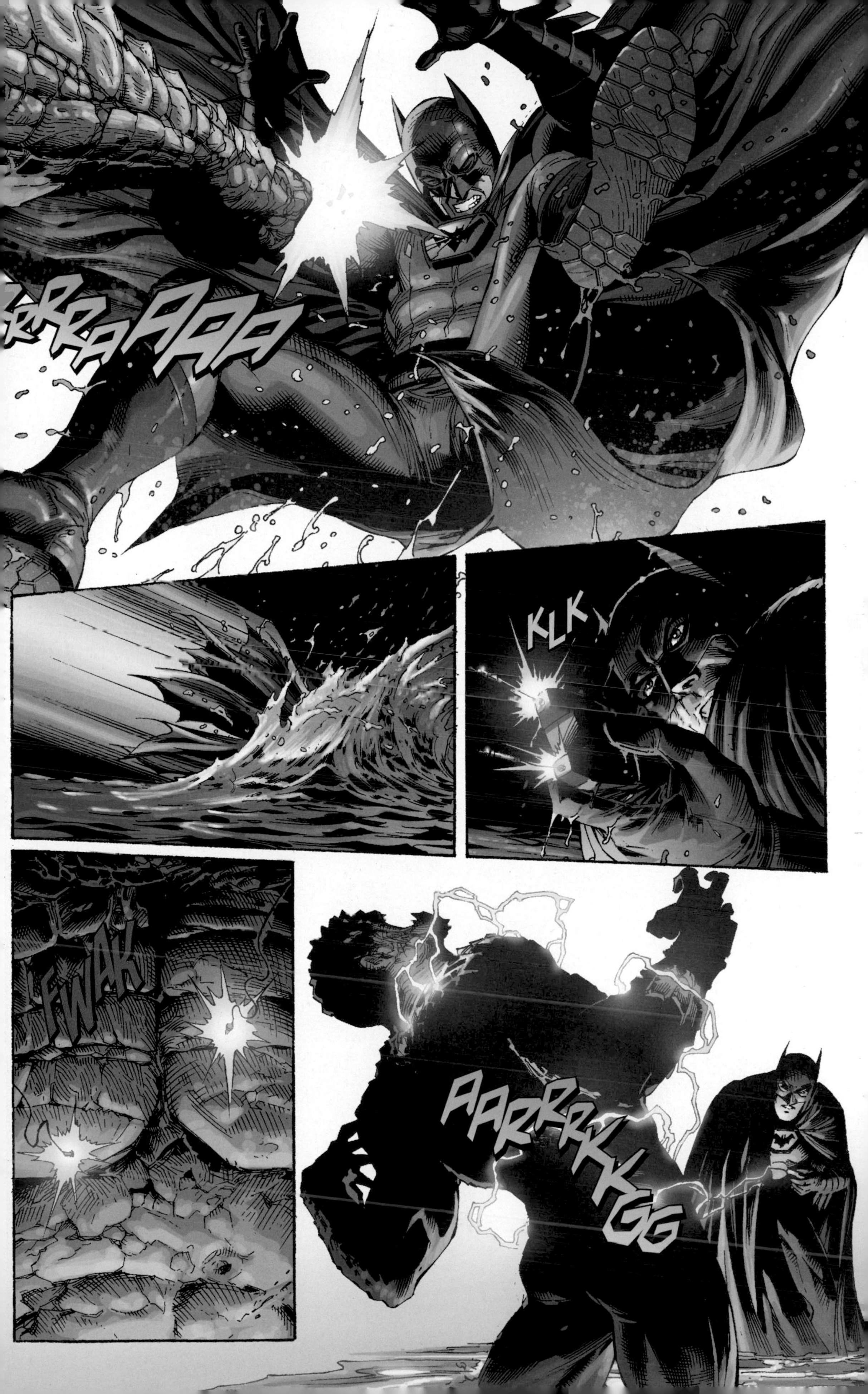
RRRAAAAA
KLK
FWAK
AARRRKKGG

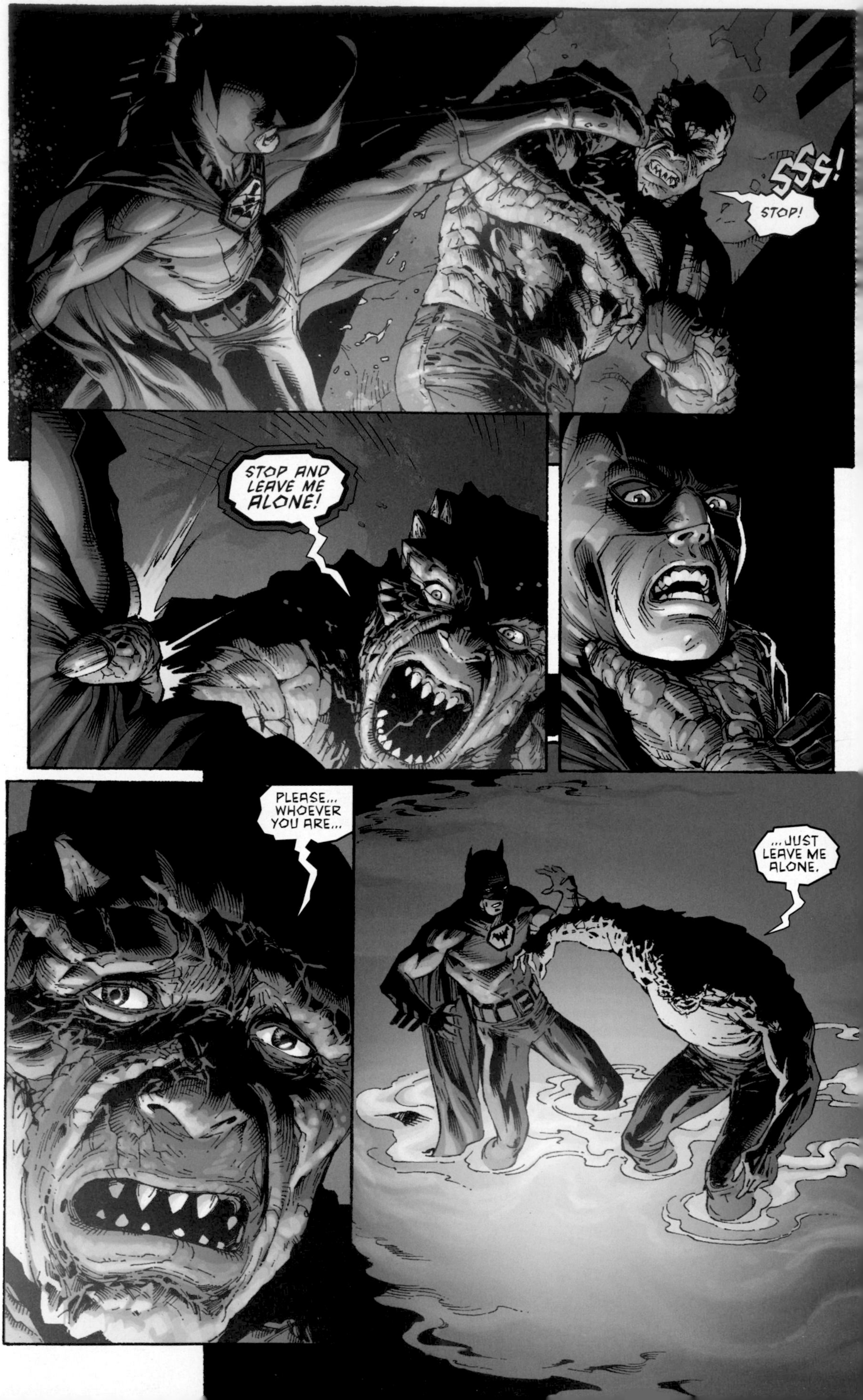
SSS!
STOP!
STOP AND LEAVE ME ALONE!
PLEASE... WHOEVER YOU ARE...
...JUST LEAVE ME ALONE.

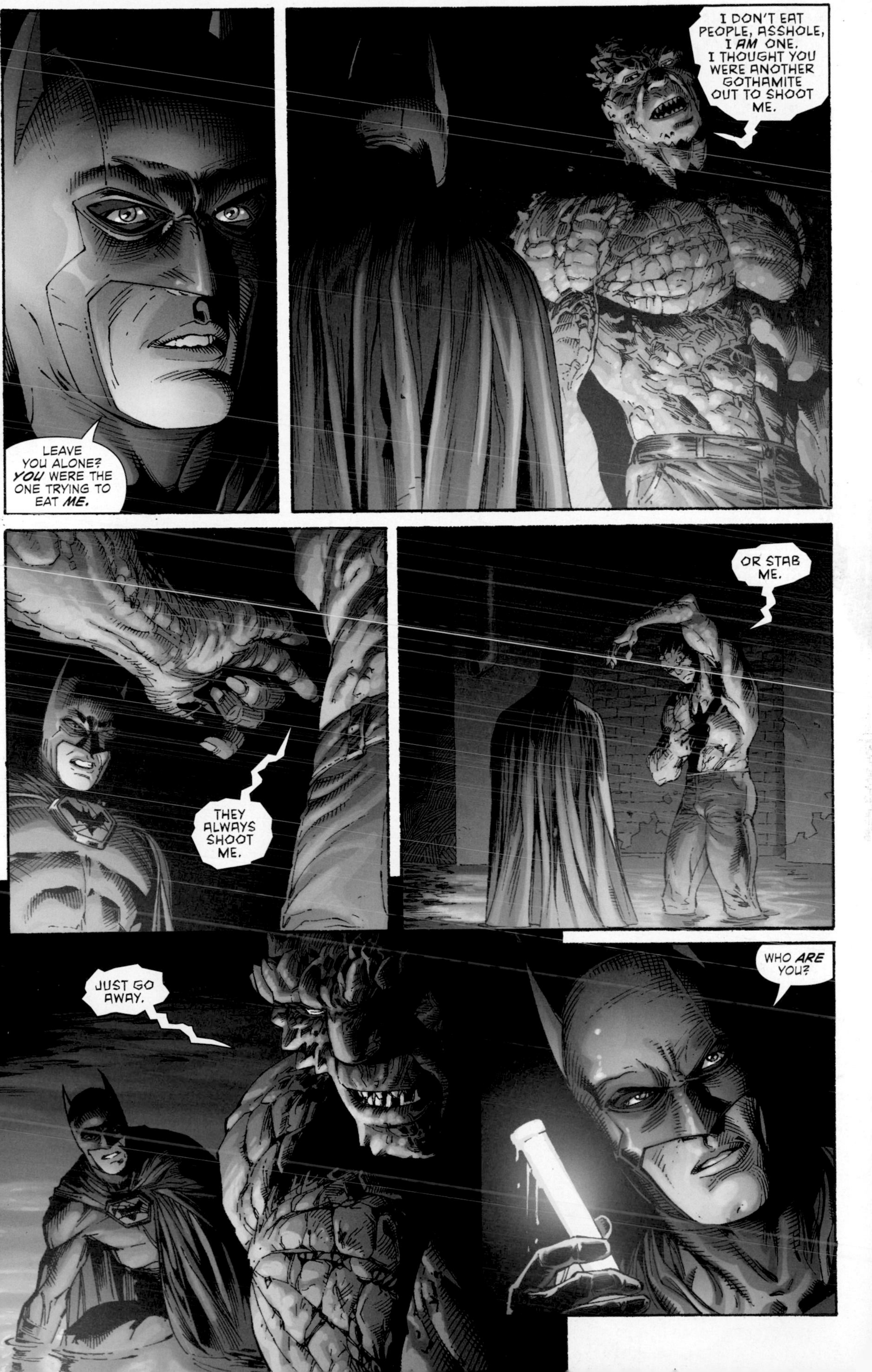
LEAVE YOU ALONE? YOU WERE THE ONE TRYING TO EAT ME.
I DON'T EAT PEOPLE, ASSHOLE, I AM ONE. I THOUGHT YOU WERE ANOTHER GOTHAMITE OUT TO SHOOT ME.
THEY ALWAYS SHOOT ME.
OR STAB ME.
JUST GO AWAY.
WHO ARE YOU?

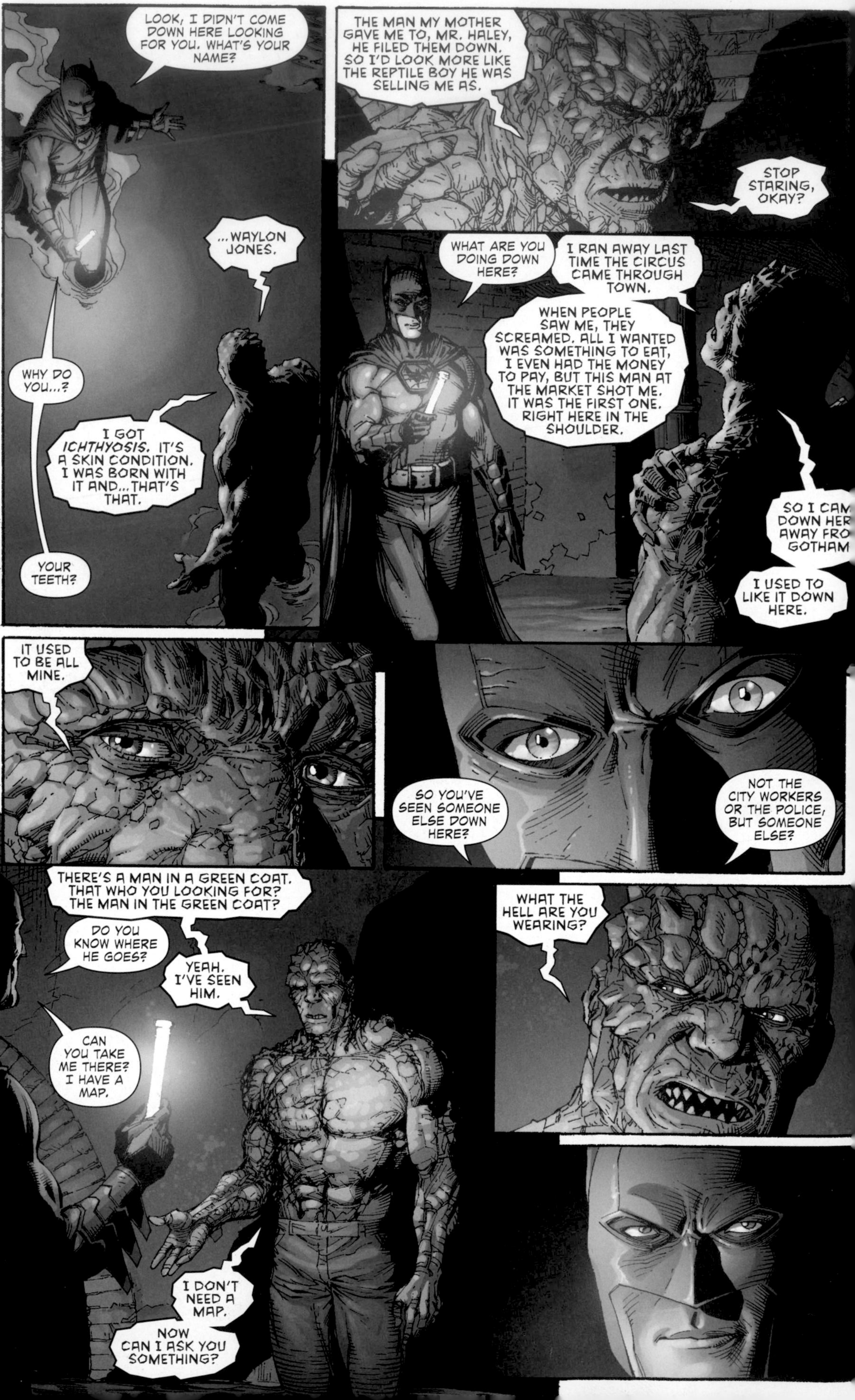
LOOK, I DIDN'T COME DOWN HERE LOOKING FOR YOU. WHAT'S YOUR NAME?
...WAYLON JONES.
WHY DO YOU...?
I GOT *ICHTHYOSIS.* IT'S A SKIN CONDITION. I WAS BORN WITH IT AND...THAT'S THAT.
YOUR TEETH?
THE MAN MY MOTHER GAVE ME TO, MR. HALEY, HE FILED THEM DOWN. SO I'D LOOK MORE LIKE THE REPTILE BOY HE WAS SELLING ME AS.
STOP STARING, OKAY?
WHAT ARE YOU DOING DOWN HERE?
I RAN AWAY LAST TIME THE CIRCUS CAME THROUGH TOWN.
WHEN PEOPLE SAW ME, THEY SCREAMED. ALL I WANTED WAS SOMETHING TO EAT, I EVEN HAD THE MONEY TO PAY, BUT THIS MAN AT THE MARKET SHOT ME. IT WAS THE FIRST ONE. RIGHT HERE IN THE SHOULDER.
I USED TO LIKE IT DOWN HERE.
IT USED TO BE ALL MINE.
SO YOU'VE SEEN SOMEONE ELSE DOWN HERE?
NOT THE CITY WORKERS OR THE POLICE, BUT SOMEONE ELSE?
THERE'S A MAN IN A GREEN COAT. THAT WHO YOU LOOKING FOR? THE MAN IN THE GREEN COAT?
DO YOU KNOW WHERE HE GOES?
YEAH. I'VE SEEN HIM.
CAN YOU TAKE ME THERE? I HAVE A MAP.
I DON'T NEED A MAP.
NOW CAN I ASK YOU SOMETHING?
WHAT THE HELL ARE YOU WEARING?

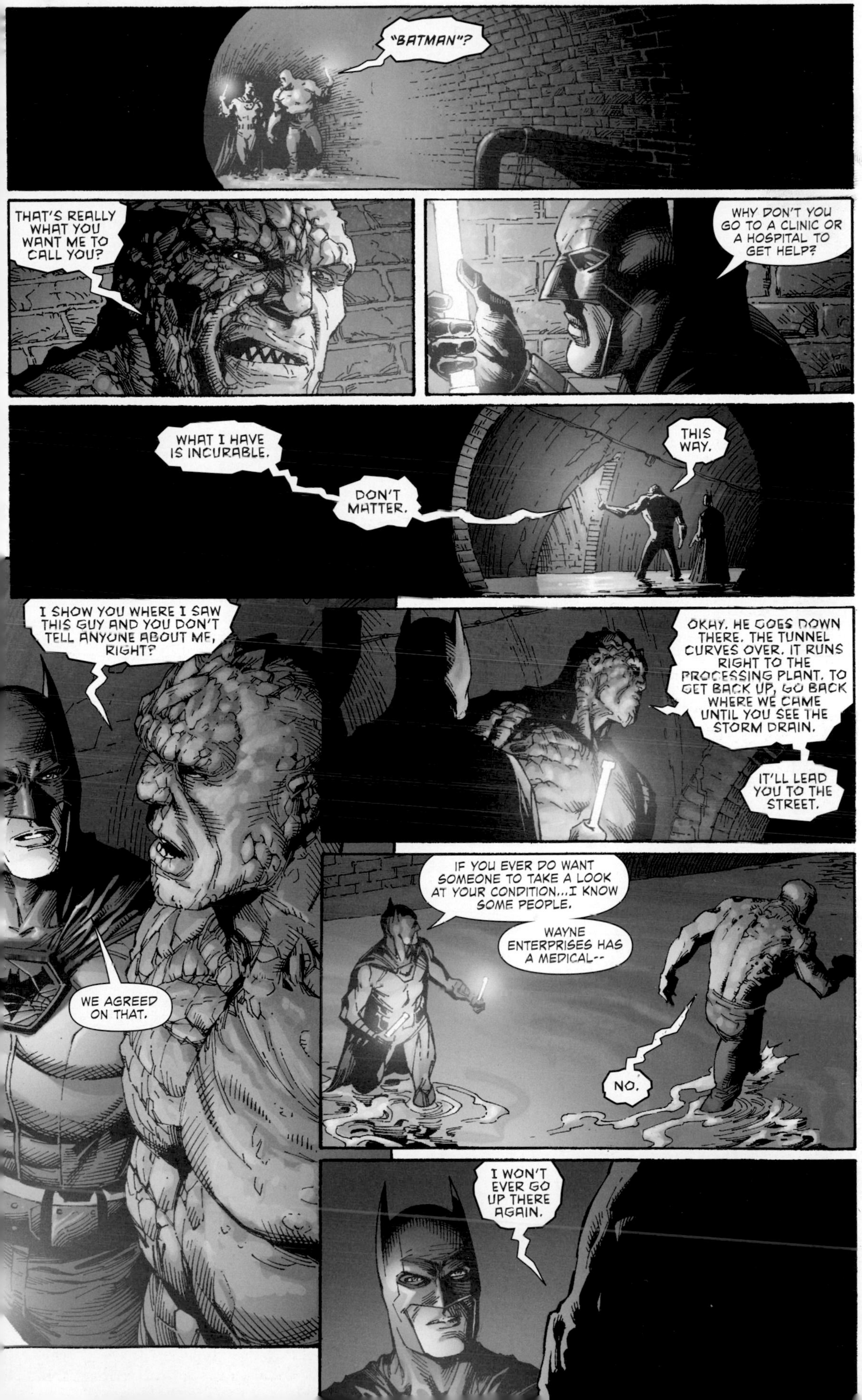

"BATMAN"?
THAT'S REALLY WHAT YOU WANT ME TO CALL YOU?
WHY DON'T YOU GO TO A CLINIC OR A HOSPITAL TO GET HELP?
WHAT I HAVE IS INCURABLE.
DON'T MATTER.
THIS WAY.
I SHOW YOU WHERE I SAW THIS GUY AND YOU DON'T TELL ANYONE ABOUT ME, RIGHT?
WE AGREED ON THAT.
OKAY. HE GOES DOWN THERE. THE TUNNEL CURVES OVER. IT RUNS RIGHT TO THE PROCESSING PLANT. TO GET BACK UP, GO BACK WHERE WE CAME UNTIL YOU SEE THE STORM DRAIN.
IT'LL LEAD YOU TO THE STREET.
IF YOU EVER DO WANT SOMEONE TO TAKE A LOOK AT YOUR CONDITION...I KNOW SOME PEOPLE.
WAYNE ENTERPRISES HAS A MEDICAL--
NO.
I WON'T EVER GO UP THERE AGAIN.

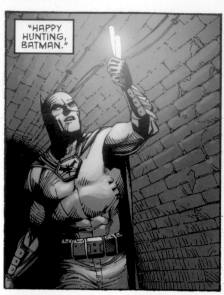

"HAPPY HUNTING, BATMAN."

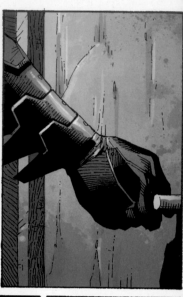

RLIP

COME ON...

SCREW IT.

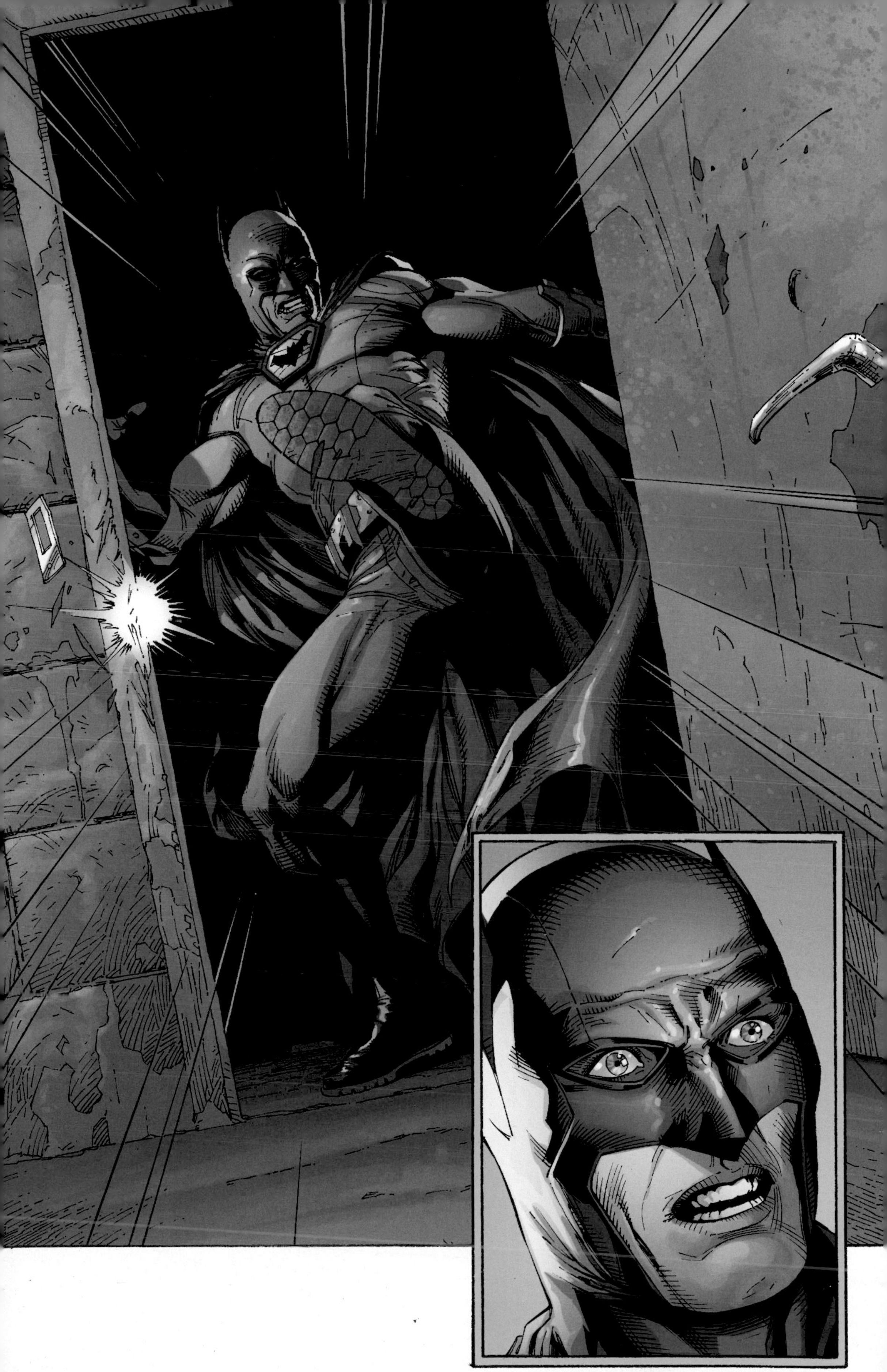

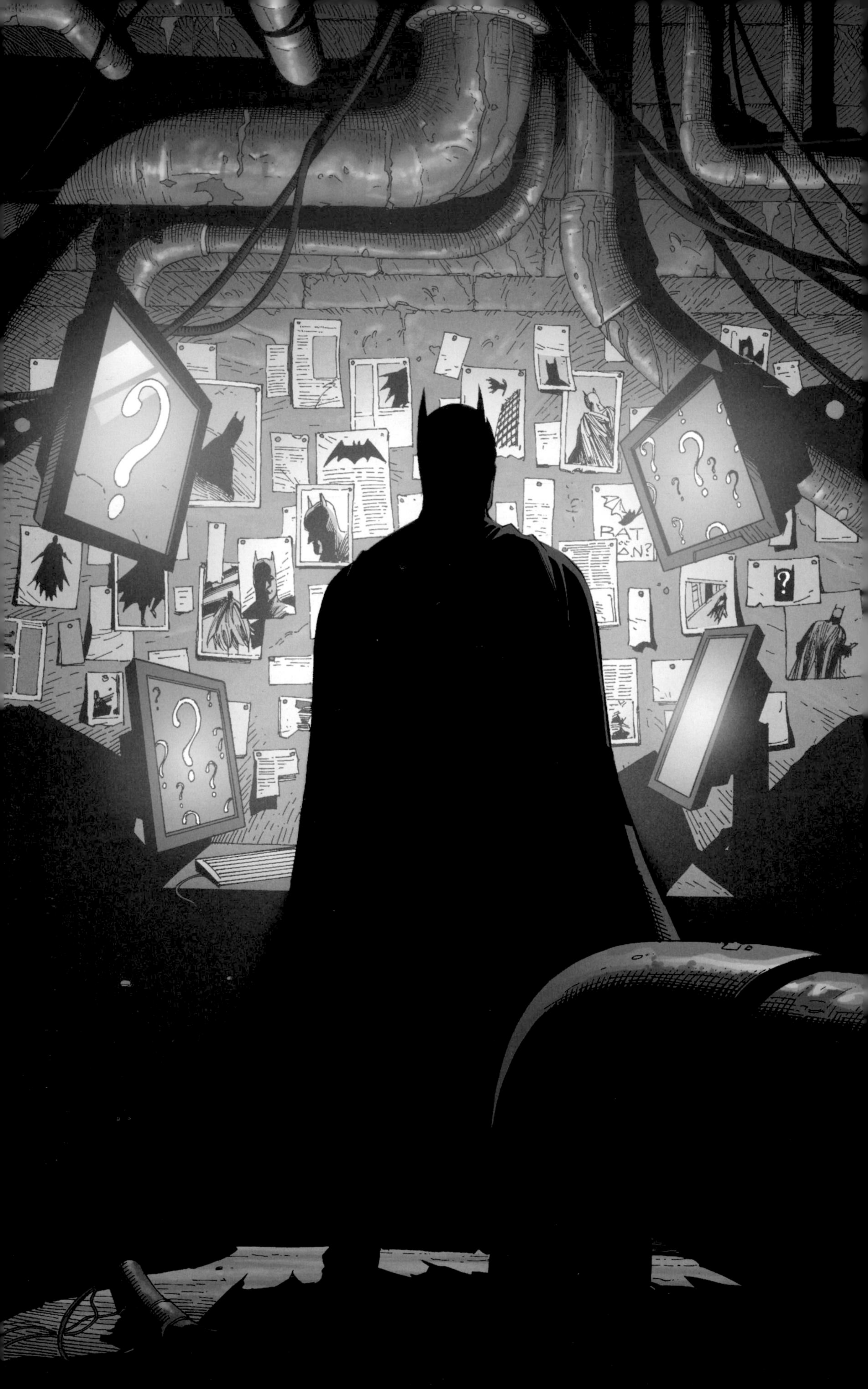
RAT

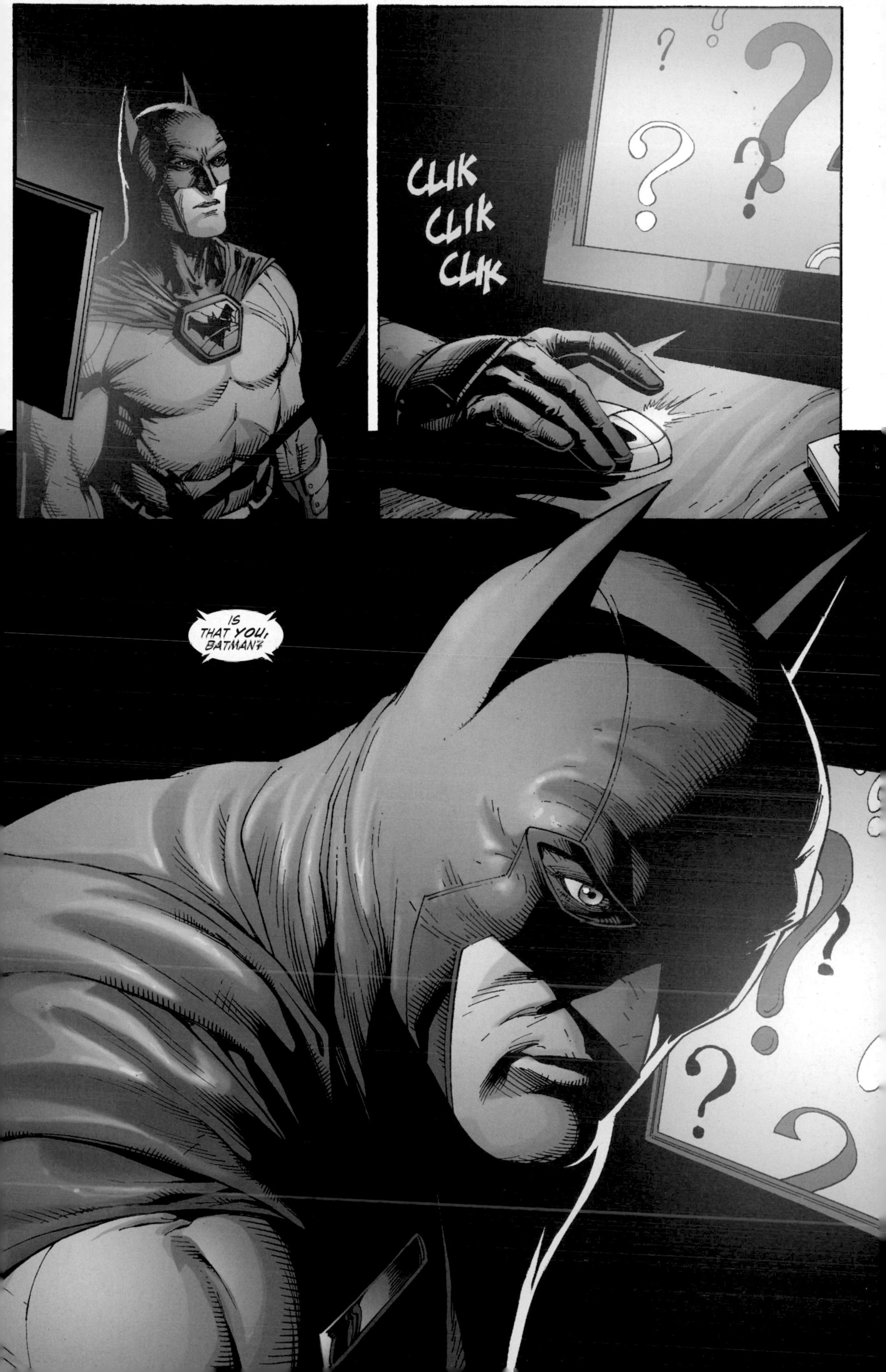
CLIK
CLIK
CLIK
IS THAT YOU, BATMAN?

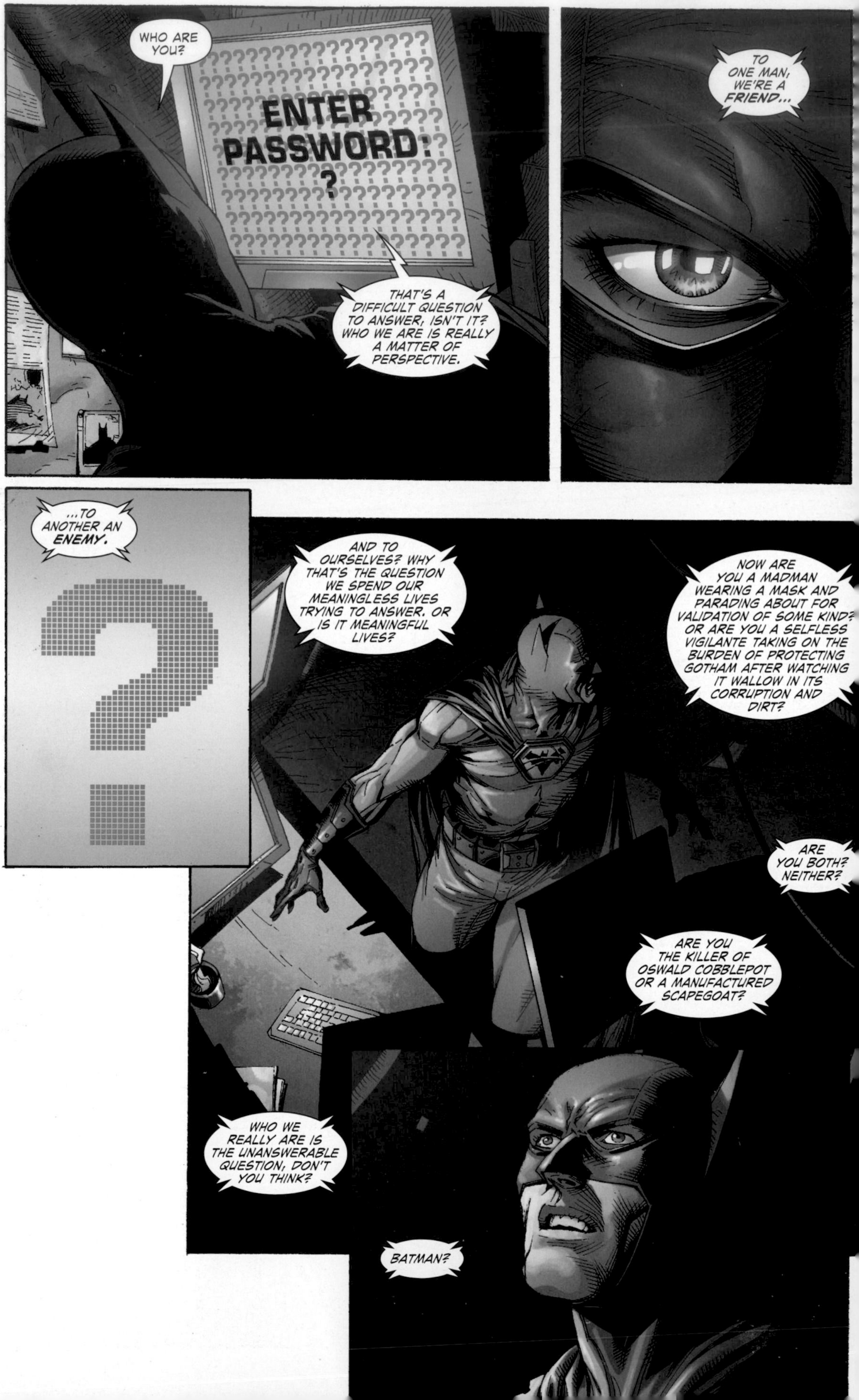
WHO ARE YOU?
ENTER PASSWORD: ?
THAT'S A DIFFICULT QUESTION TO ANSWER, ISN'T IT? WHO WE ARE IS REALLY A MATTER OF PERSPECTIVE.
TO ONE MAN, WE'RE A FRIEND...
...TO ANOTHER AN ENEMY.
AND TO OURSELVES? WHY THAT'S THE QUESTION WE SPEND OUR MEANINGLESS LIVES TRYING TO ANSWER. OR IS IT MEANINGFUL LIVES?
NOW ARE YOU A MADMAN WEARING A MASK AND PARADING ABOUT FOR VALIDATION OF SOME KIND? OR ARE YOU A SELFLESS VIGILANTE TAKING ON THE BURDEN OF PROTECTING GOTHAM AFTER WATCHING IT WALLOW IN ITS CORRUPTION AND DIRT?
ARE YOU BOTH? NEITHER?
ARE YOU THE KILLER OF OSWALD COBBLEPOT OR A MANUFACTURED SCAPEGOAT?
WHO WE REALLY ARE IS THE UNANSWERABLE QUESTION, DON'T YOU THINK?
BATMAN?

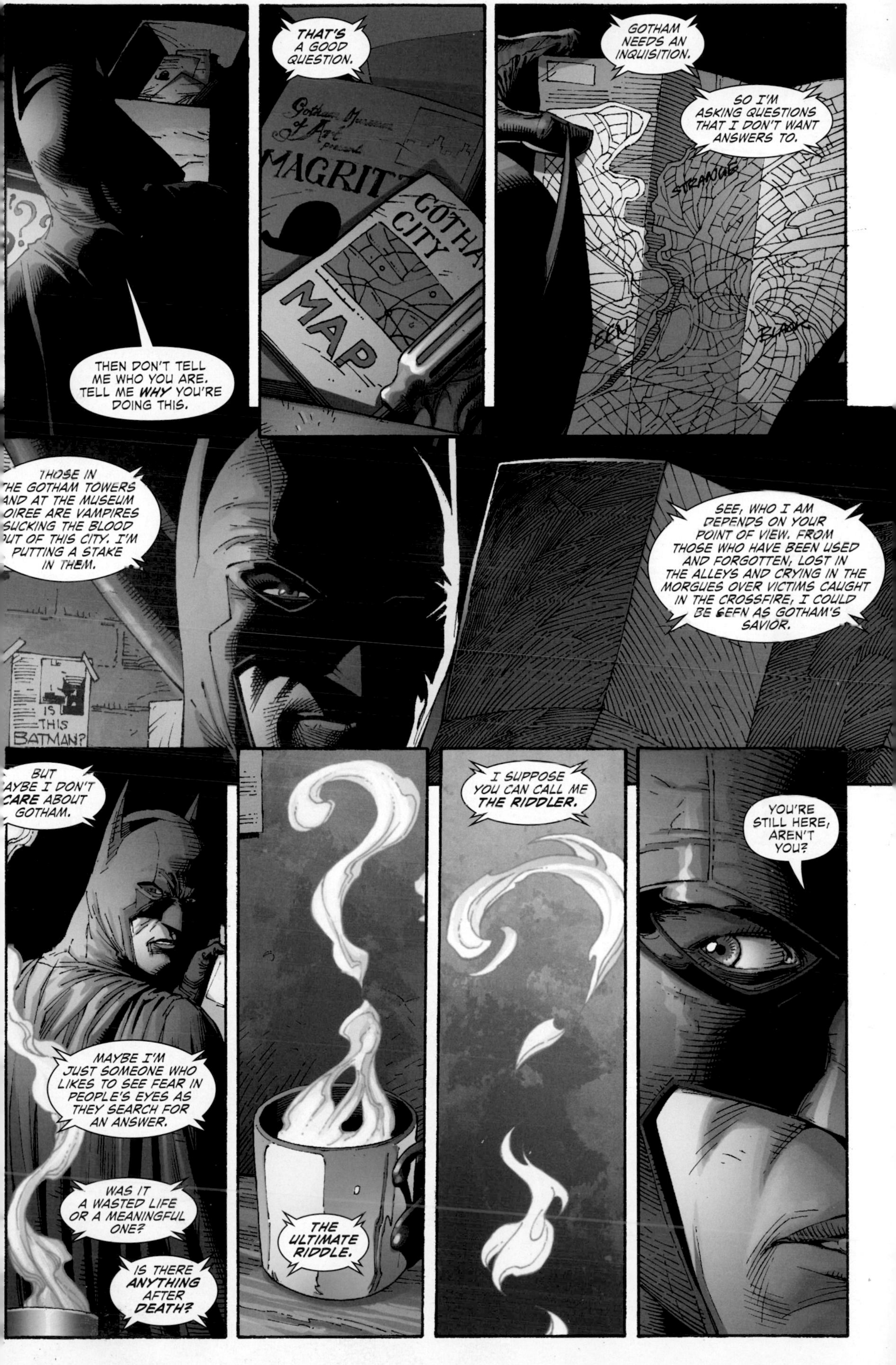
THEN DON'T TELL ME WHO YOU ARE. TELL ME **WHY** YOU'RE DOING THIS.
THAT'S A GOOD QUESTION.
MAGRITT
GOTHA CITY
MAP
GOTHAM NEEDS AN INQUISITION.
SO I'M ASKING QUESTIONS THAT I DON'T WANT ANSWERS TO.
THOSE IN THE GOTHAM TOWERS AND AT THE MUSEUM OIREE ARE VAMPIRES SUCKING THE BLOOD OUT OF THIS CITY. I'M PUTTING A STAKE IN THEM.
IS THIS BATMAN?
SEE, WHO I AM DEPENDS ON YOUR POINT OF VIEW. FROM THOSE WHO HAVE BEEN USED AND FORGOTTEN, LOST IN THE ALLEYS AND CRYING IN THE MORGUES OVER VICTIMS CAUGHT IN THE CROSSFIRE, I COULD BE SEEN AS GOTHAM'S SAVIOR.
*BUT AYBE I DON'T **CARE** ABOUT GOTHAM.*
MAYBE I'M JUST SOMEONE WHO LIKES TO SEE FEAR IN PEOPLE'S EYES AS THEY SEARCH FOR AN ANSWER.
WAS IT A WASTED LIFE OR A MEANINGFUL ONE?
*IS THERE **ANYTHING** AFTER **DEATH?***
THE ULTIMATE RIDDLE.
*I SUPPOSE YOU CAN CALL ME **THE RIDDLER.***
YOU'RE STILL HERE, AREN'T YOU?

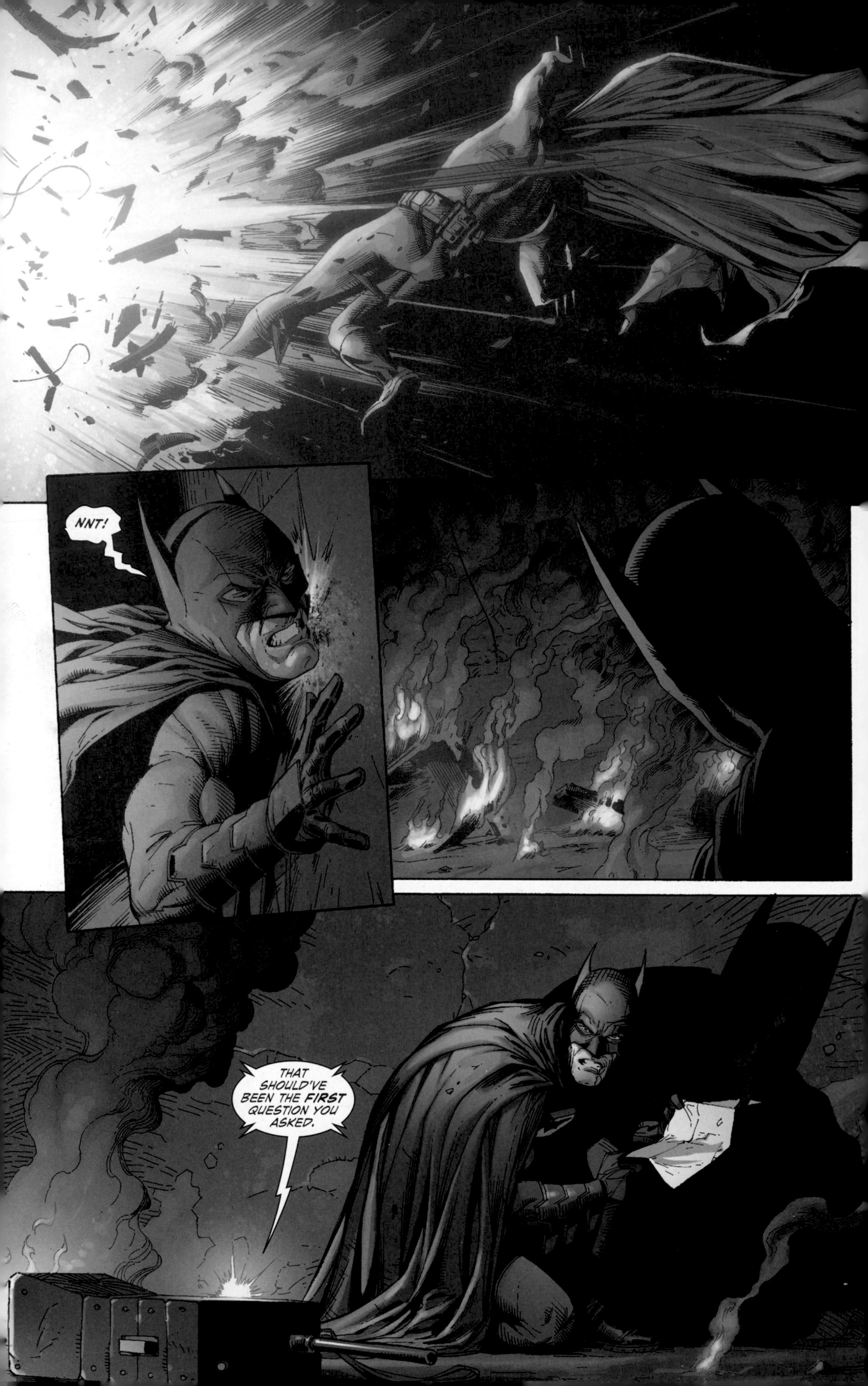
NNT!
THAT SHOULD'VE BEEN THE **FIRST** QUESTION YOU ASKED.

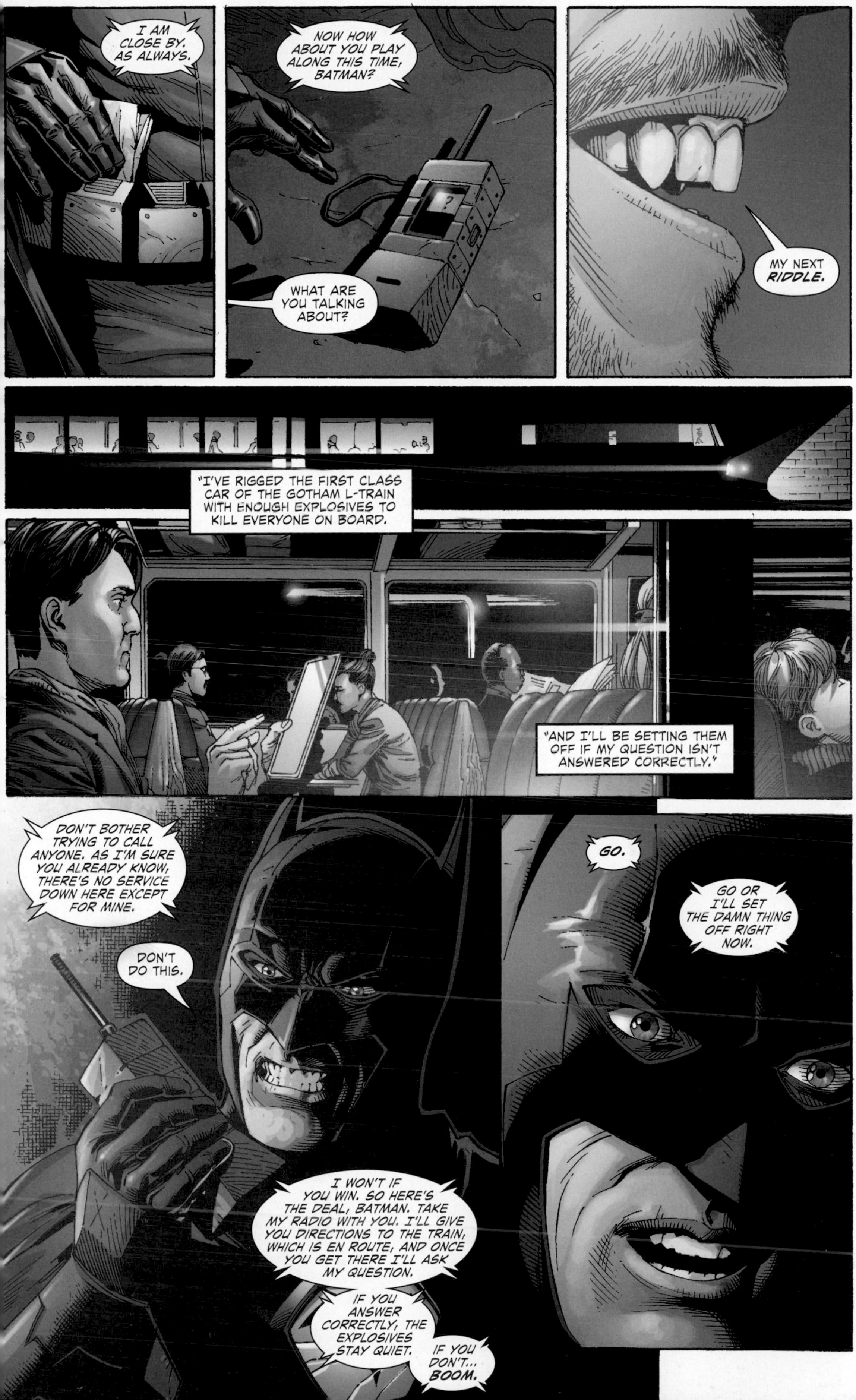
I AM CLOSE BY. AS ALWAYS.
NOW HOW ABOUT YOU PLAY ALONG THIS TIME, BATMAN?
WHAT ARE YOU TALKING ABOUT?
MY NEXT RIDDLE.
"I'VE RIGGED THE FIRST CLASS CAR OF THE GOTHAM L-TRAIN WITH ENOUGH EXPLOSIVES TO KILL EVERYONE ON BOARD.
"AND I'LL BE SETTING THEM OFF IF MY QUESTION ISN'T ANSWERED CORRECTLY."
DON'T BOTHER TRYING TO CALL ANYONE. AS I'M SURE YOU ALREADY KNOW, THERE'S NO SERVICE DOWN HERE EXCEPT FOR MINE.
DON'T DO THIS.
GO.
GO OR I'LL SET THE DAMN THING OFF RIGHT NOW.
I WON'T IF YOU WIN. SO HERE'S THE DEAL, BATMAN. TAKE MY RADIO WITH YOU. I'LL GIVE YOU DIRECTIONS TO THE TRAIN, WHICH IS EN ROUTE, AND ONCE YOU GET THERE I'LL ASK MY QUESTION.
IF YOU ANSWER CORRECTLY, THE EXPLOSIVES STAY QUIET.
IF YOU DON'T... BOOM.

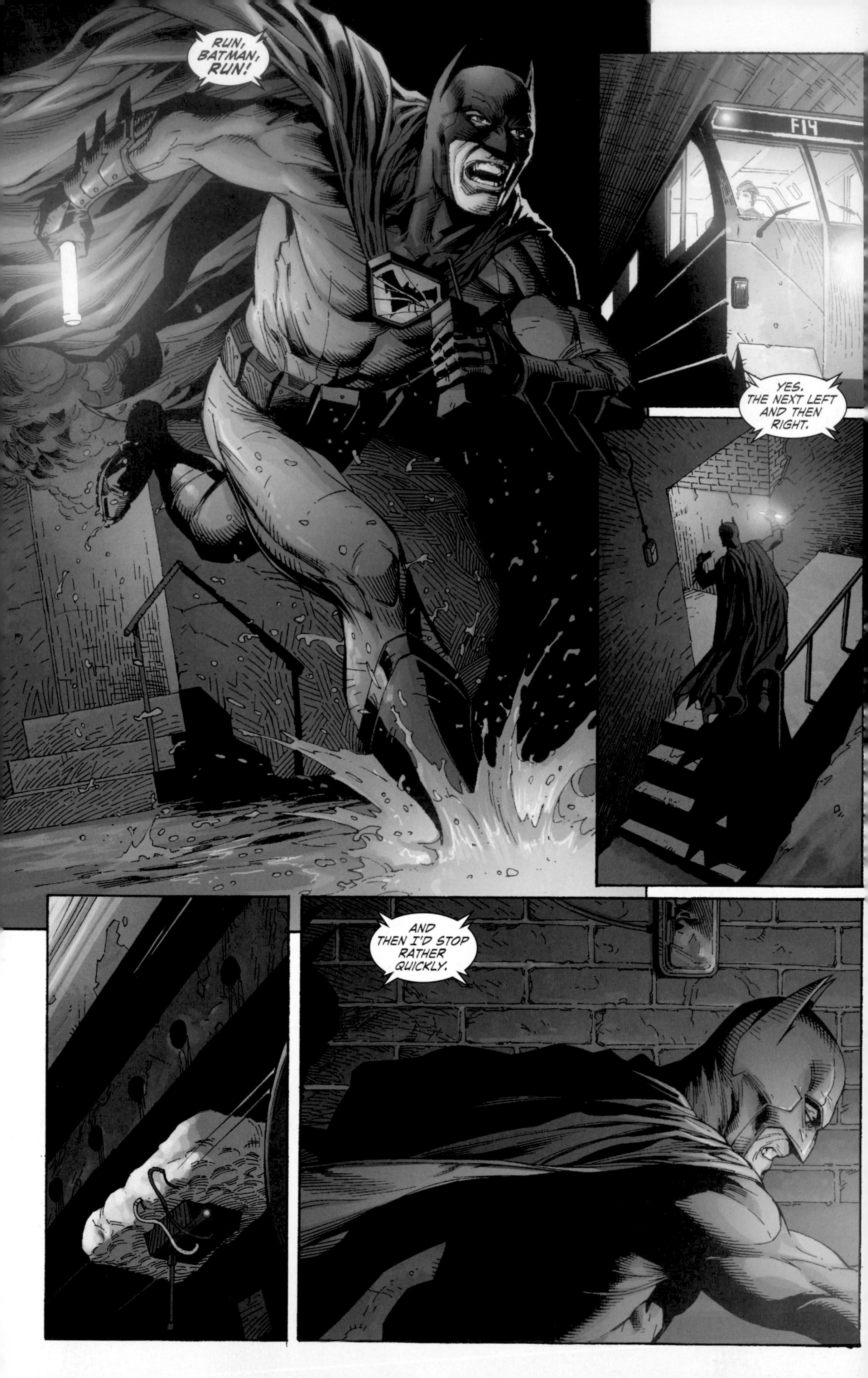
RUN, BATMAN, RUN!
F14
YES. THE NEXT LEFT AND THEN RIGHT.
AND THEN I'D STOP RATHER QUICKLY.

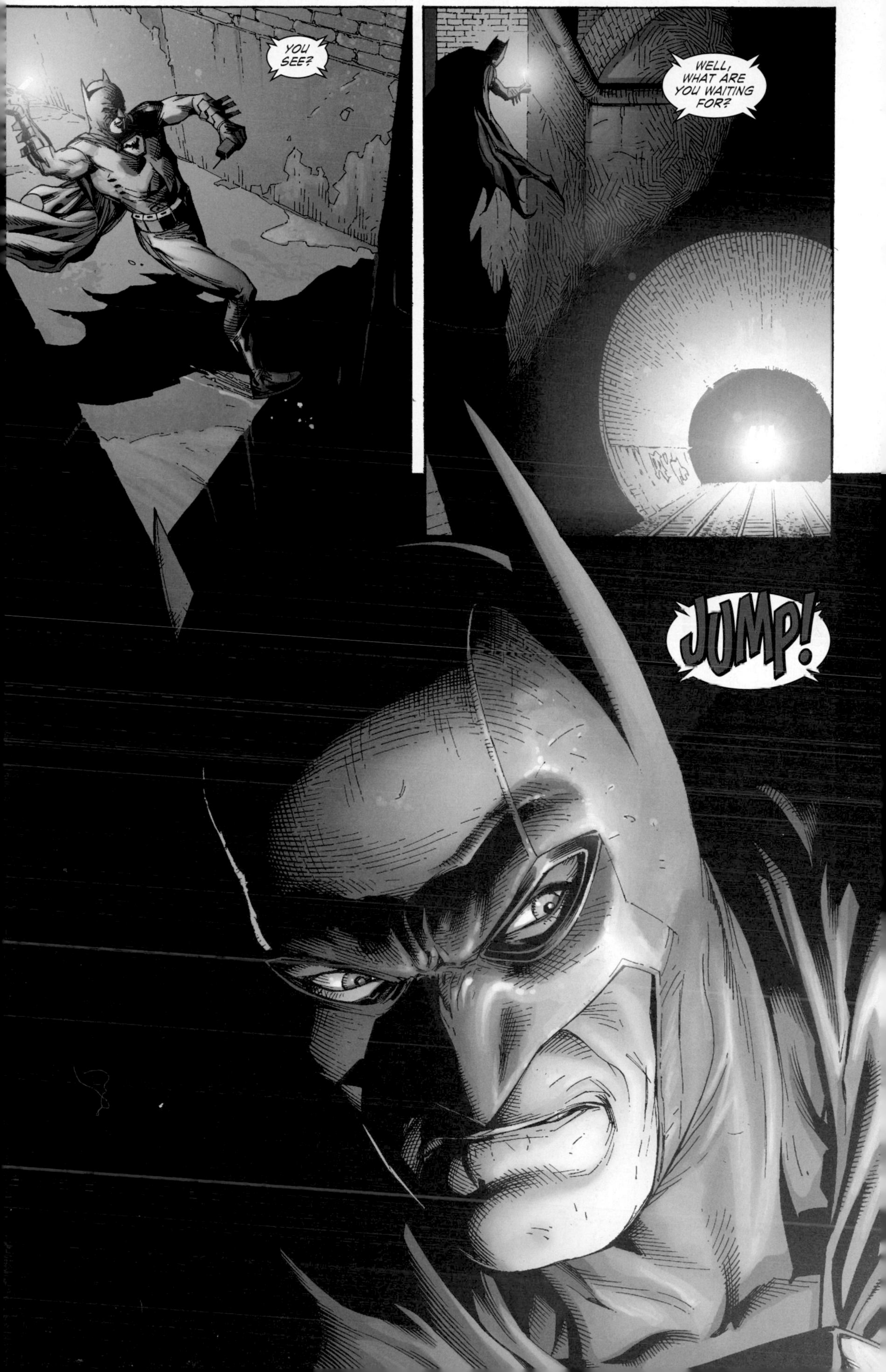
YOU SEE?
WELL, WHAT ARE YOU WAITING FOR?
JUMP!

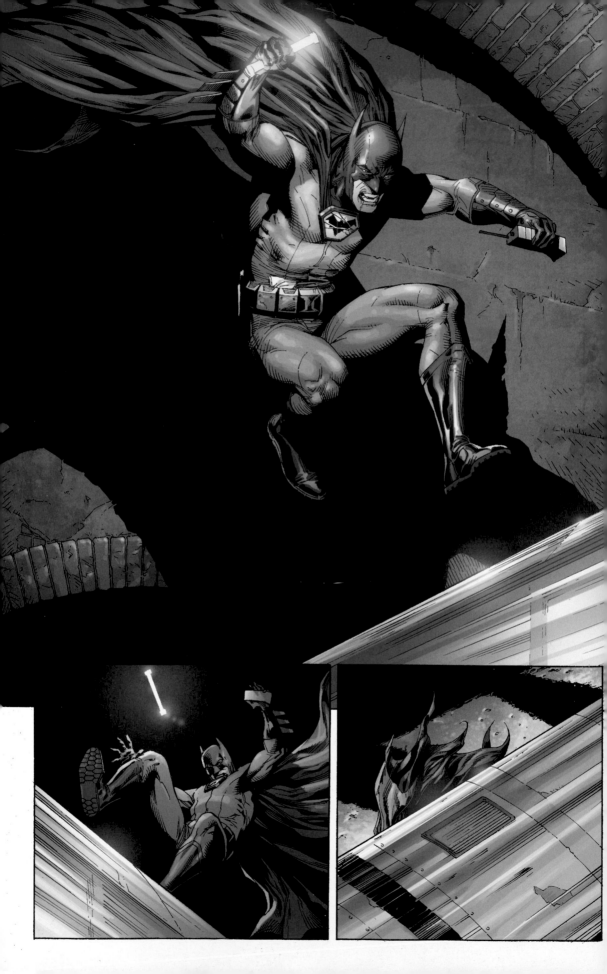

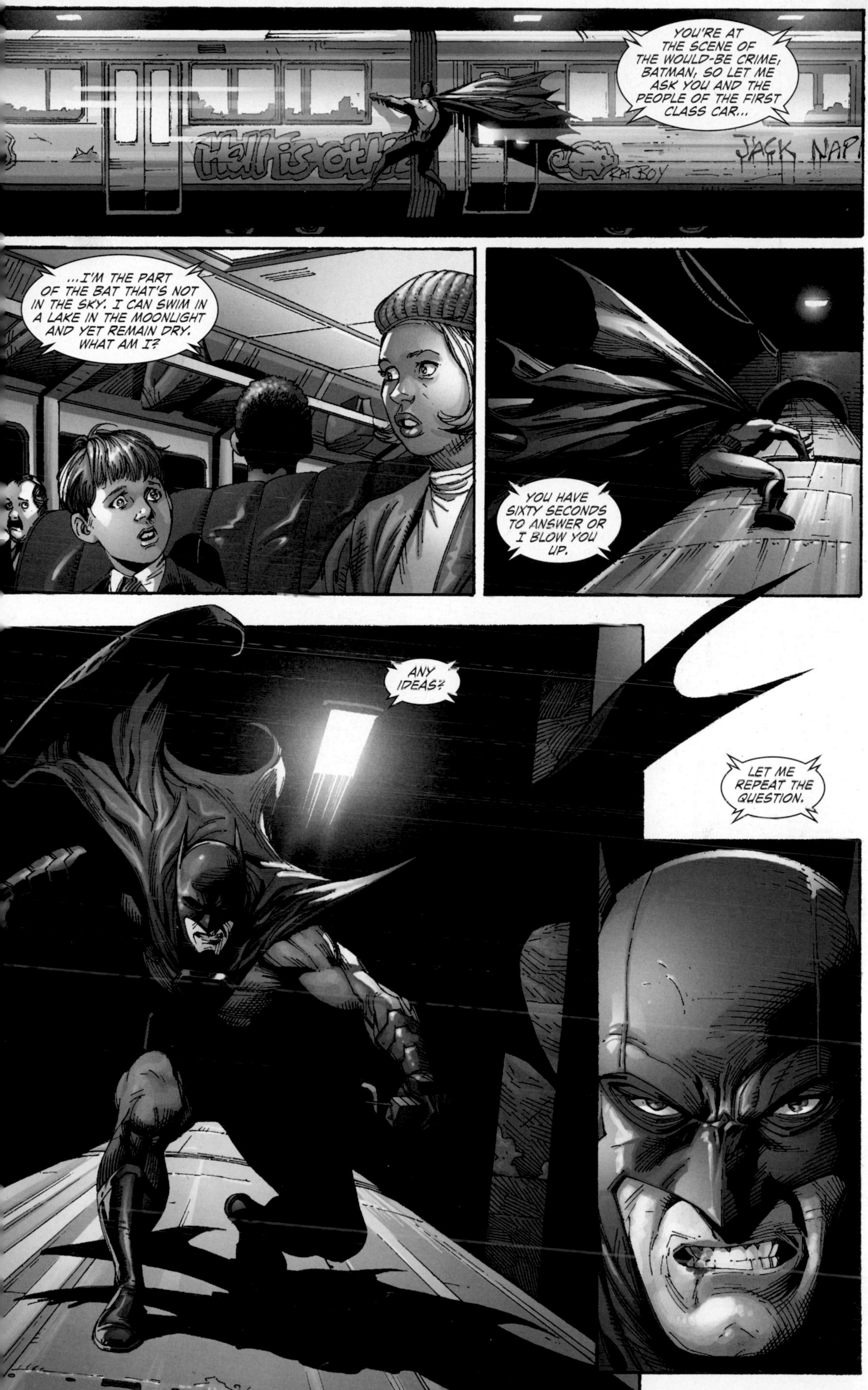
YOU'RE AT THE SCENE OF THE WOULD-BE CRIME, BATMAN, SO LET ME ASK YOU AND THE PEOPLE OF THE FIRST CLASS CAR...
JACK NAP
RAT BOY
...I'M THE PART OF THE BAT THAT'S NOT IN THE SKY. I CAN SWIM IN A LAKE IN THE MOONLIGHT AND YET REMAIN DRY. WHAT AM I?
YOU HAVE SIXTY SECONDS TO ANSWER OR I BLOW YOU UP.
ANY IDEAS?
LET ME REPEAT THE QUESTION.

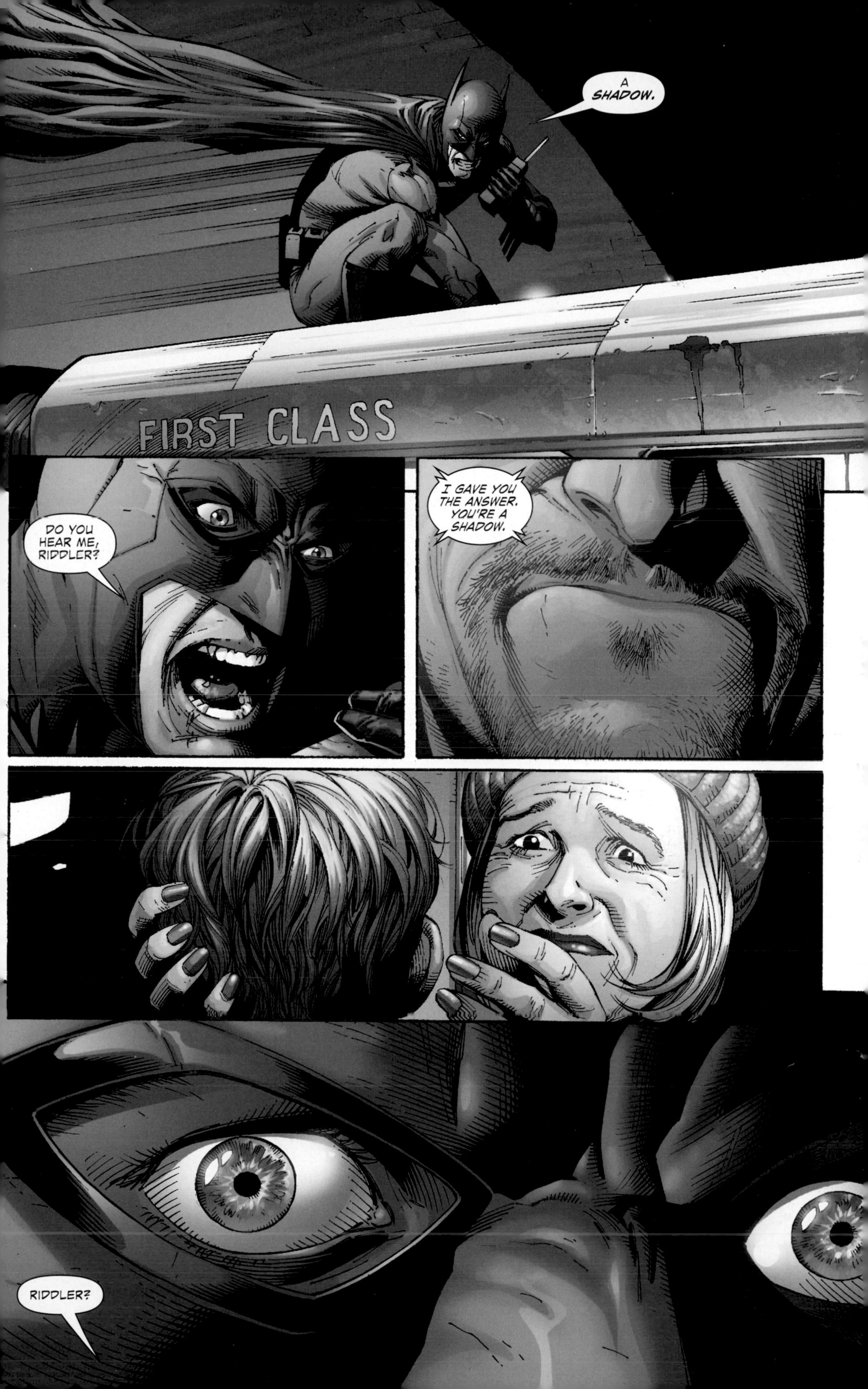
A SHADOW.
FIRST CLASS
DO YOU HEAR ME, RIDDLER?
I GAVE YOU THE ANSWER. YOU'RE A SHADOW.
RIDDLER?

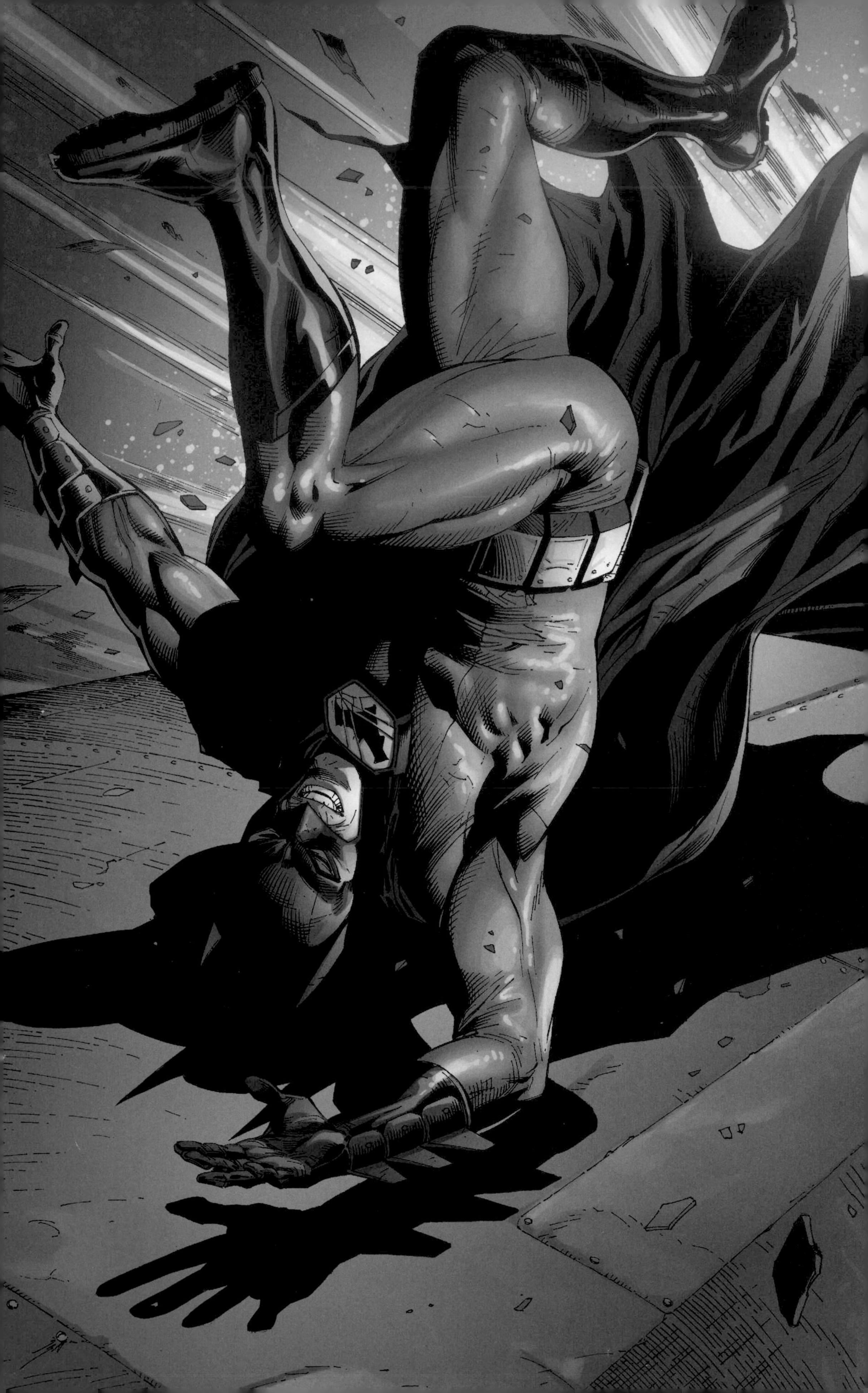

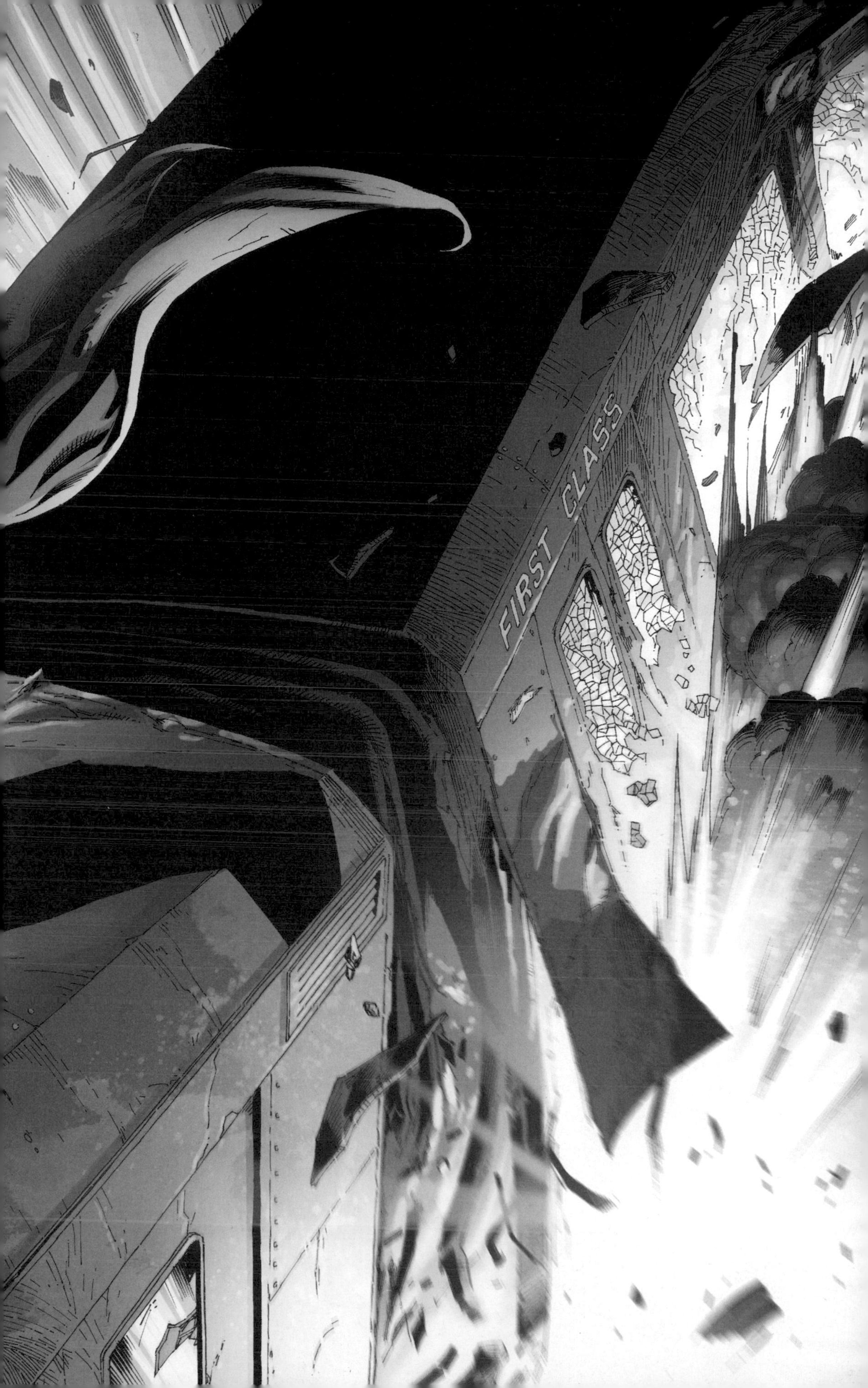
FIRST CLASS

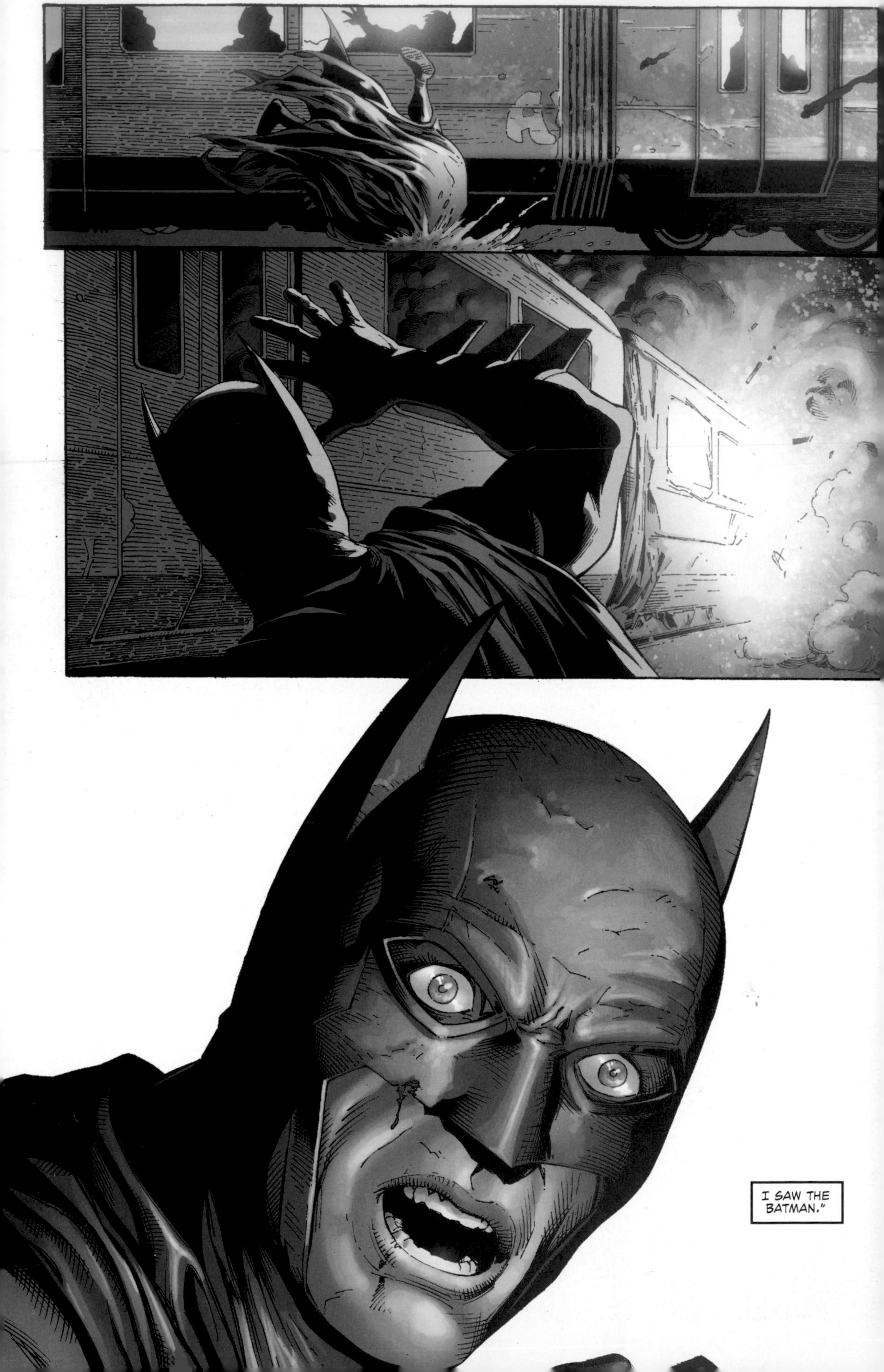
I SAW THE BATMAN."

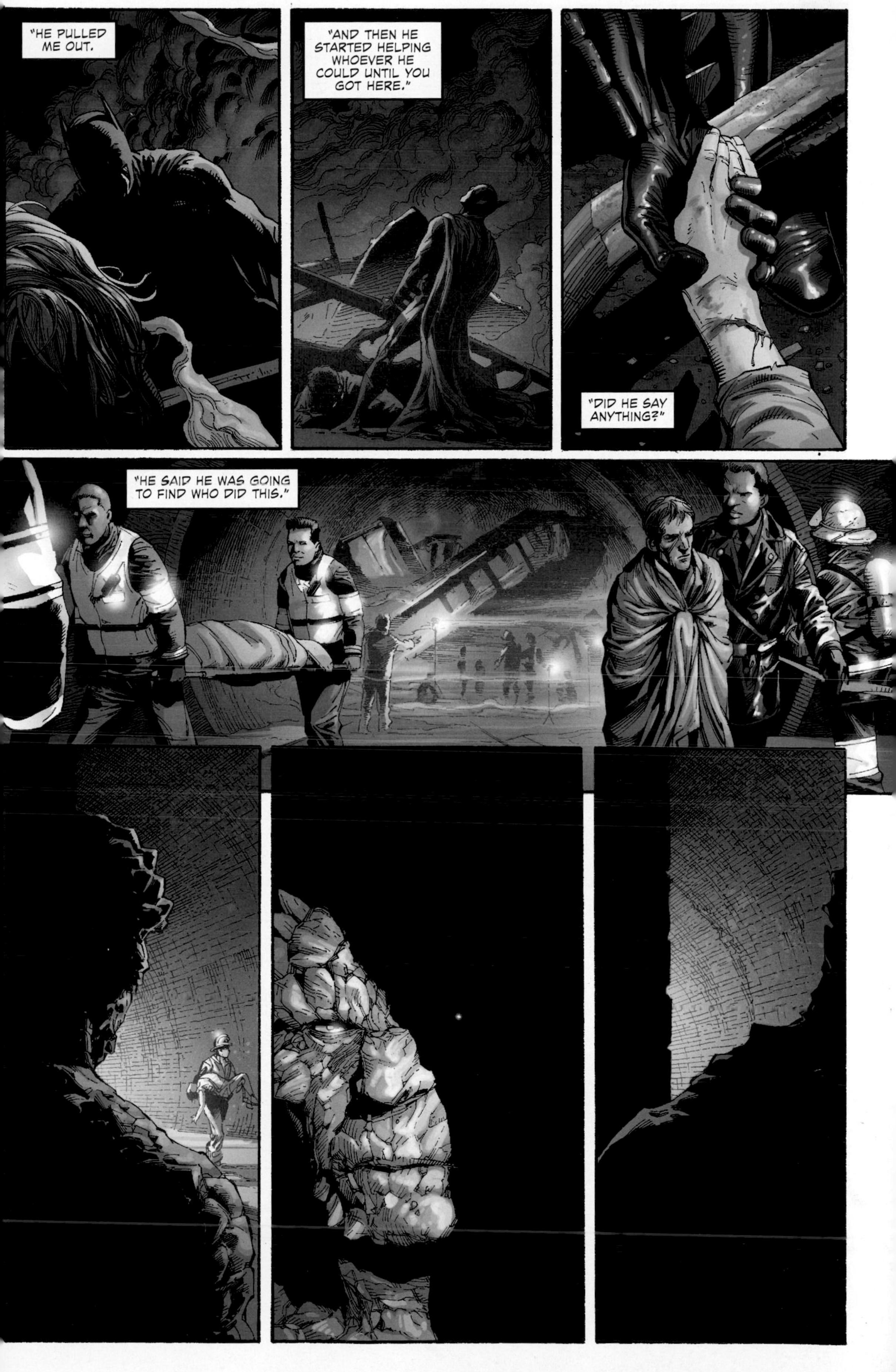
"HE PULLED ME OUT.
"AND THEN HE STARTED HELPING WHOEVER HE COULD UNTIL YOU GOT HERE."
"DID HE SAY ANYTHING?"
"HE SAID HE WAS GOING TO FIND WHO DID THIS."

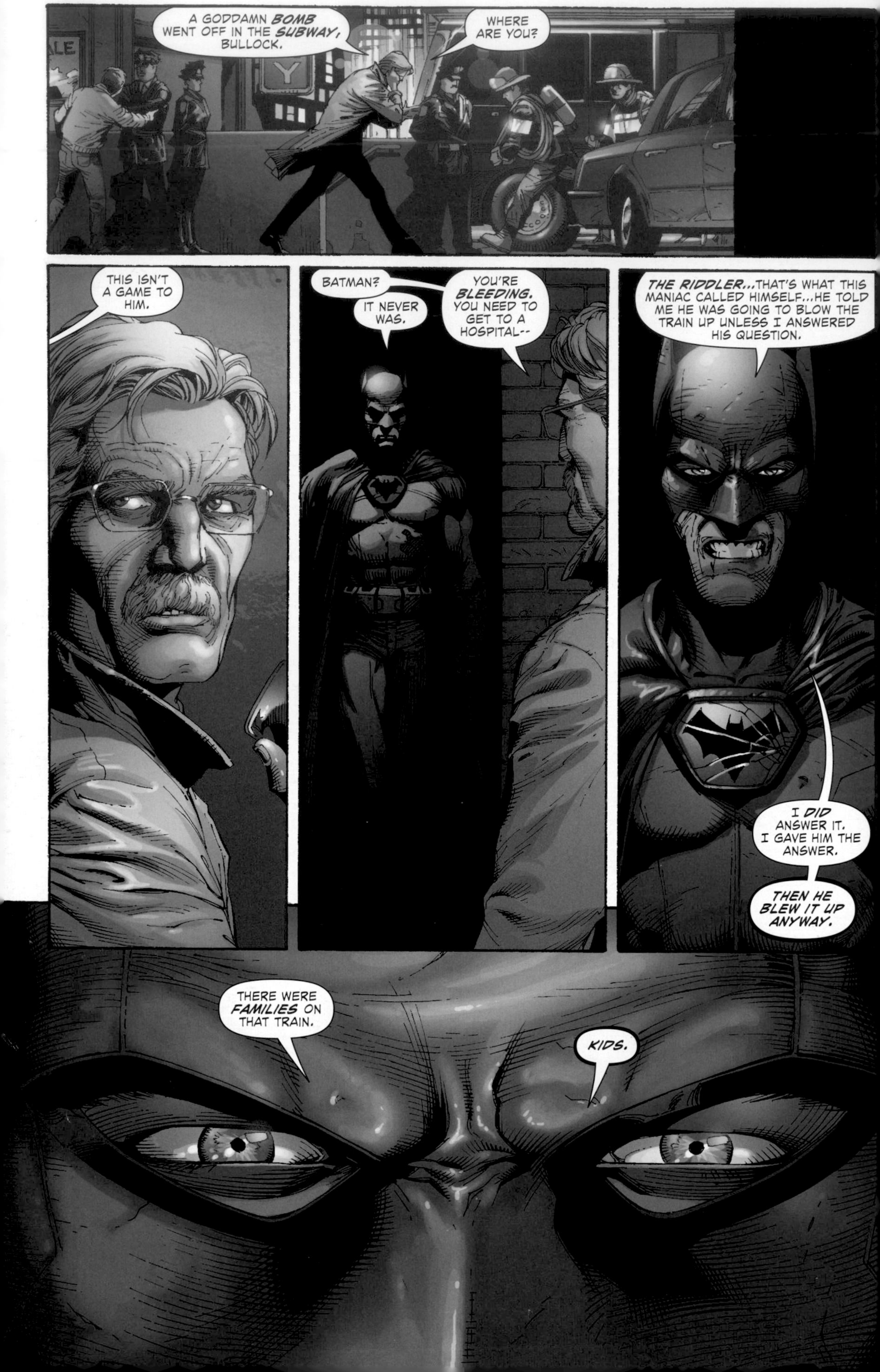
A GODDAMN *BOMB* WENT OFF IN THE *SUBWAY*, BULLOCK.
WHERE ARE YOU?
THIS ISN'T A GAME TO HIM.
BATMAN?
IT NEVER WAS.
YOU'RE *BLEEDING.* YOU NEED TO GET TO A HOSPITAL--
*THE RIDDLER...*THAT'S WHAT THIS MANIAC CALLED HIMSELF...HE TOLD ME HE WAS GOING TO BLOW THE TRAIN UP UNLESS I ANSWERED HIS QUESTION.
I *DID* ANSWER IT. I GAVE HIM THE ANSWER.
THEN HE BLEW IT UP ANYWAY.
THERE WERE *FAMILIES* ON THAT TRAIN.
KIDS.

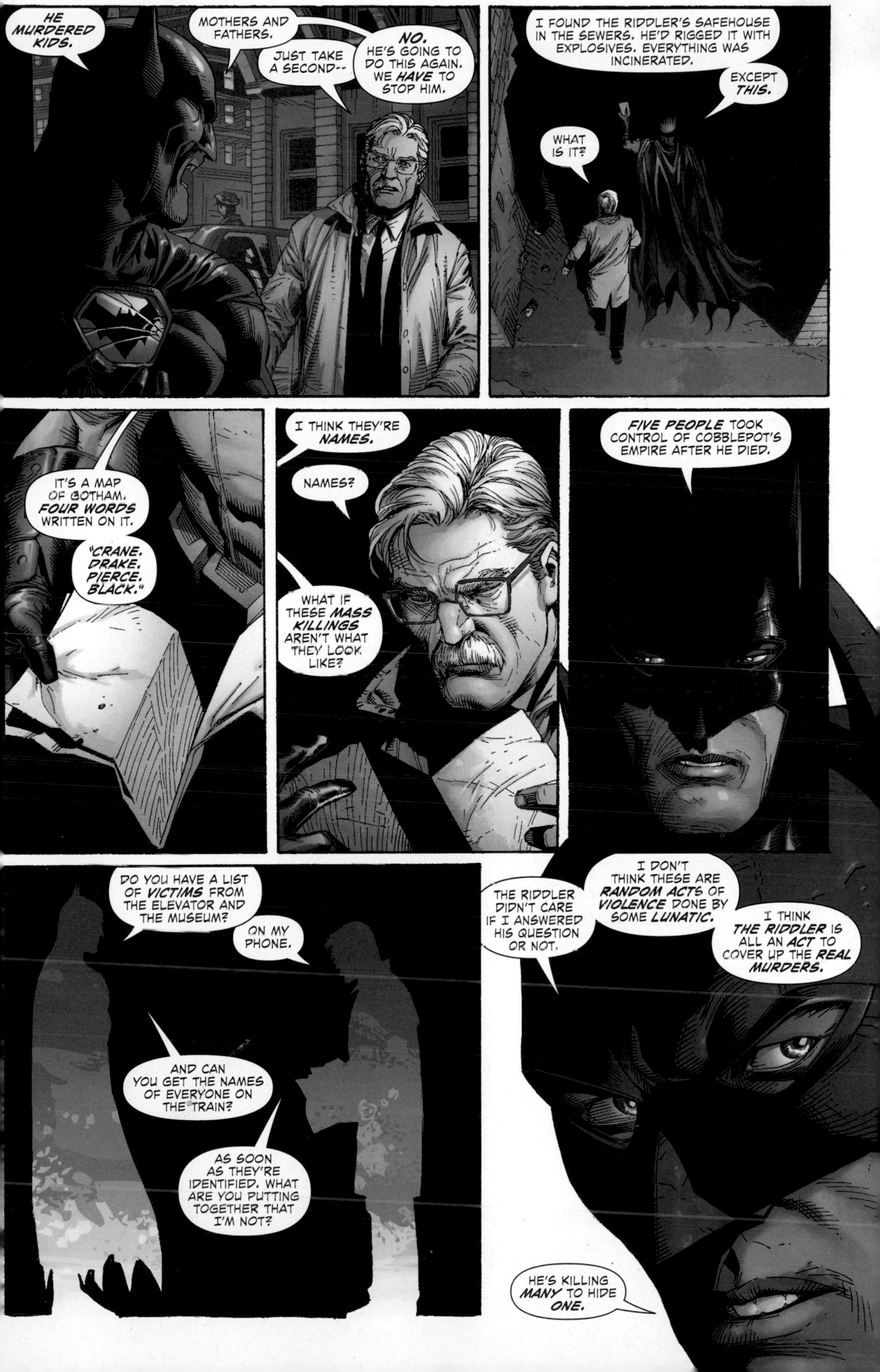
HE MURDERED KIDS.
MOTHERS AND FATHERS.
JUST TAKE A SECOND--
NO. HE'S GOING TO DO THIS AGAIN. WE HAVE TO STOP HIM.
I FOUND THE RIDDLER'S SAFEHOUSE IN THE SEWERS. HE'D RIGGED IT WITH EXPLOSIVES. EVERYTHING WAS INCINERATED.
EXCEPT THIS.
WHAT IS IT?
IT'S A MAP OF GOTHAM. FOUR WORDS WRITTEN ON IT.
"CRANE. DRAKE. PIERCE. BLACK."
I THINK THEY'RE NAMES.
NAMES?
WHAT IF THESE MASS KILLINGS AREN'T WHAT THEY LOOK LIKE?
FIVE PEOPLE TOOK CONTROL OF COBBLEPOT'S EMPIRE AFTER HE DIED.
DO YOU HAVE A LIST OF VICTIMS FROM THE ELEVATOR AND THE MUSEUM?
ON MY PHONE.
AND CAN YOU GET THE NAMES OF EVERYONE ON THE TRAIN?
AS SOON AS THEY'RE IDENTIFIED. WHAT ARE YOU PUTTING TOGETHER THAT I'M NOT?
THE RIDDLER DIDN'T CARE IF I ANSWERED HIS QUESTION OR NOT.
I DON'T THINK THESE ARE RANDOM ACTS OF VIOLENCE DONE BY SOME LUNATIC.
I THINK THE RIDDLER IS ALL AN ACT TO COVER UP THE REAL MURDERS.
HE'S KILLING MANY TO HIDE ONE.

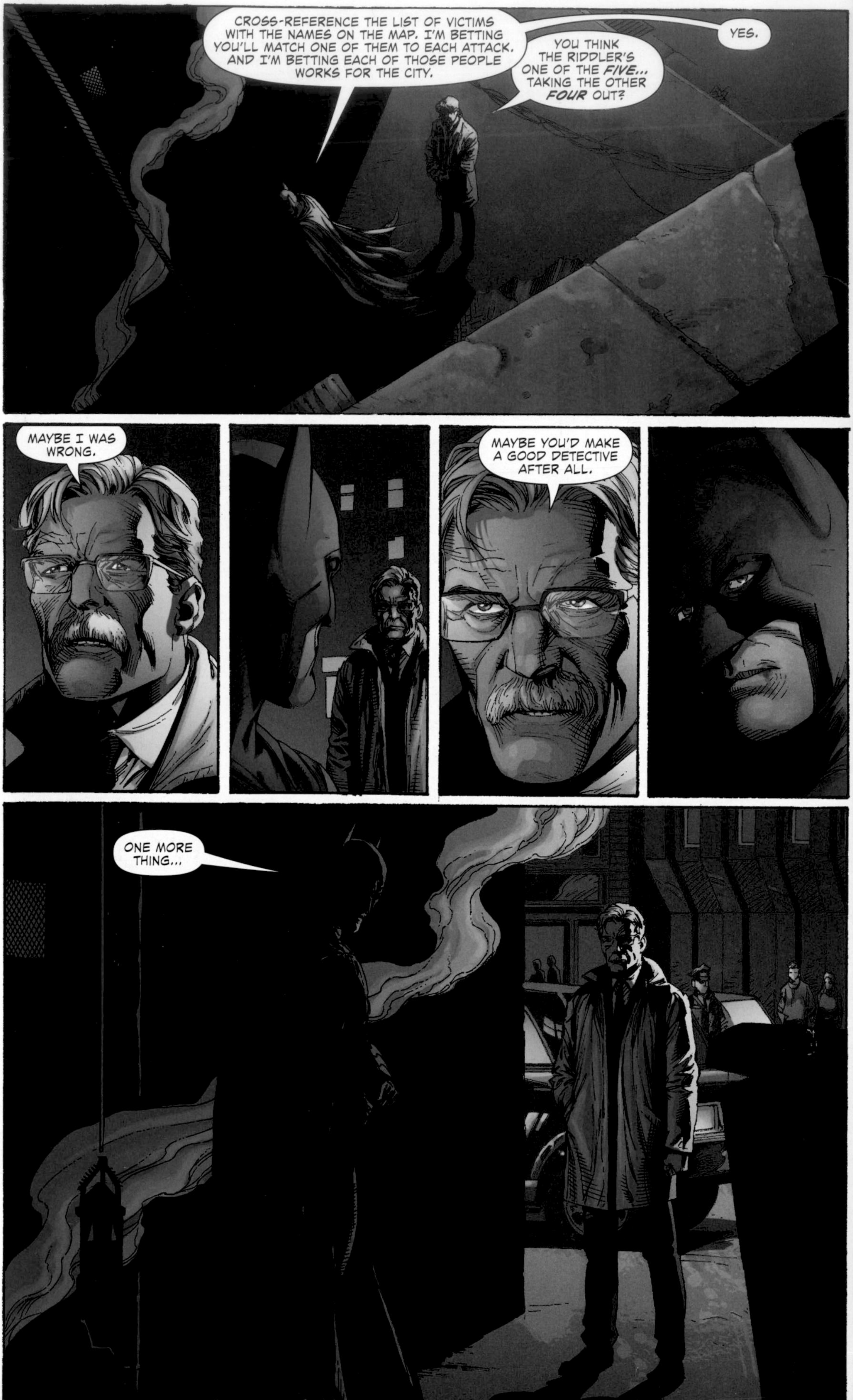
CROSS-REFERENCE THE LIST OF VICTIMS WITH THE NAMES ON THE MAP. I'M BETTING YOU'LL MATCH ONE OF THEM TO EACH ATTACK. AND I'M BETTING EACH OF THOSE PEOPLE WORKS FOR THE CITY.
YOU THINK THE RIDDLER'S ONE OF THE *FIVE...* TAKING THE OTHER *FOUR* OUT?
YES.
MAYBE I WAS WRONG.
MAYBE YOU'D MAKE A GOOD DETECTIVE AFTER ALL.
ONE MORE THING...

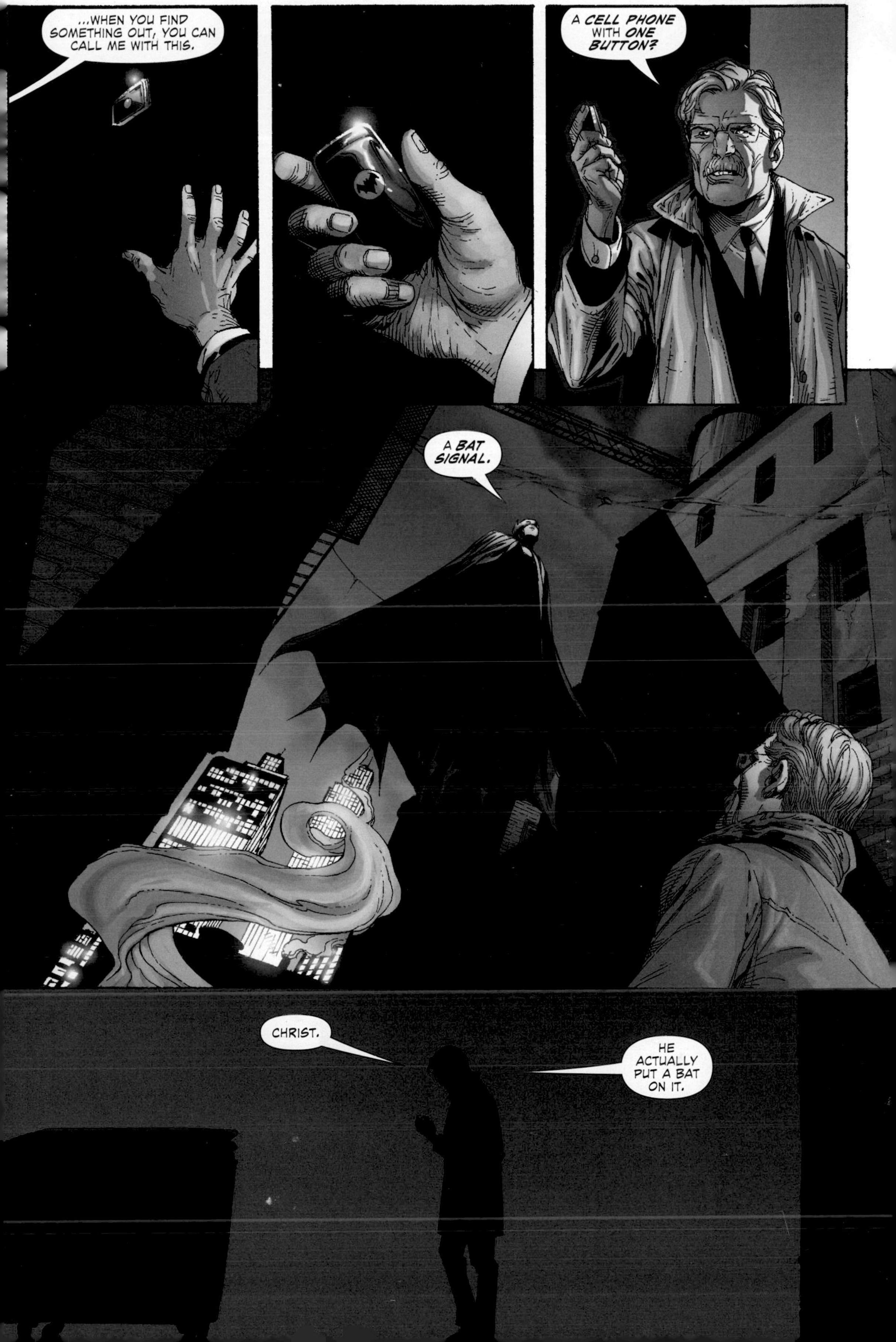
...WHEN YOU FIND SOMETHING OUT, YOU CAN CALL ME WITH THIS.
A CELL PHONE WITH ONE BUTTON?
A BAT SIGNAL.
CHRIST.
HE ACTUALLY PUT A BAT ON IT.

THIS WAS SENT TO MY OFFICE EARLIER TODAY.

AND YOU OPENED IT?

AFTER I MADE SURE IT WASN'T TICKING.

BLIMEY, JESS. YOU SHOULD'VE CALLED THE BOMB SQUAD OR SOMETHIN'.

I CAN'T TRUST ANYONE WITH THIS, ALFRED.

"I'LL STOP ASKING QUESTIONS IF YOU ARREST HIM."

I'LL STOP asKiNG QueStioNS F yoU ARReST HiM

ARREST WHO?

BATMAN.

BATMAN? WHAT DOES HE WANT WITH BATMAN...?

...AND WHY COME HERE WITH THIS?

ALFRED...

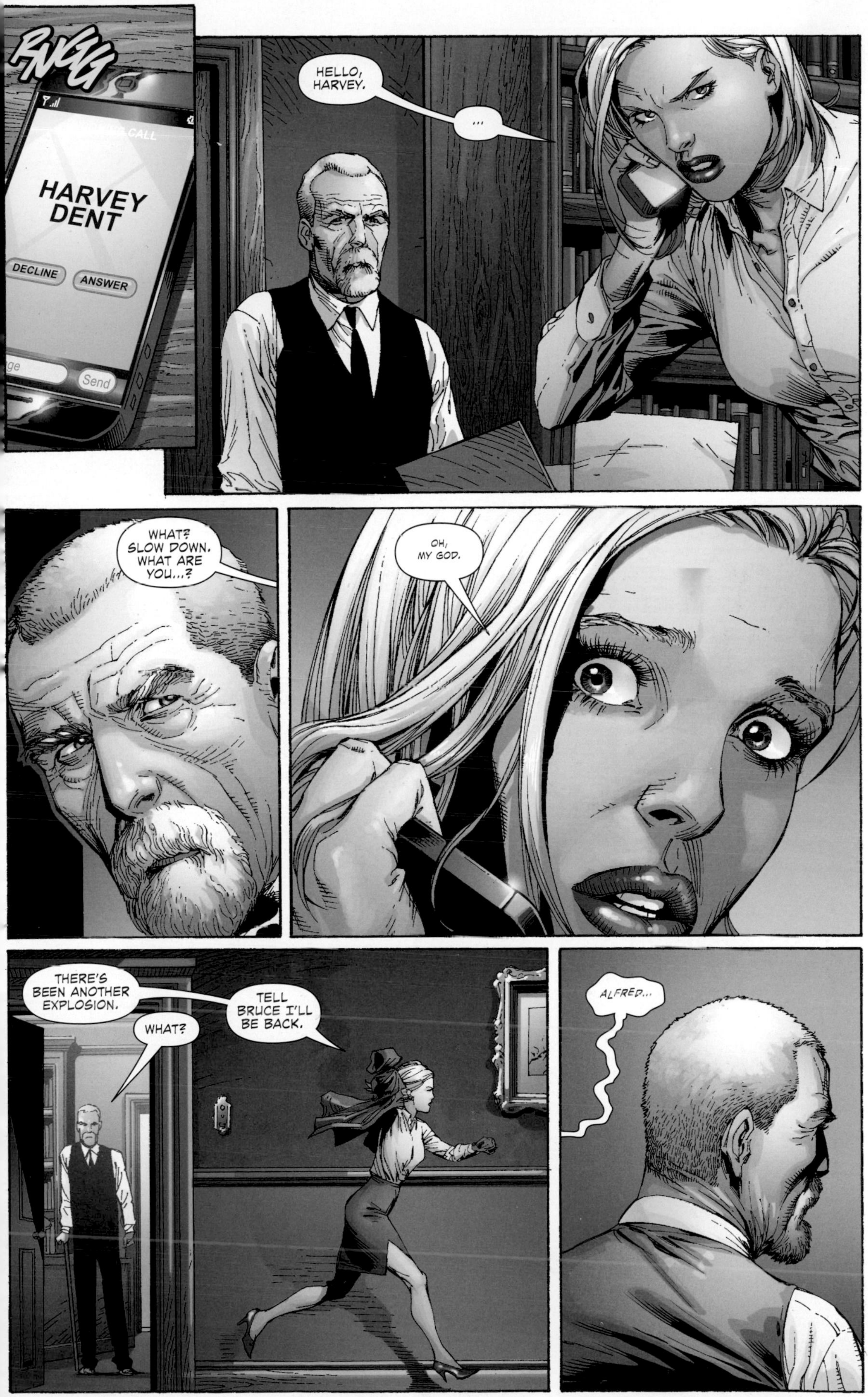
RNGGG
HARVEY DENT
DECLINE
ANSWER
Send
HELLO, HARVEY.
...
WHAT? SLOW DOWN. WHAT ARE YOU...?
OH, MY GOD.
THERE'S BEEN ANOTHER EXPLOSION.
WHAT?
TELL BRUCE I'LL BE BACK.
ALFRED...

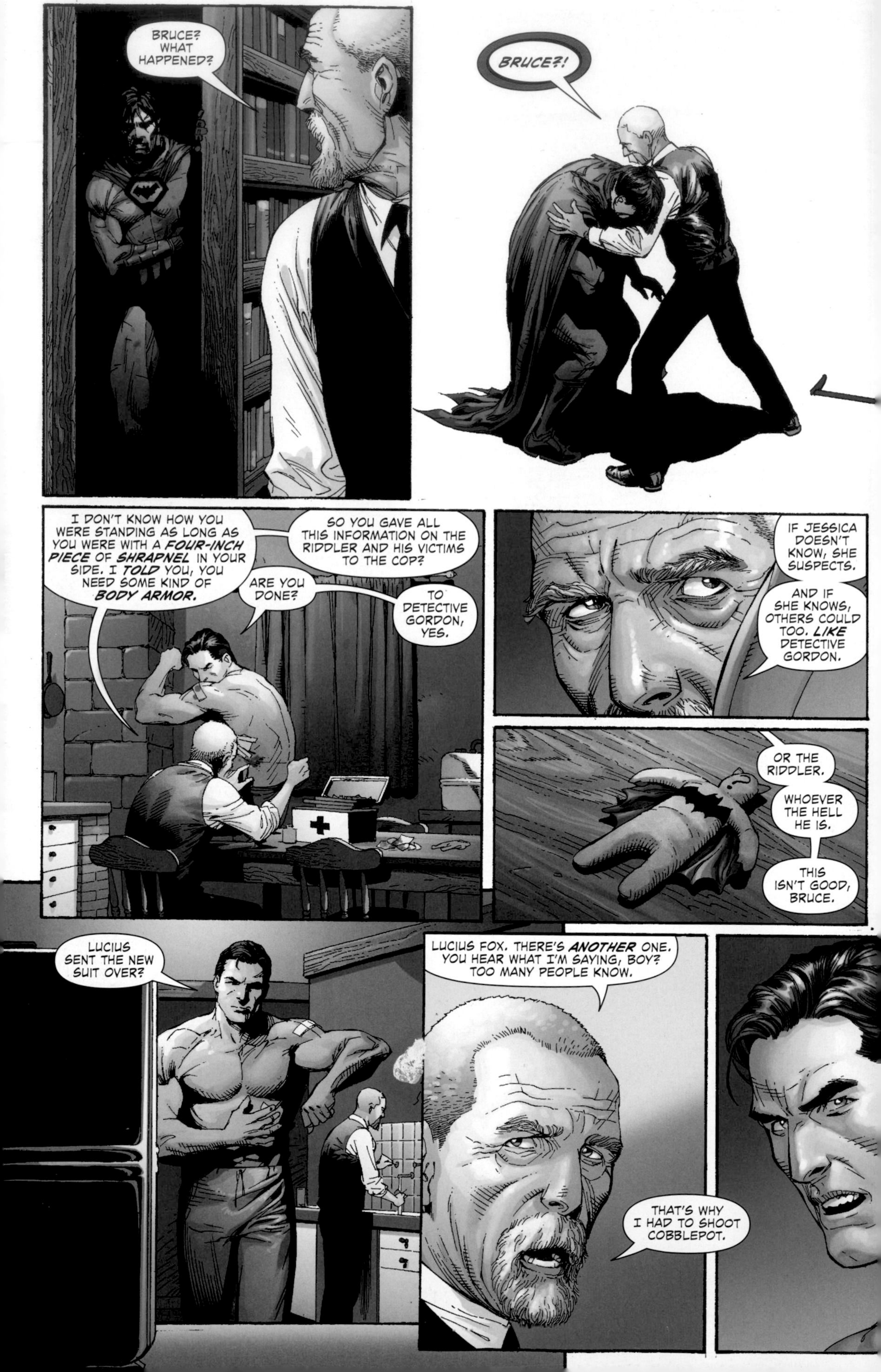
BRUCE? WHAT HAPPENED?
BRUCE?!
I DON'T KNOW HOW YOU WERE STANDING AS LONG AS YOU WERE WITH A FOUR-INCH PIECE OF SHRAPNEL IN YOUR SIDE. I TOLD YOU, YOU NEED SOME KIND OF BODY ARMOR.
ARE YOU DONE?
SO YOU GAVE ALL THIS INFORMATION ON THE RIDDLER AND HIS VICTIMS TO THE COP?
TO DETECTIVE GORDON, YES.
IF JESSICA DOESN'T KNOW, SHE SUSPECTS.
AND IF SHE KNOWS, OTHERS COULD TOO. LIKE DETECTIVE GORDON.
OR THE RIDDLER.
WHOEVER THE HELL HE IS.
THIS ISN'T GOOD, BRUCE.
LUCIUS SENT THE NEW SUIT OVER?
LUCIUS FOX. THERE'S ANOTHER ONE. YOU HEAR WHAT I'M SAYING, BOY? TOO MANY PEOPLE KNOW.
THAT'S WHY I HAD TO SHOOT COBBLEPOT.

YOU TOLD ME YOU SHOT HIM BECAUSE YOU THOUGHT HE WAS GOING TO KILL ME.

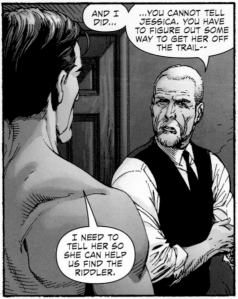

AND I DID...

...YOU CANNOT TELL JESSICA. YOU HAVE TO FIGURE OUT SOME WAY TO GET HER OFF THE TRAIL--

I NEED TO TELL HER SO SHE CAN HELP US FIND THE RIDDLER.

YOU CAN'T HAVE HER *AND* BATMAN, BRUCE.

YOU MADE THAT CHOICE A LONG TIME AGO, NOT *ME.*

YOU'RE NOT A *MAN* ANYMORE.

YOU'RE A *WEAPON.*

IS *THAT* WHAT YOU TURNED ME INTO?

THAT'S WHAT YOU *ASKED* TO BE TURNED INTO.

WEAPONS ARE DESIGNED TO *HURT* PEOPLE. YOU DON'T WANT TO HURT *HER.*

BATMAN?

VZZD

I'VE MATCHED THE NAMES.

AND SOMETHING *ELSE...*

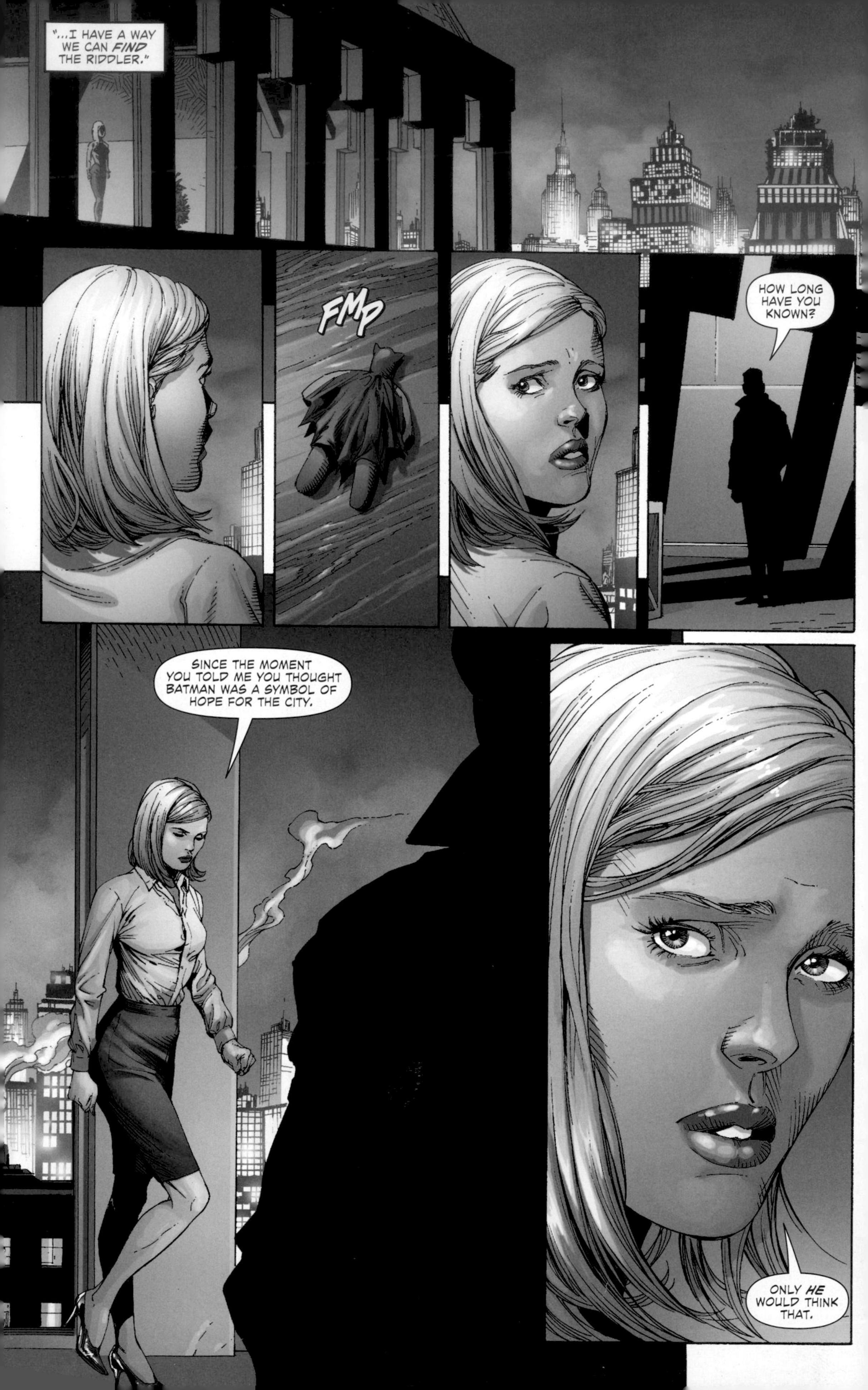
"...I HAVE A WAY WE CAN FIND THE RIDDLER."
FMP
HOW LONG HAVE YOU KNOWN?
SINCE THE MOMENT YOU TOLD ME YOU THOUGHT BATMAN WAS A SYMBOL OF HOPE FOR THE CITY.
ONLY HE WOULD THINK THAT.

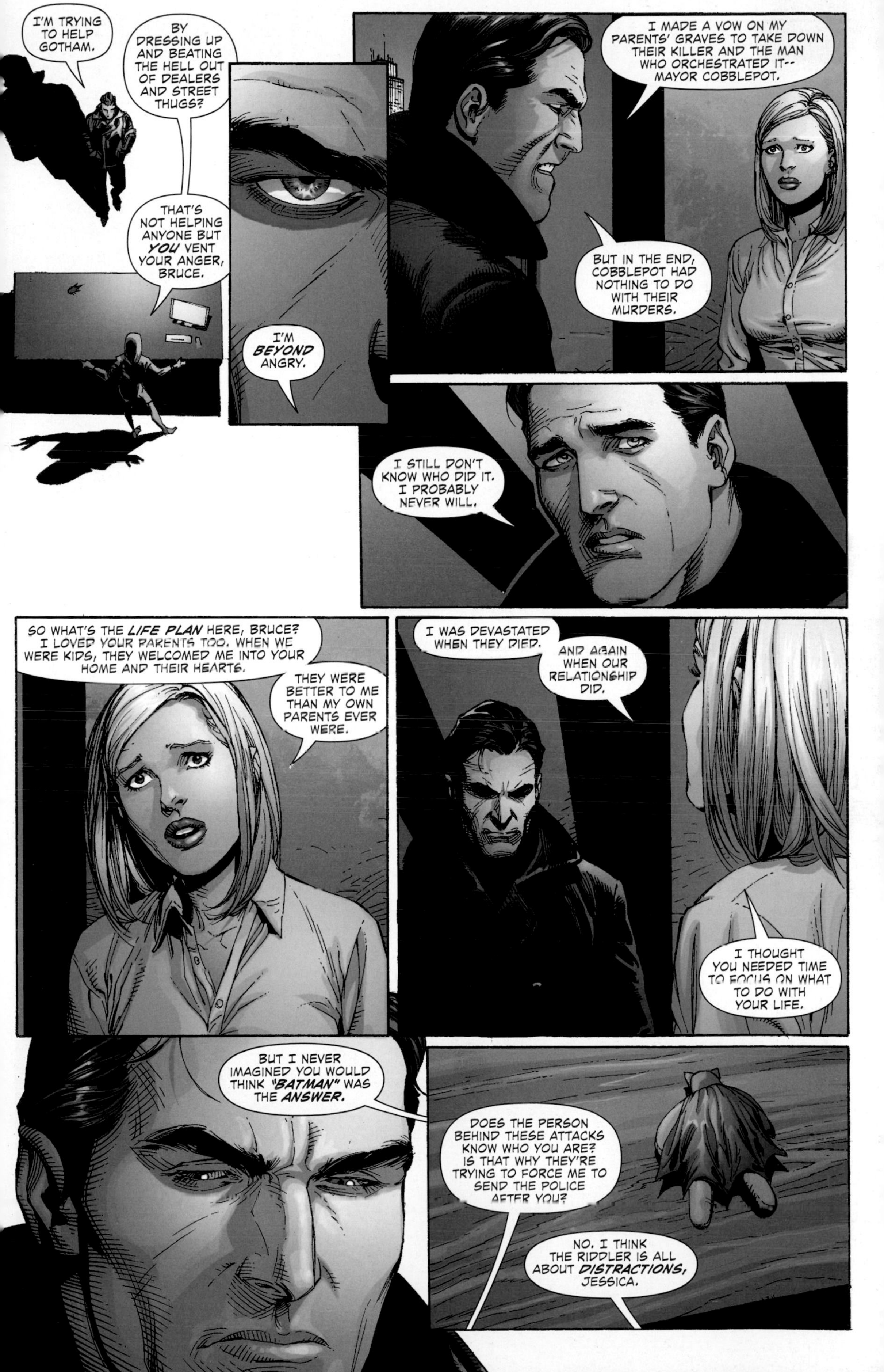
I'M TRYING TO HELP GOTHAM.
BY DRESSING UP AND BEATING THE HELL OUT OF DEALERS AND STREET THUGS?
THAT'S NOT HELPING ANYONE BUT *YOU* VENT YOUR ANGER, BRUCE.
I'M *BEYOND* ANGRY.
I MADE A VOW ON MY PARENTS' GRAVES TO TAKE DOWN THEIR KILLER AND THE MAN WHO ORCHESTRATED IT-- MAYOR COBBLEPOT.
BUT IN THE END, COBBLEPOT HAD NOTHING TO DO WITH THEIR MURDERS.
I STILL DON'T KNOW WHO DID IT. I PROBABLY NEVER WILL.
SO WHAT'S THE *LIFE PLAN* HERE, BRUCE? I LOVED YOUR PARENTS TOO. WHEN WE WERE KIDS, THEY WELCOMED ME INTO YOUR HOME AND THEIR HEARTS.
THEY WERE BETTER TO ME THAN MY OWN PARENTS EVER WERE.
I WAS DEVASTATED WHEN THEY DIED.
AND AGAIN WHEN OUR RELATIONSHIP DID.
I THOUGHT YOU NEEDED TIME TO FOCUS ON WHAT TO DO WITH YOUR LIFE.
BUT I NEVER IMAGINED YOU WOULD THINK *"BATMAN"* WAS THE *ANSWER.*
DOES THE PERSON BEHIND THESE ATTACKS KNOW WHO YOU ARE? IS THAT WHY THEY'RE TRYING TO FORCE ME TO SEND THE POLICE AFTER YOU?
NO. I THINK THE RIDDLER IS ALL ABOUT *DISTRACTIONS,* JESSICA.

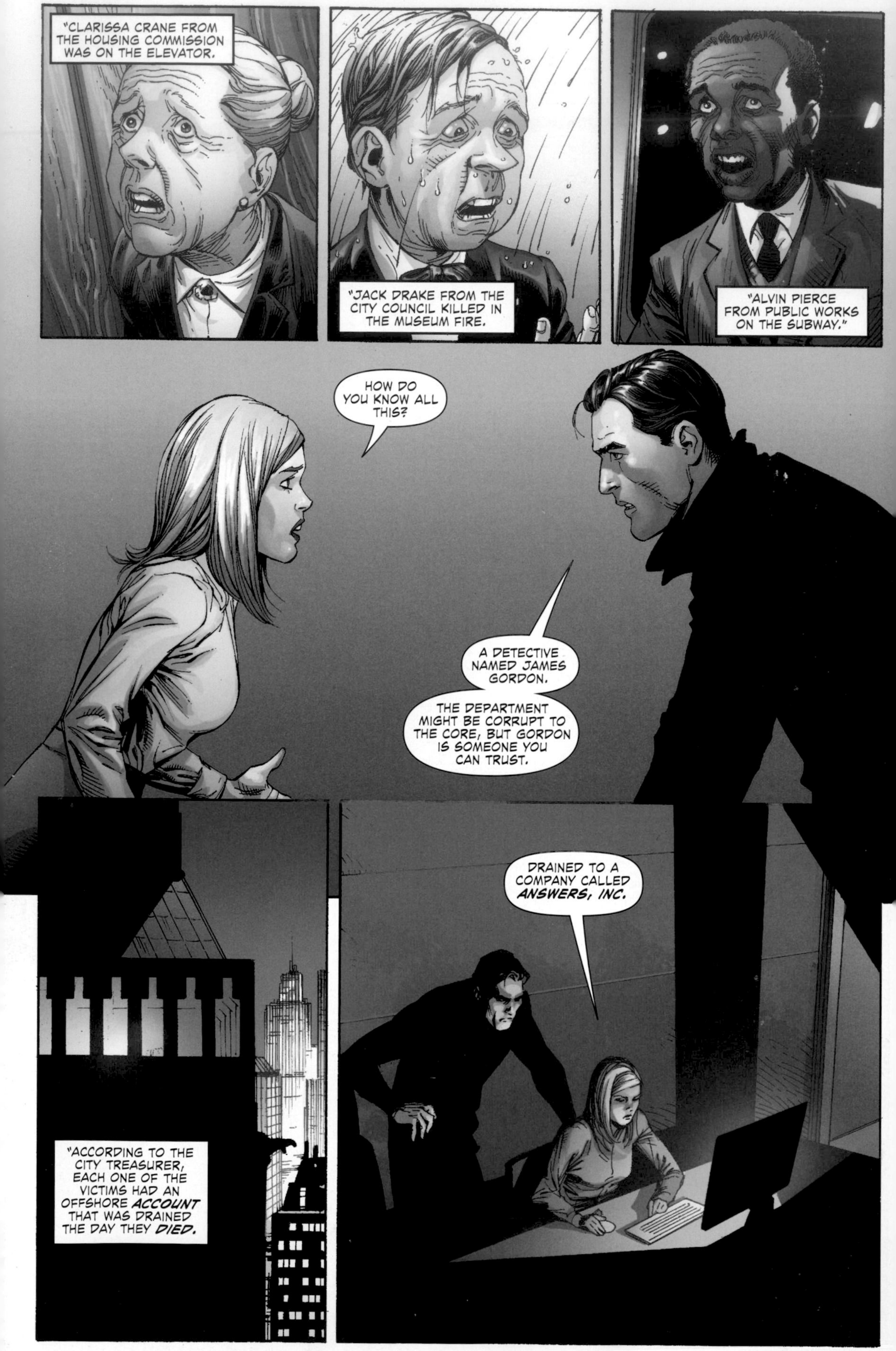
"CLARISSA CRANE FROM THE HOUSING COMMISSION WAS ON THE ELEVATOR.
"JACK DRAKE FROM THE CITY COUNCIL KILLED IN THE MUSEUM FIRE.
"ALVIN PIERCE FROM PUBLIC WORKS ON THE SUBWAY."
HOW DO YOU KNOW ALL THIS?
A DETECTIVE NAMED JAMES GORDON.
THE DEPARTMENT MIGHT BE CORRUPT TO THE CORE, BUT GORDON IS SOMEONE YOU CAN TRUST.
"ACCORDING TO THE CITY TREASURER, EACH ONE OF THE VICTIMS HAD AN OFFSHORE ACCOUNT THAT WAS DRAINED THE DAY THEY DIED.
DRAINED TO A COMPANY CALLED ANSWERS, INC.

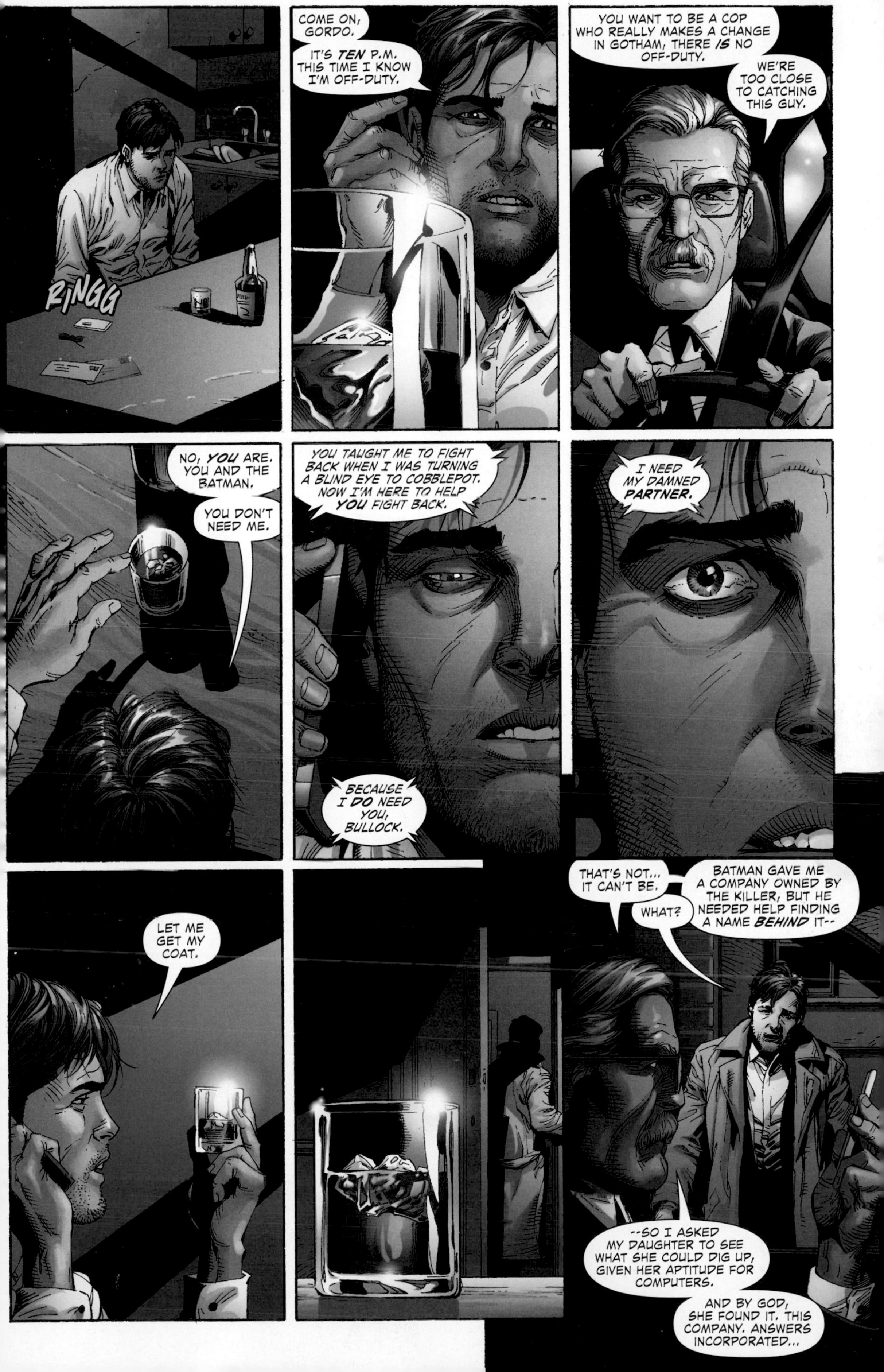
RINGG
COME ON, GORDO.
IT'S TEN P.M. THIS TIME I KNOW I'M OFF-DUTY.
YOU WANT TO BE A COP WHO REALLY MAKES A CHANGE IN GOTHAM, THERE IS NO OFF-DUTY.
WE'RE TOO CLOSE TO CATCHING THIS GUY.
NO, YOU ARE. YOU AND THE BATMAN.
YOU DON'T NEED ME.
YOU TAUGHT ME TO FIGHT BACK WHEN I WAS TURNING A BLIND EYE TO COBBLEPOT. NOW I'M HERE TO HELP YOU FIGHT BACK.
BECAUSE I DO NEED YOU, BULLOCK.
I NEED MY DAMNED PARTNER.
LET ME GET MY COAT.
THAT'S NOT... IT CAN'T BE.
WHAT?
BATMAN GAVE ME A COMPANY OWNED BY THE KILLER, BUT HE NEEDED HELP FINDING A NAME BEHIND IT--
--SO I ASKED MY DAUGHTER TO SEE WHAT SHE COULD DIG UP, GIVEN HER APTITUDE FOR COMPUTERS.
AND BY GOD, SHE FOUND IT. THIS COMPANY. ANSWERS INCORPORATED...

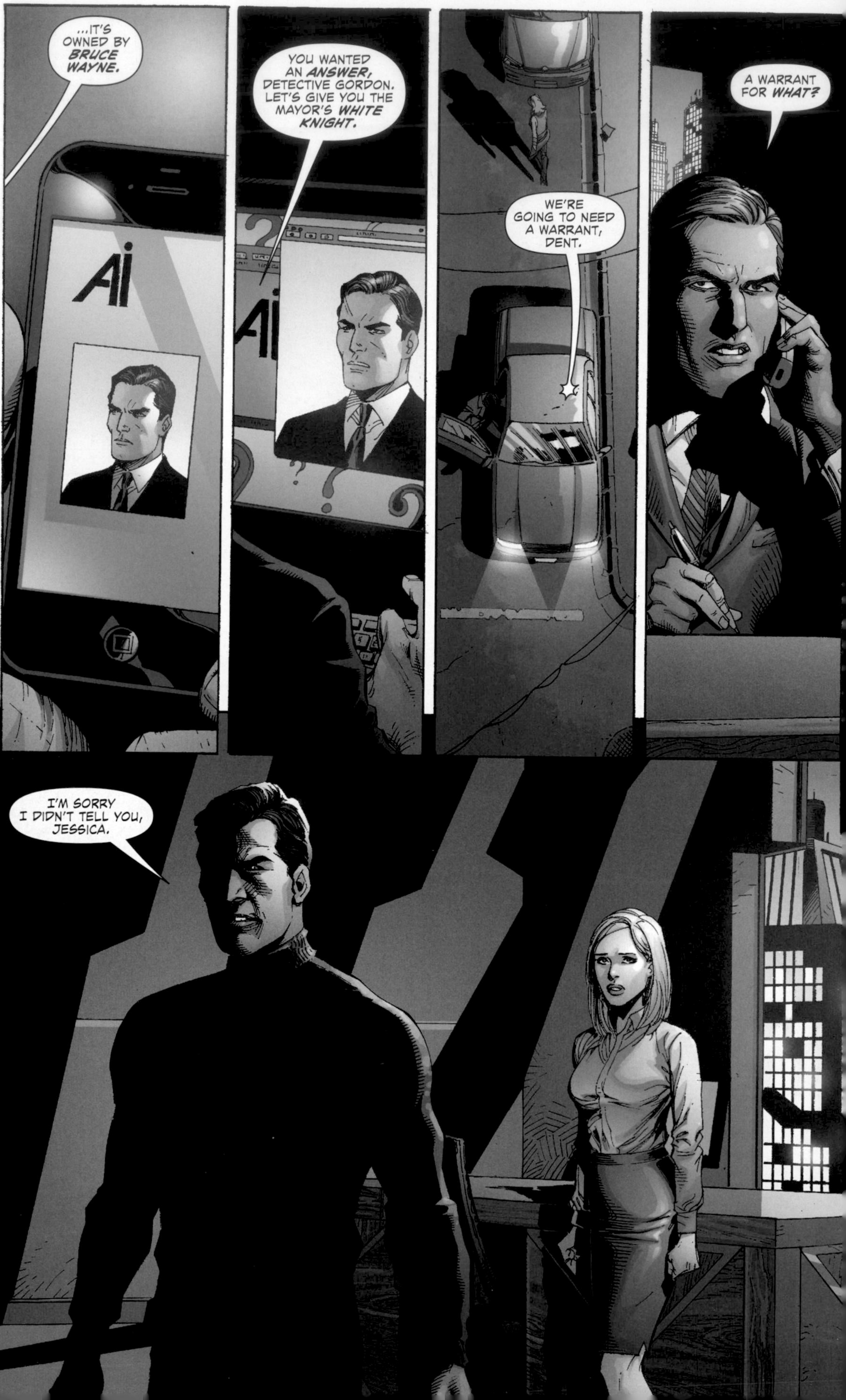
...IT'S OWNED BY *BRUCE WAYNE.*
YOU WANTED AN *ANSWER,* DETECTIVE GORDON. LET'S GIVE YOU THE MAYOR'S *WHITE KNIGHT.*
WE'RE GOING TO NEED A WARRANT, DENT.
A WARRANT FOR *WHAT?*
I'M SORRY I DIDN'T TELL YOU, JESSICA.

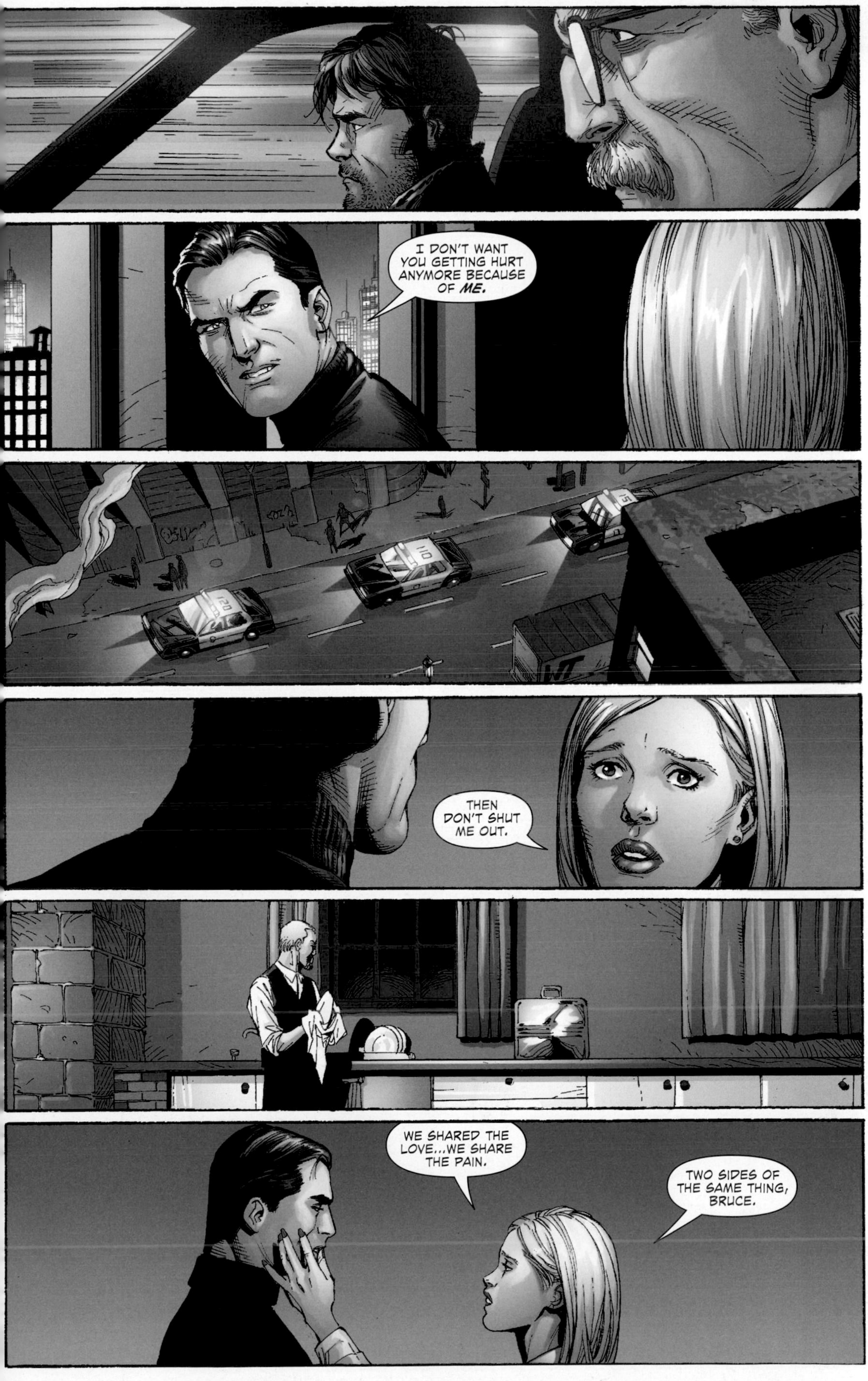
I DON'T WANT YOU GETTING HURT ANYMORE BECAUSE OF *ME.*
THEN DON'T SHUT ME OUT.
WE SHARED THE LOVE...WE SHARE THE PAIN.
TWO SIDES OF THE SAME THING, BRUCE.

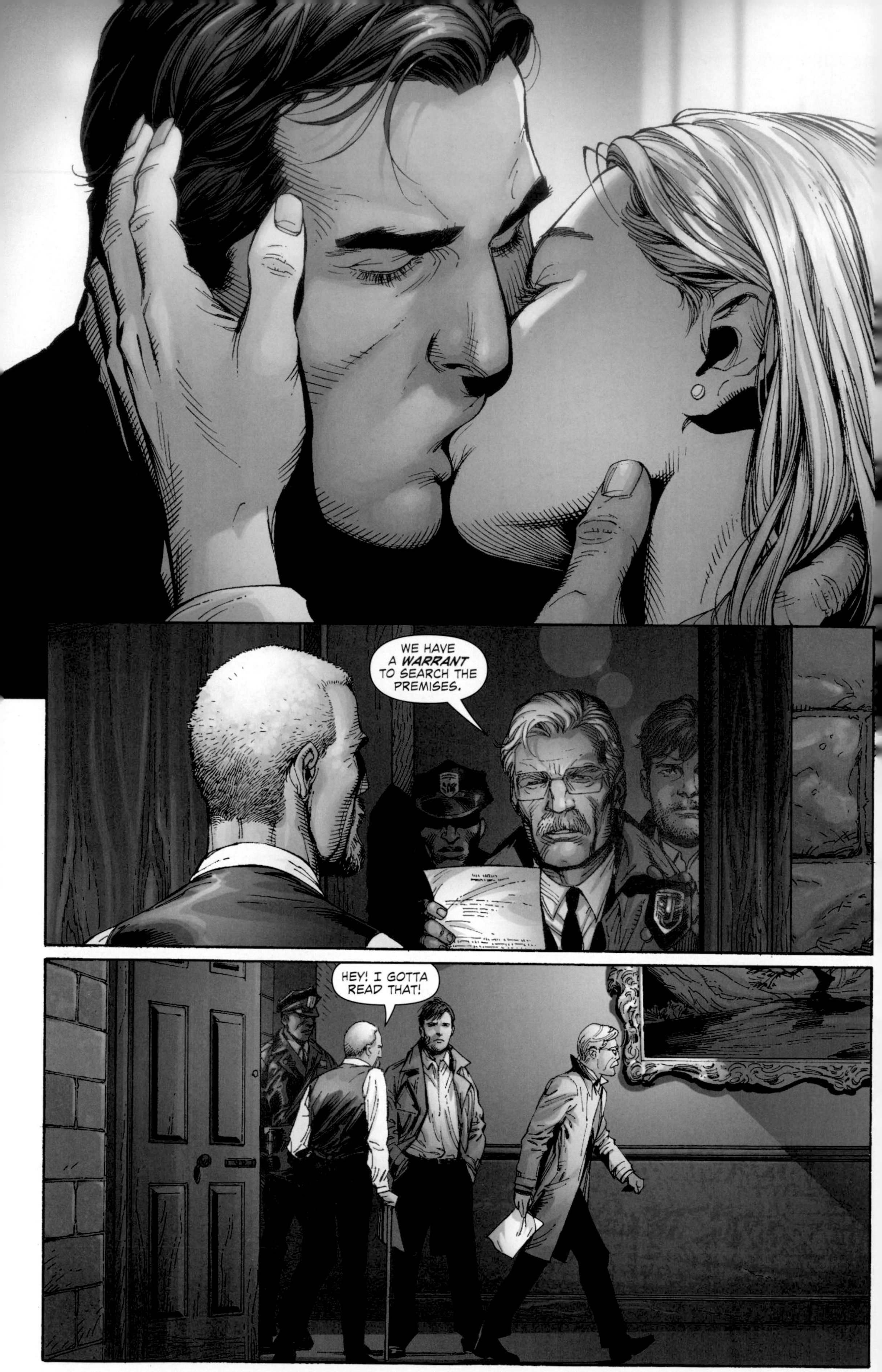
WE HAVE A WARRANT TO SEARCH THE PREMISES.
HEY! I GOTTA READ THAT!

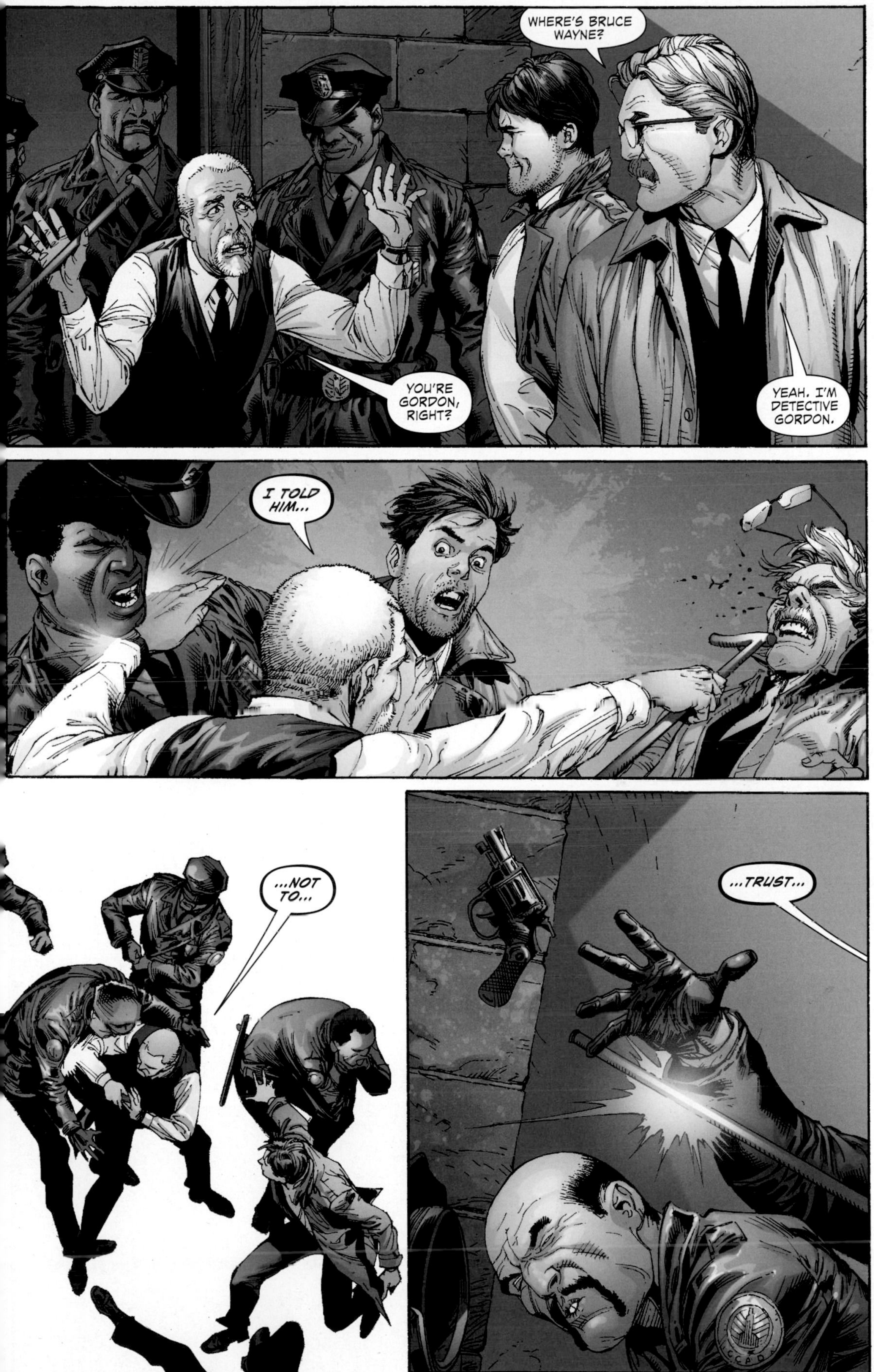
WHERE'S BRUCE WAYNE?
YOU'RE GORDON, RIGHT?
YEAH. I'M DETECTIVE GORDON.
I TOLD HIM...
...NOT TO...
...TRUST...

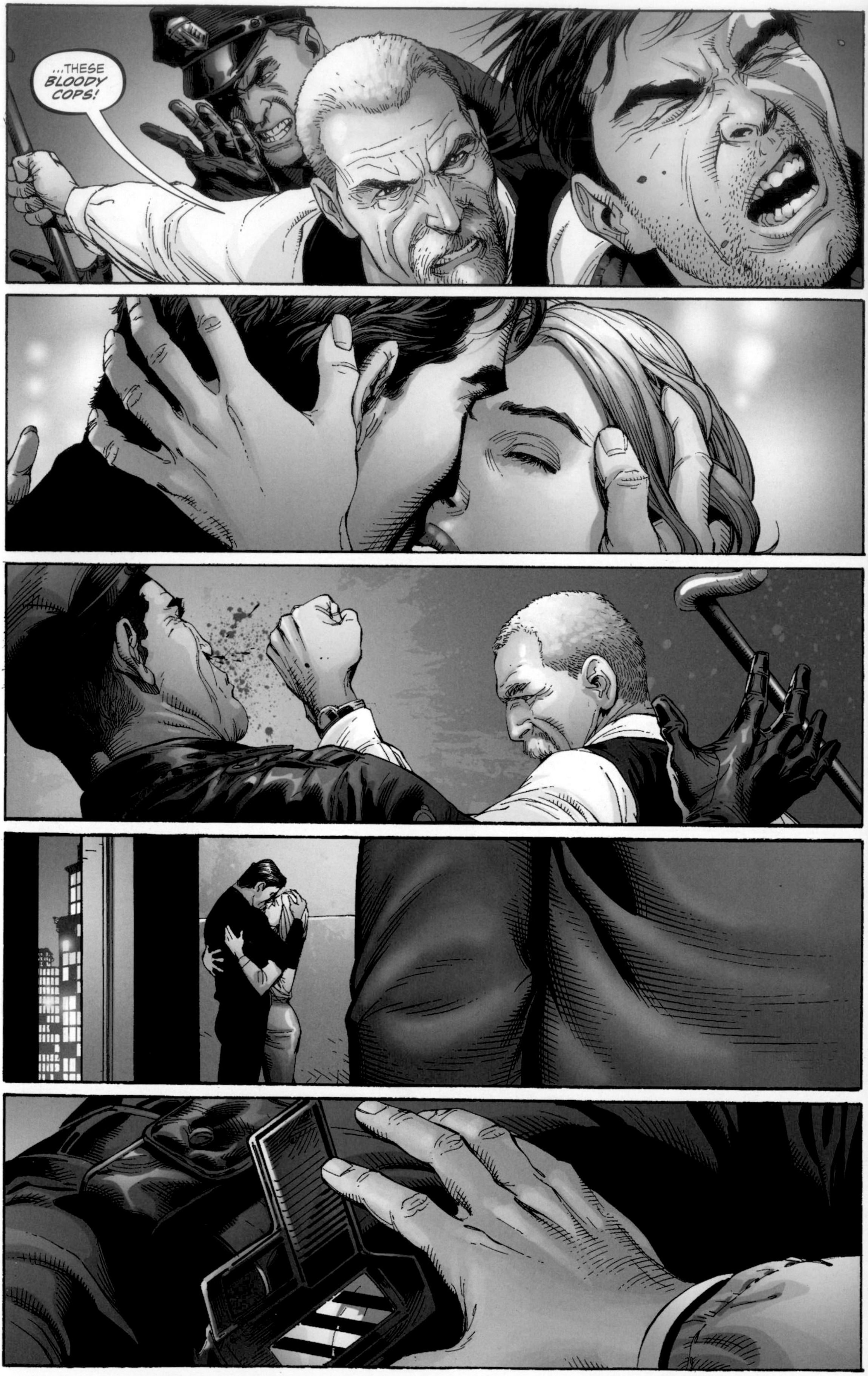
...THESE BLOODY COPS!

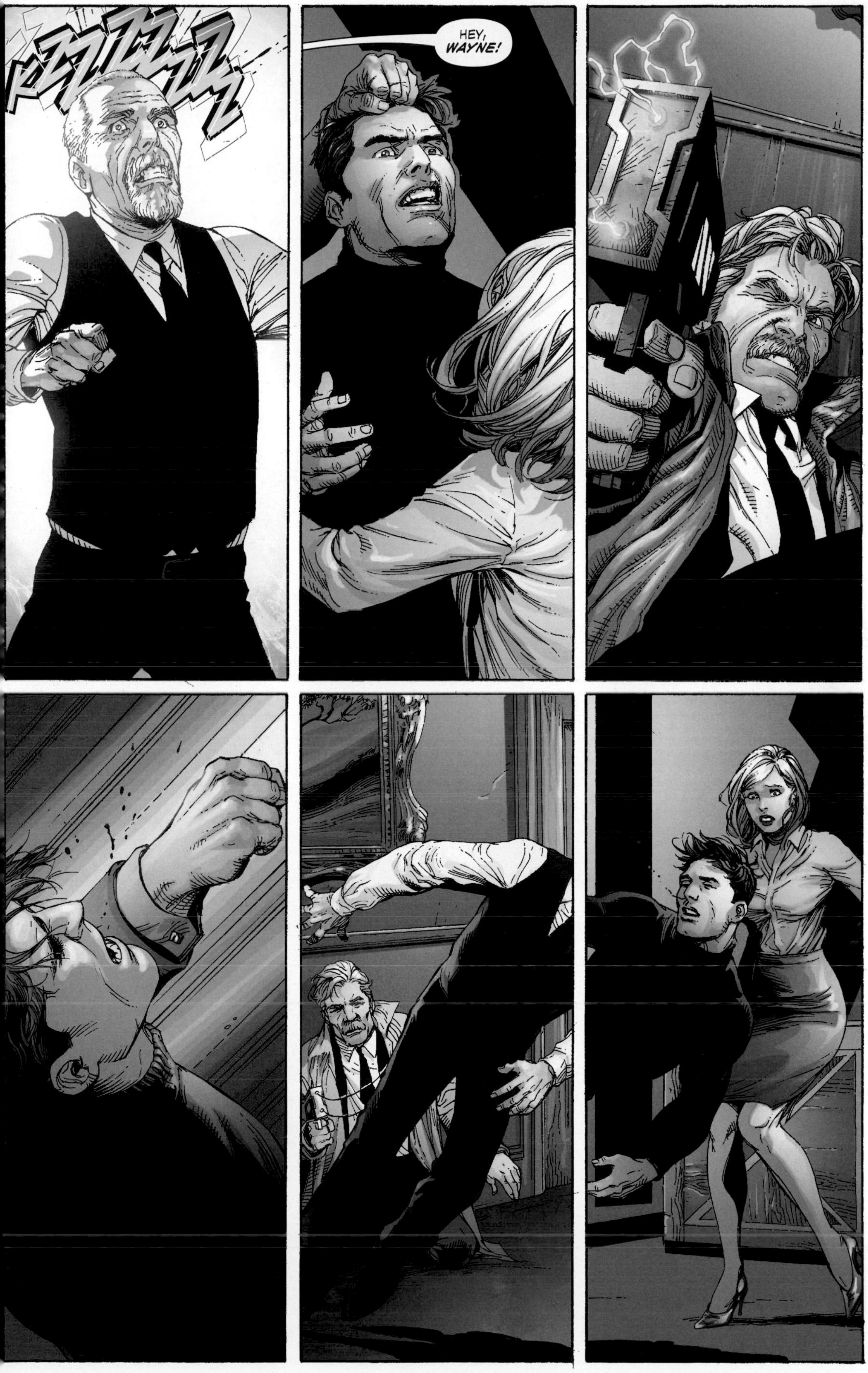
KZZZZZZZ
HEY, WAYNE!

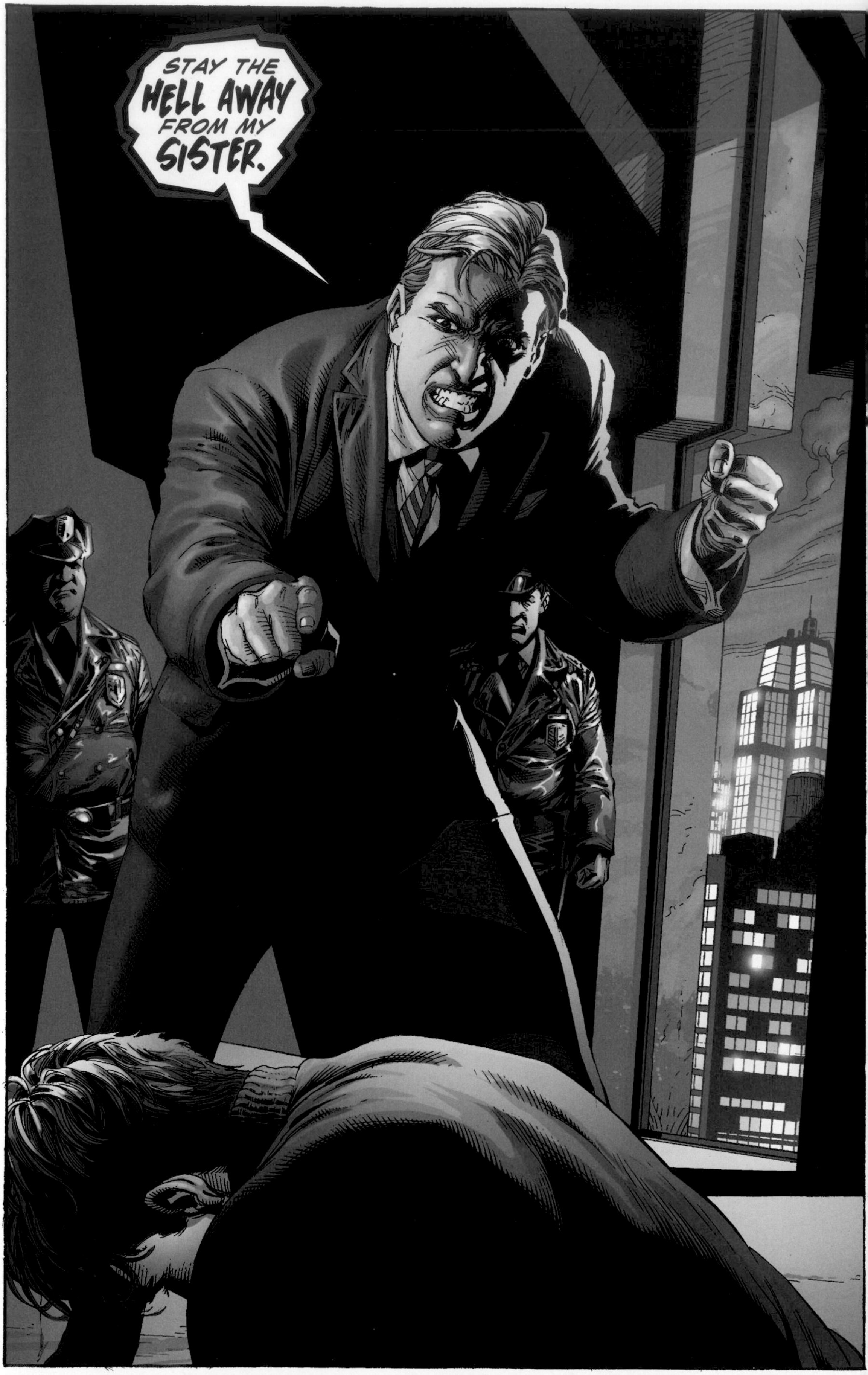
STAY THE HELL AWAY FROM MY SISTER.

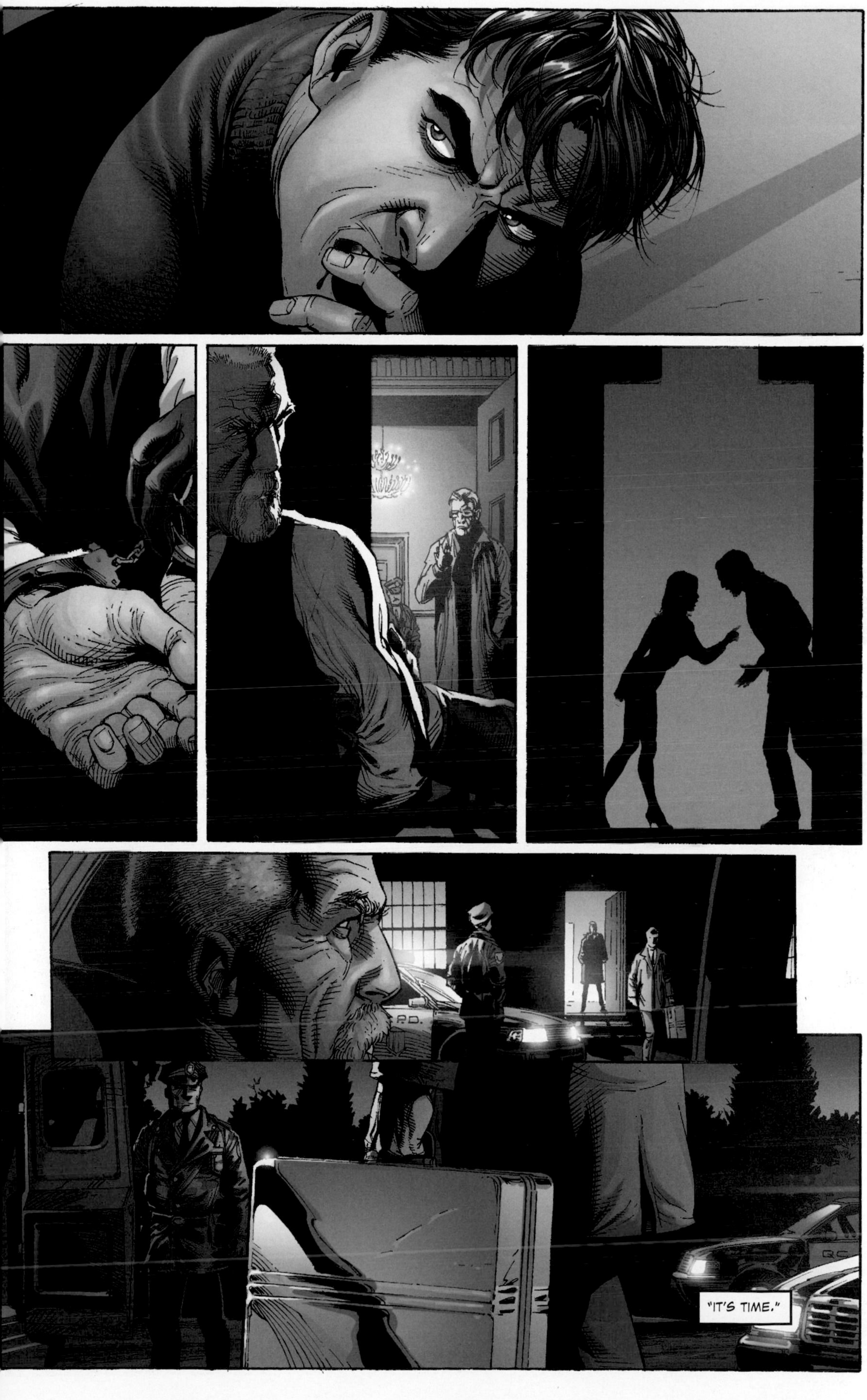
"IT'S TIME."

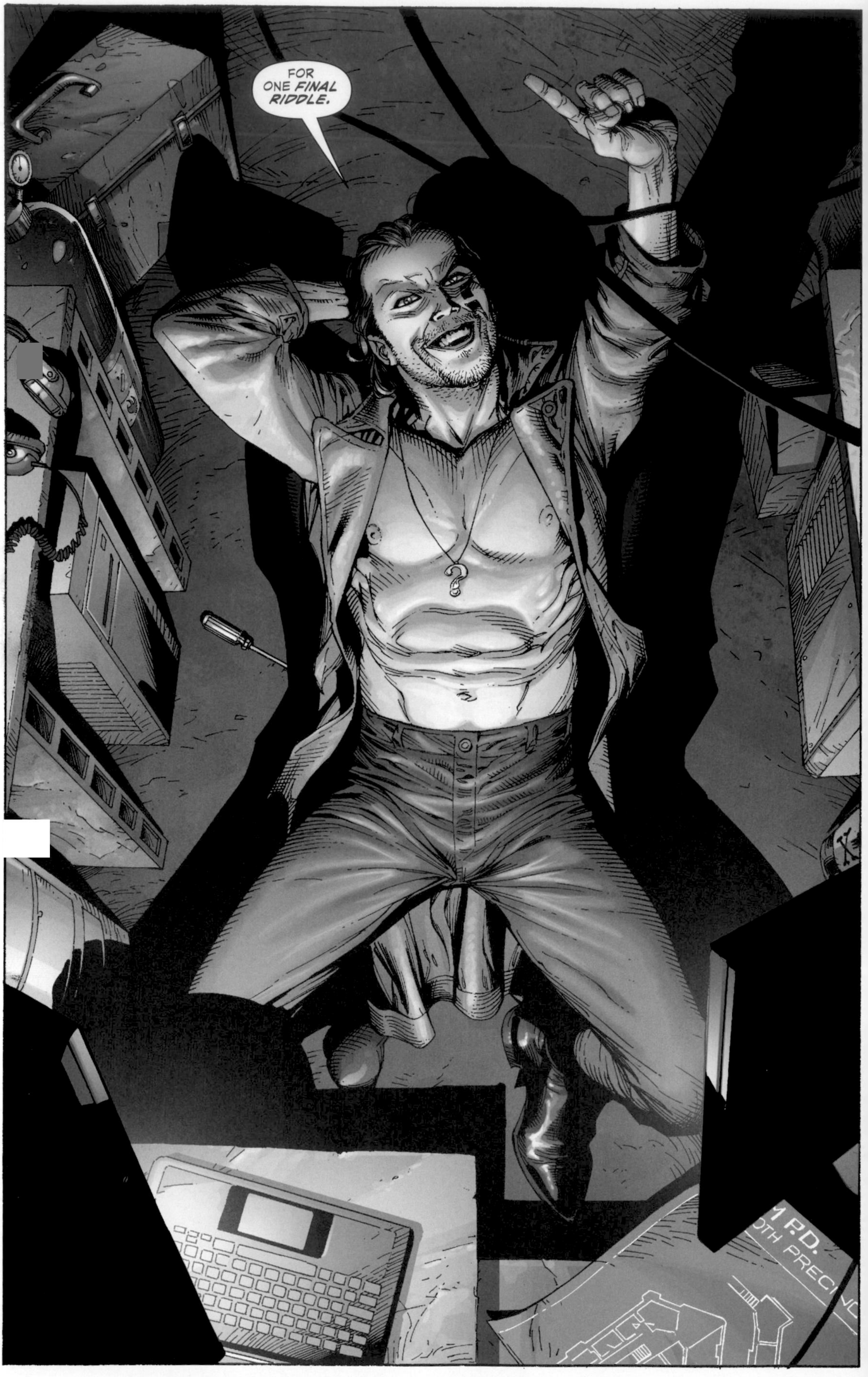
FOR ONE FINAL RIDDLE.

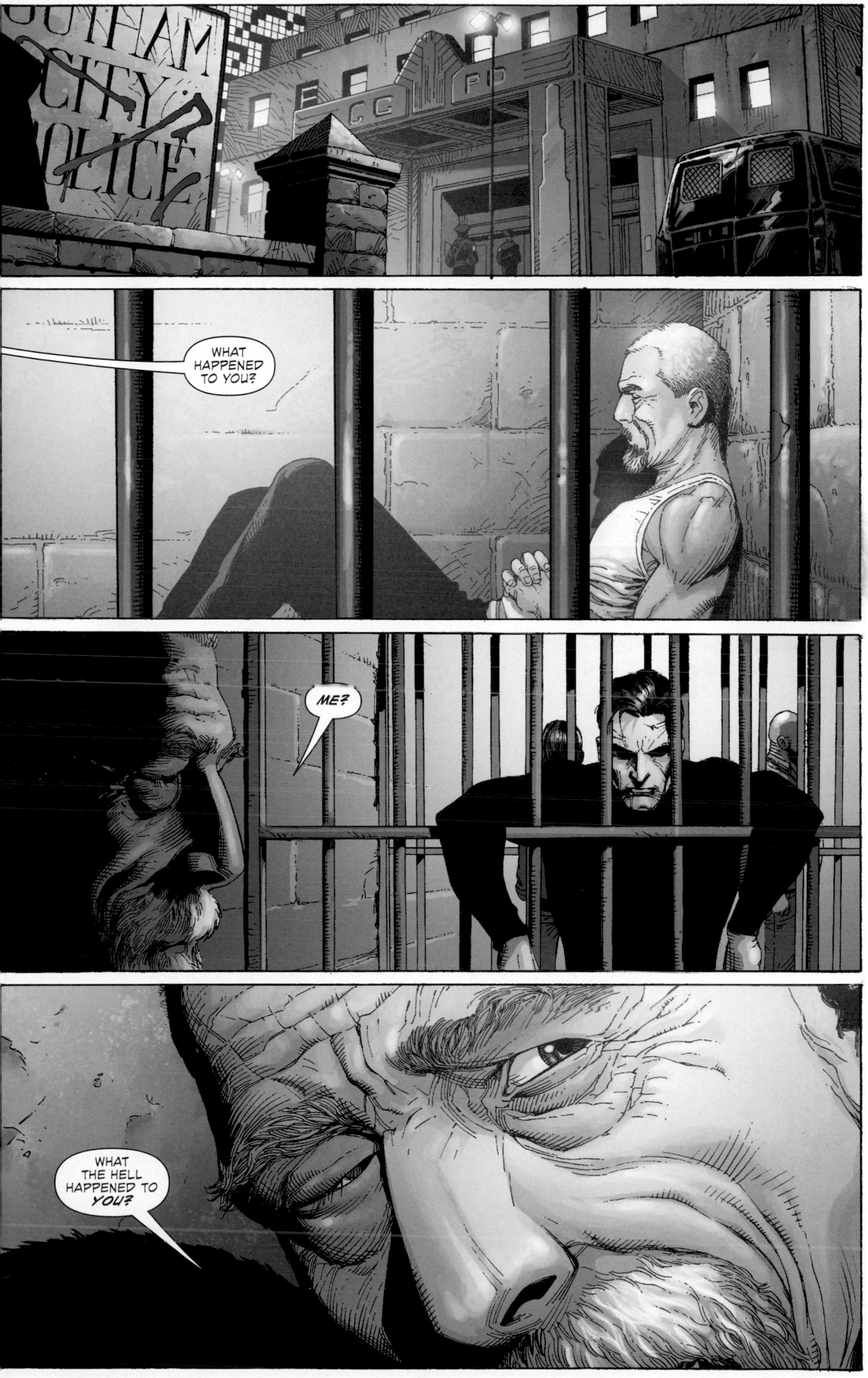
WHAT HAPPENED TO YOU?
ME?
WHAT THE HELL HAPPENED TO YOU?

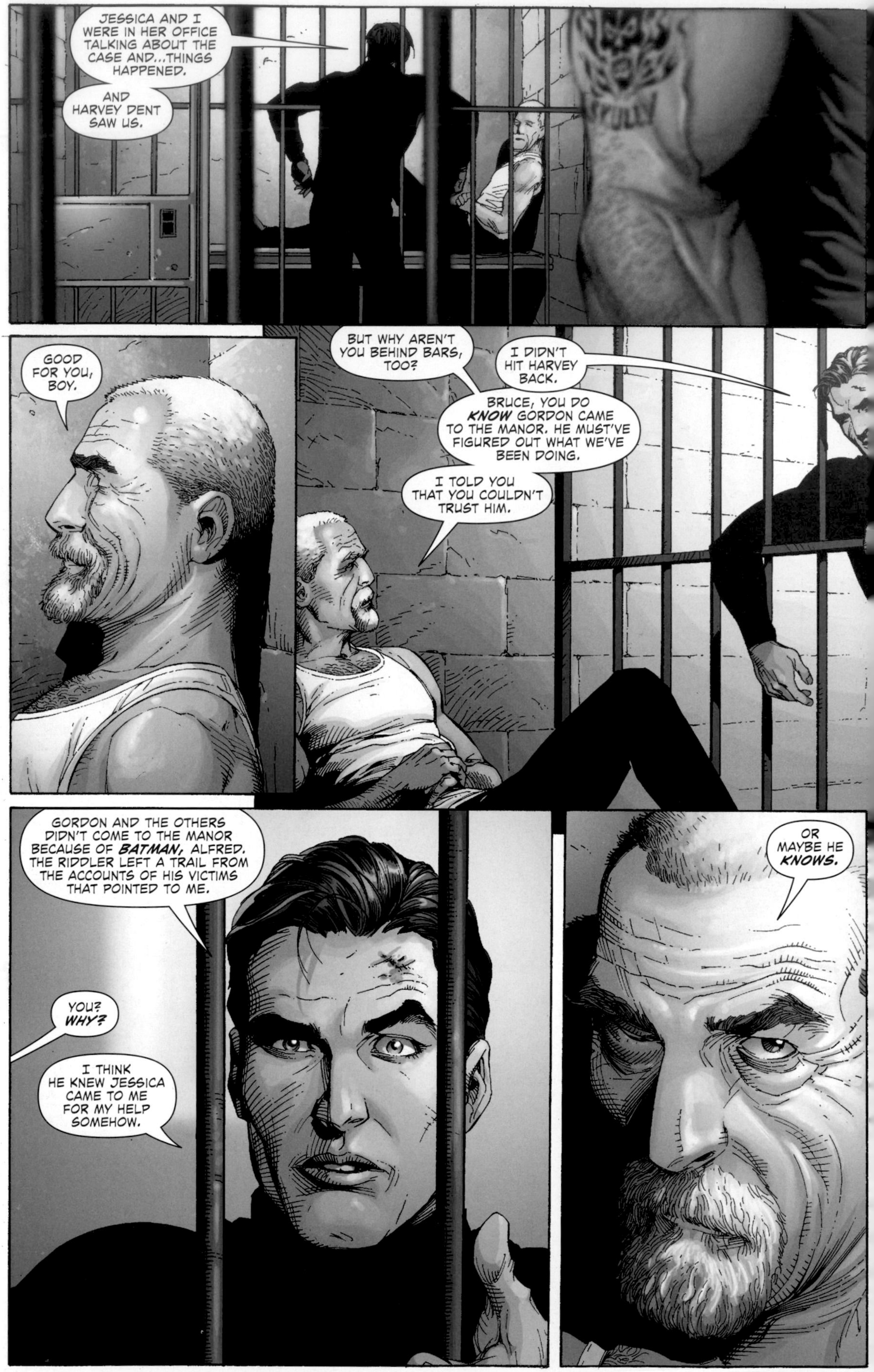
JESSICA AND I WERE IN HER OFFICE TALKING ABOUT THE CASE AND...THINGS HAPPENED.
AND HARVEY DENT SAW US.
GOOD FOR YOU, BOY.
BUT WHY AREN'T YOU BEHIND BARS, TOO?
I DIDN'T HIT HARVEY BACK.
BRUCE, YOU DO KNOW GORDON CAME TO THE MANOR. HE MUST'VE FIGURED OUT WHAT WE'VE BEEN DOING.
I TOLD YOU THAT YOU COULDN'T TRUST HIM.
GORDON AND THE OTHERS DIDN'T COME TO THE MANOR BECAUSE OF BATMAN, ALFRED. THE RIDDLER LEFT A TRAIL FROM THE ACCOUNTS OF HIS VICTIMS THAT POINTED TO ME.
YOU? WHY?
I THINK HE KNEW JESSICA CAME TO ME FOR MY HELP SOMEHOW.
OR MAYBE HE KNOWS.

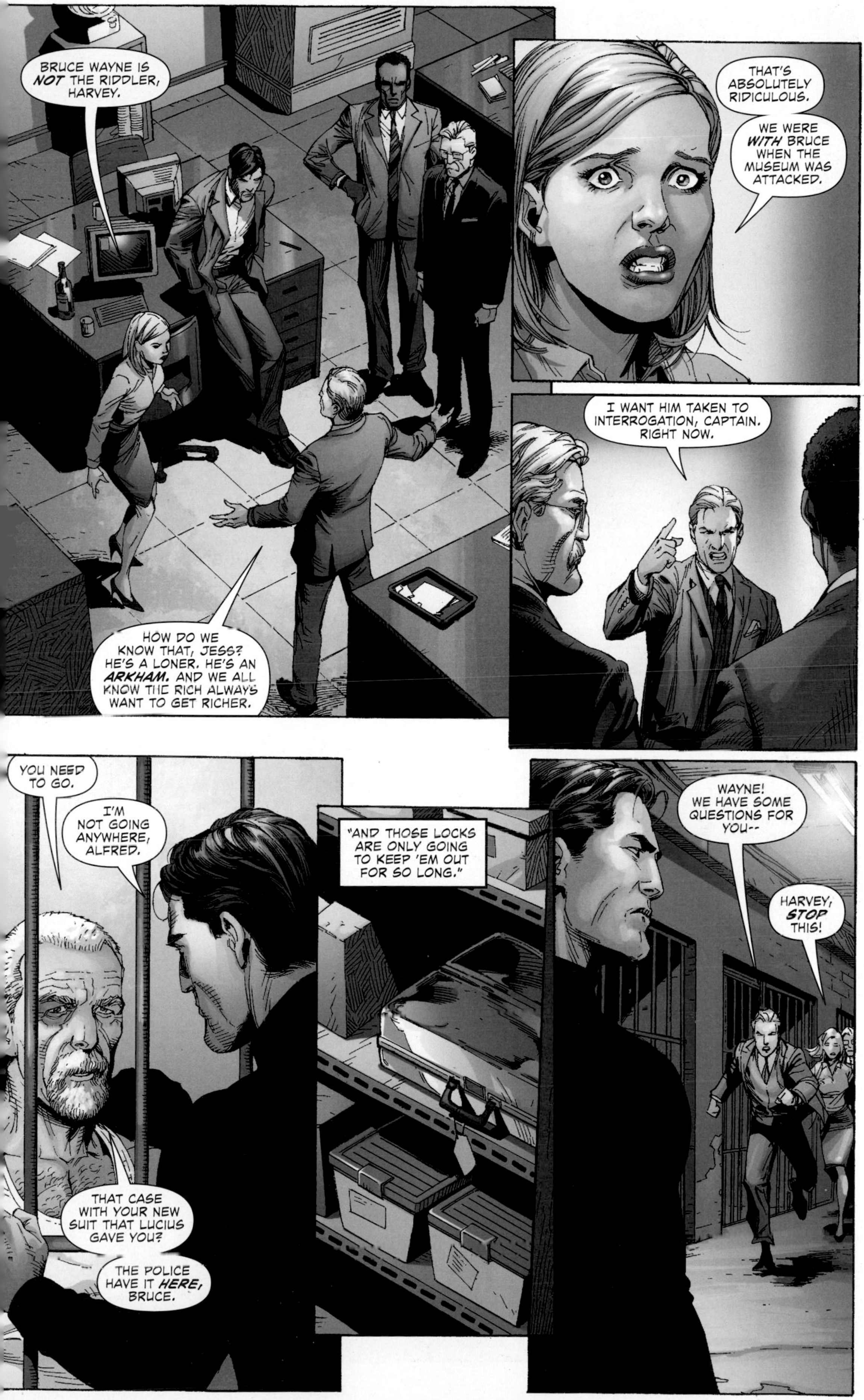
BRUCE WAYNE IS NOT THE RIDDLER, HARVEY.
HOW DO WE KNOW THAT, JESS? HE'S A LONER. HE'S AN ARKHAM. AND WE ALL KNOW THE RICH ALWAYS WANT TO GET RICHER.
THAT'S ABSOLUTELY RIDICULOUS.
WE WERE WITH BRUCE WHEN THE MUSEUM WAS ATTACKED.
I WANT HIM TAKEN TO INTERROGATION, CAPTAIN. RIGHT NOW.
YOU NEED TO GO.
I'M NOT GOING ANYWHERE, ALFRED.
THAT CASE WITH YOUR NEW SUIT THAT LUCIUS GAVE YOU?
THE POLICE HAVE IT HERE, BRUCE.
"AND THOSE LOCKS ARE ONLY GOING TO KEEP 'EM OUT FOR SO LONG."
WAYNE! WE HAVE SOME QUESTIONS FOR YOU--
HARVEY, STOP THIS!

THE POWER'S OUT.

THANKS TO ME.

GOOD EVENING, LADIES AND GENTLEMEN.

OFFICERS.

MR. DISTRICT ATTORNEY. MAYOR DENT.

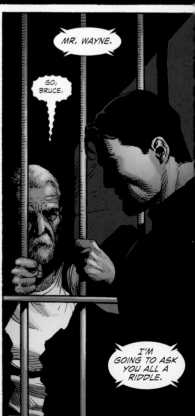

MR. WAYNE.

GO, BRUCE.

I'M GOING TO ASK YOU ALL A RIDDLE.

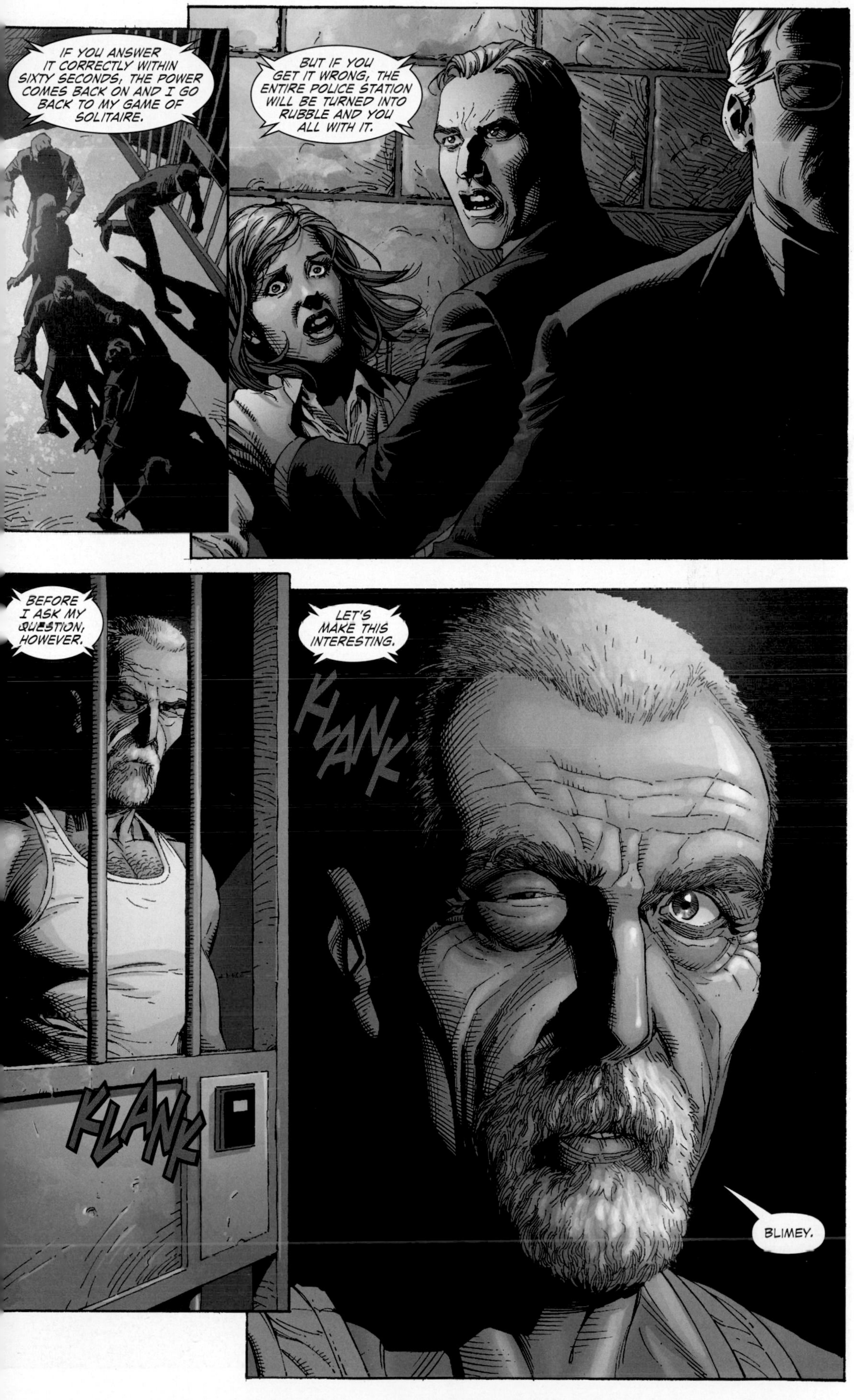
IF YOU ANSWER IT CORRECTLY WITHIN SIXTY SECONDS, THE POWER COMES BACK ON AND I GO BACK TO MY GAME OF SOLITAIRE.
BUT IF YOU GET IT WRONG, THE ENTIRE POLICE STATION WILL BE TURNED INTO RUBBLE AND YOU ALL WITH IT.
BEFORE I ASK MY QUESTION, HOWEVER.
LET'S MAKE THIS INTERESTING.
KLANK
KLANK
BLIMEY.

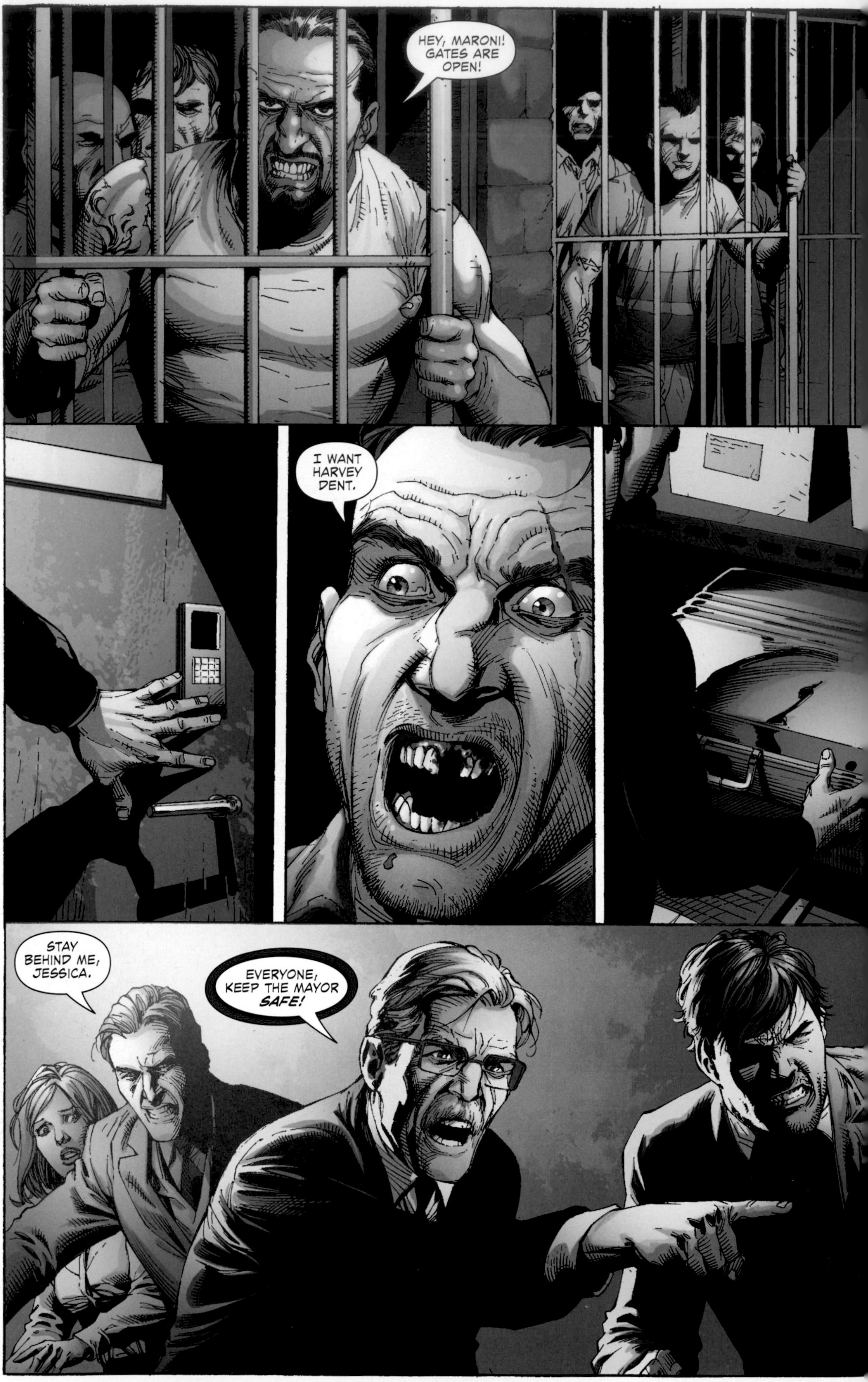
HEY, MARONI! GATES ARE OPEN!
I WANT HARVEY DENT.
STAY BEHIND ME, JESSICA.
EVERYONE, KEEP THE MAYOR *SAFE!*

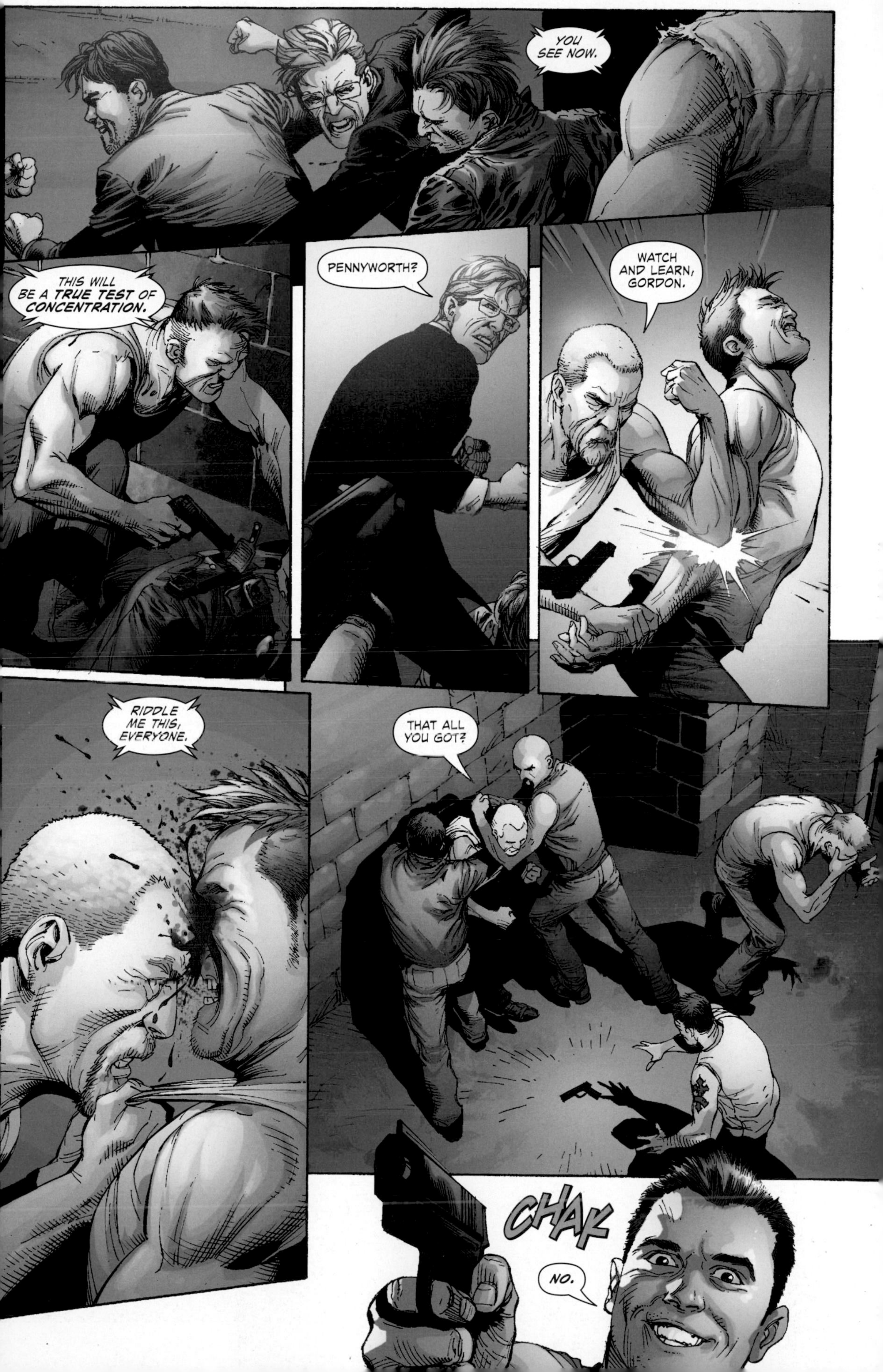

YOU SEE NOW.
THIS WILL BE A TRUE TEST OF CONCENTRATION.
PENNYWORTH?
WATCH AND LEARN, GORDON.
RIDDLE ME THIS, EVERYONE.
THAT ALL YOU GOT?
CHAK
NO.

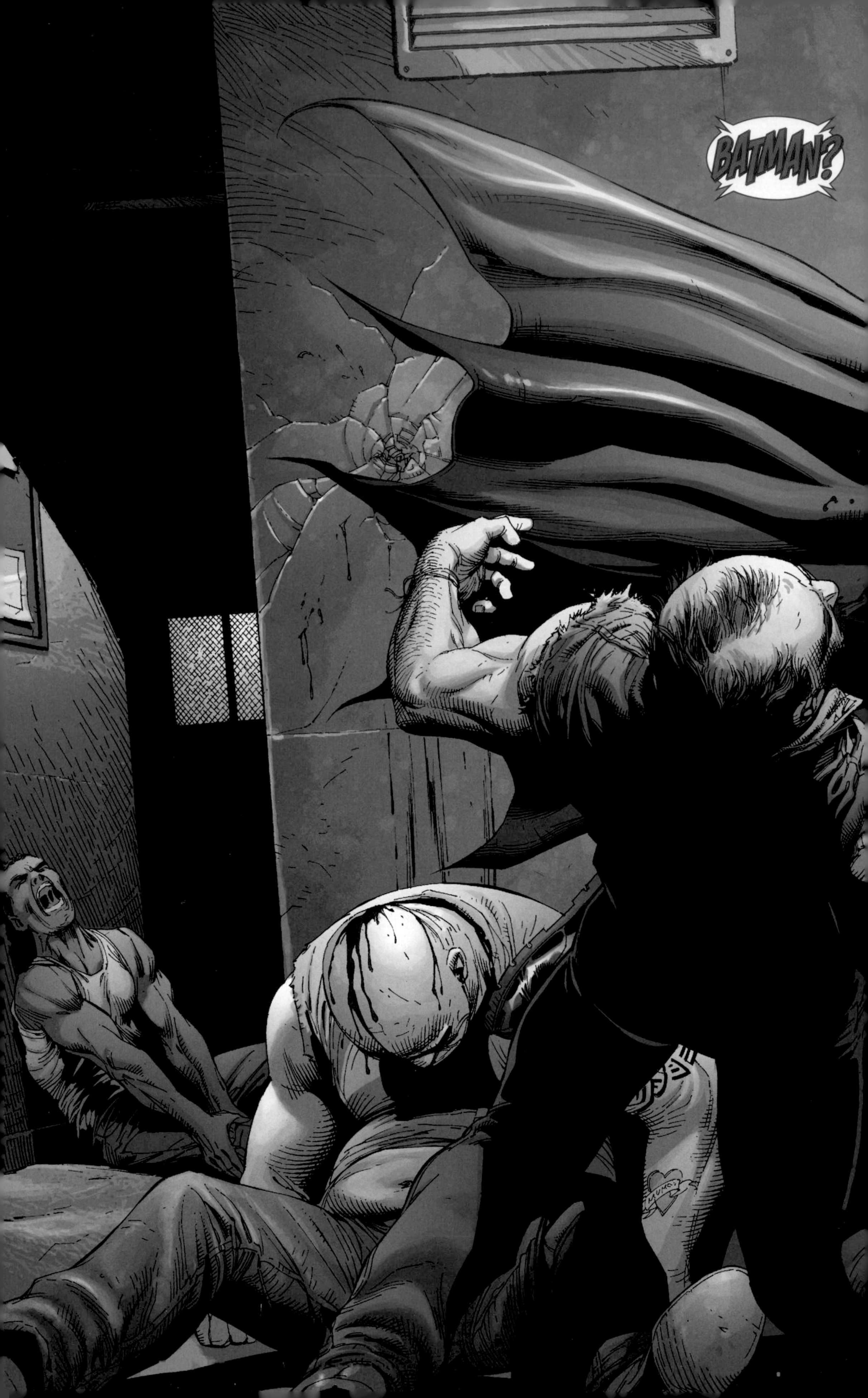
BATMAN?

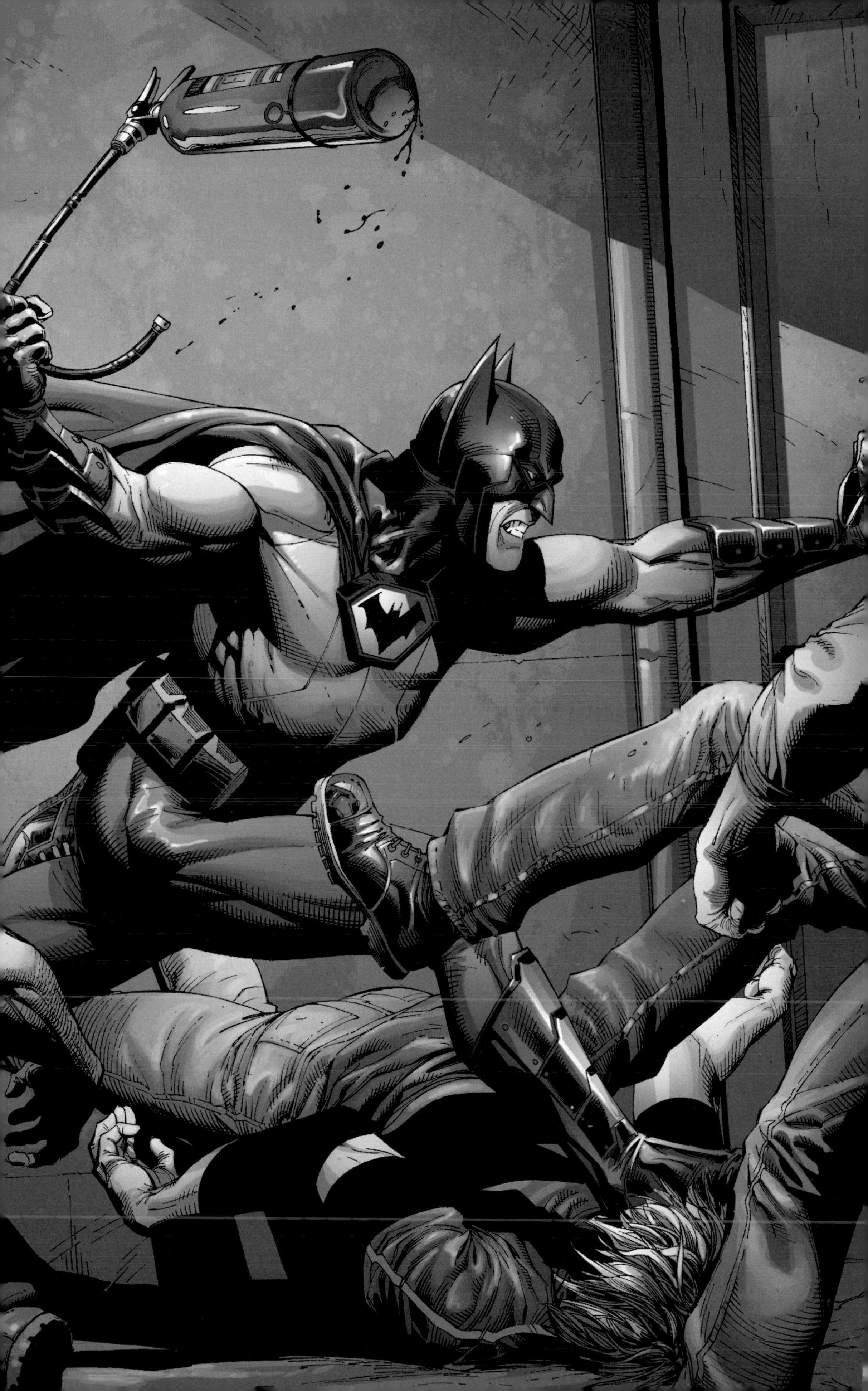

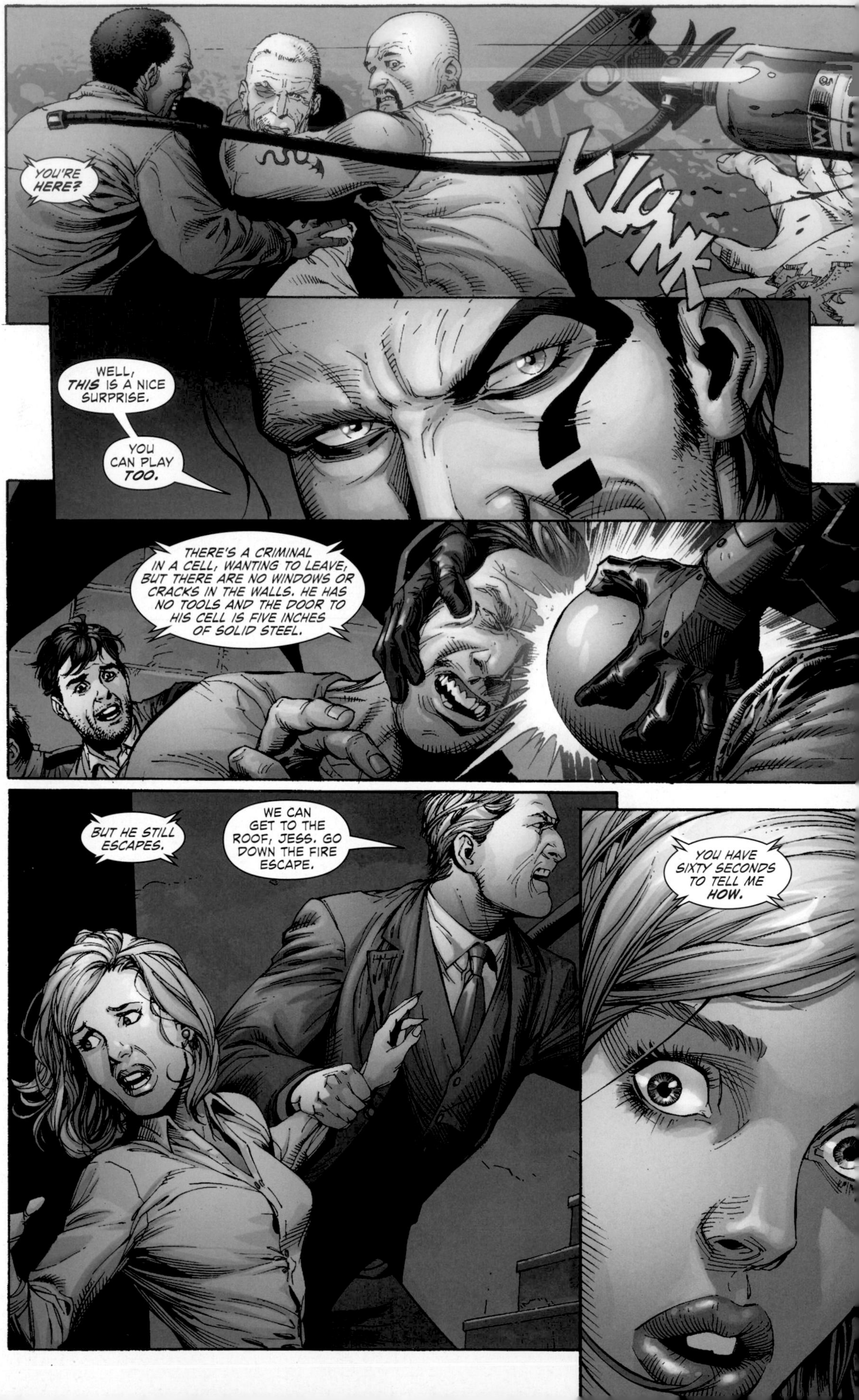
YOU'RE HERE?
KLUNK
WELL, THIS IS A NICE SURPRISE.
YOU CAN PLAY TOO.
THERE'S A CRIMINAL IN A CELL, WANTING TO LEAVE; BUT THERE ARE NO WINDOWS OR CRACKS IN THE WALLS. HE HAS NO TOOLS AND THE DOOR TO HIS CELL IS FIVE INCHES OF SOLID STEEL.
BUT HE STILL ESCAPES.
WE CAN GET TO THE ROOF, JESS. GO DOWN THE FIRE ESCAPE.
YOU HAVE SIXTY SECONDS TO TELL ME HOW.

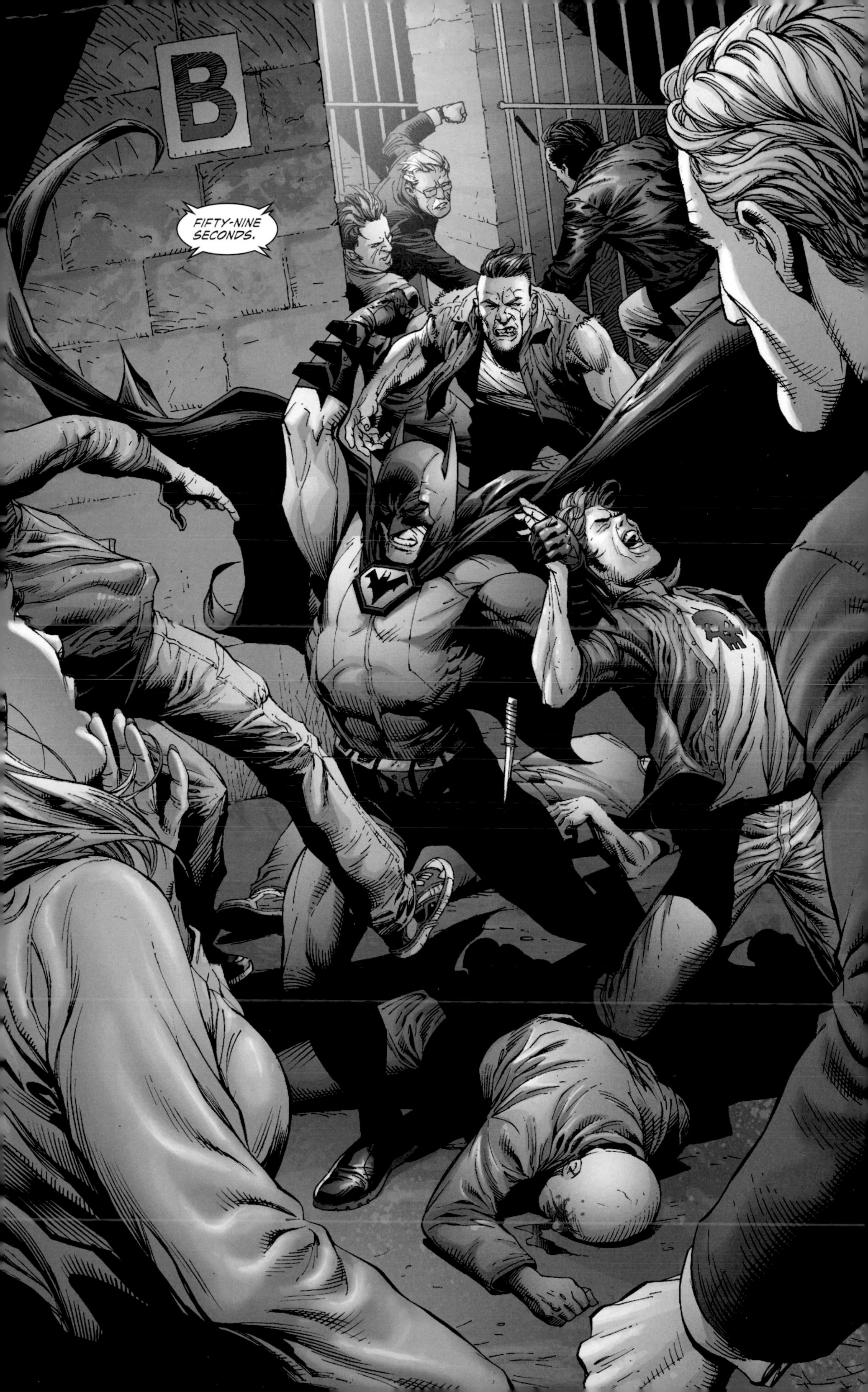
FIFTY-NINE SECONDS.

COME ON, JESS!

BRUCE IS DOWN THERE, ALFRED.

AND WE'LL GET HELP ONCE I GET YOU OUT OF--

--NNK.

HARVEY?

I'M CUTTING A DEAL, DENT. LITERALLY.

TWENTY SECONDS.

BATMAN, THE ANSWER--

"THE DOOR WASN'T LOCKED." BUT IT DOESN'T MATTER IF WE ANSWER IT.

HE'S GOING TO BLOW THE PRECINCT UP ANYWAY.

MARONI'S GOT THE D.A.!

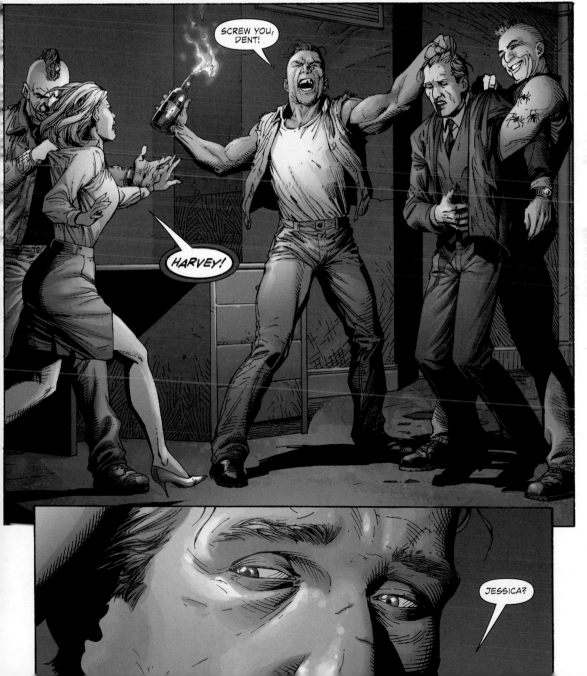

SCREW YOU, DENT!

HARVEY!

JESSICA?

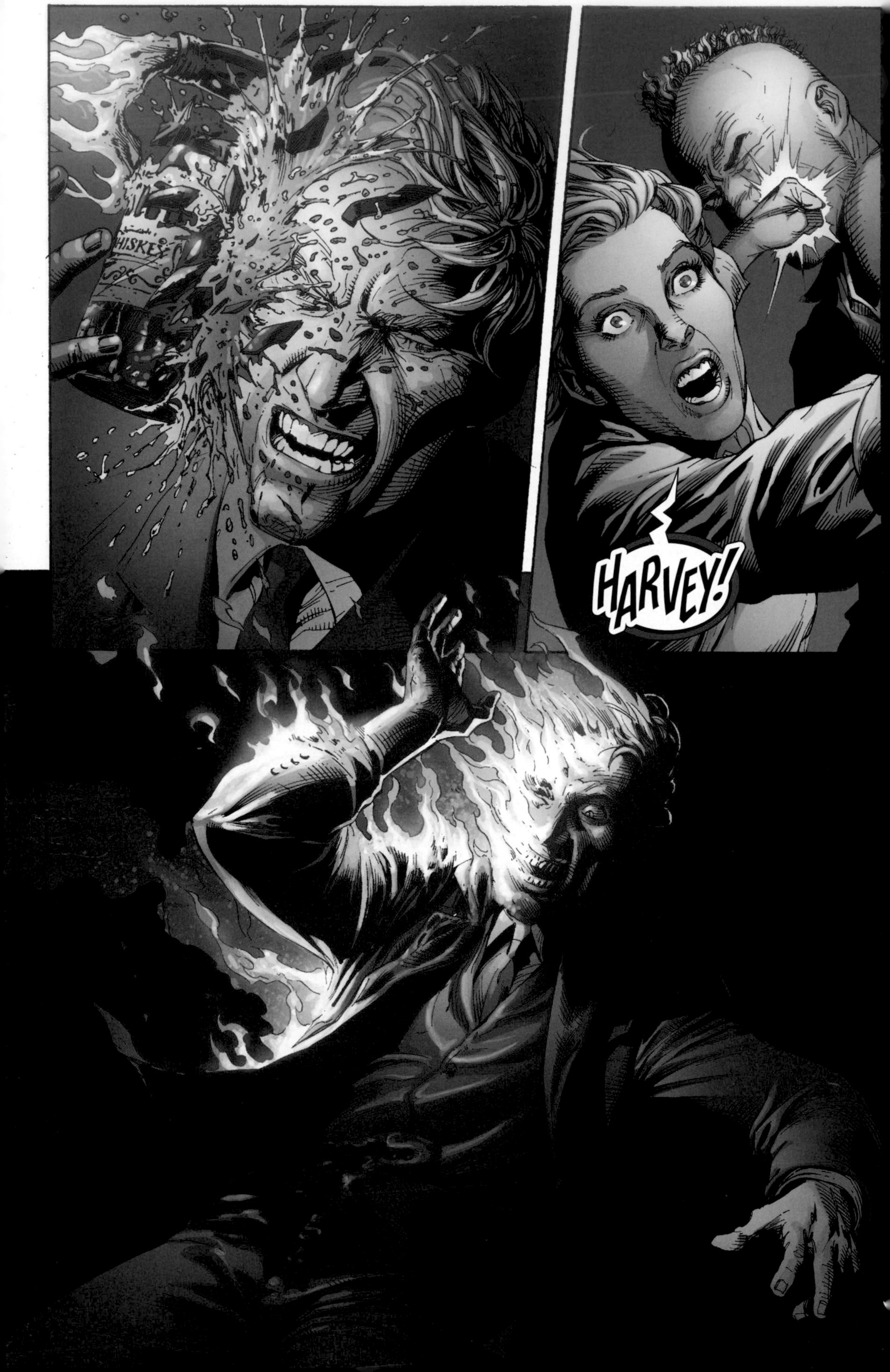
HISKEY
HARVEY!

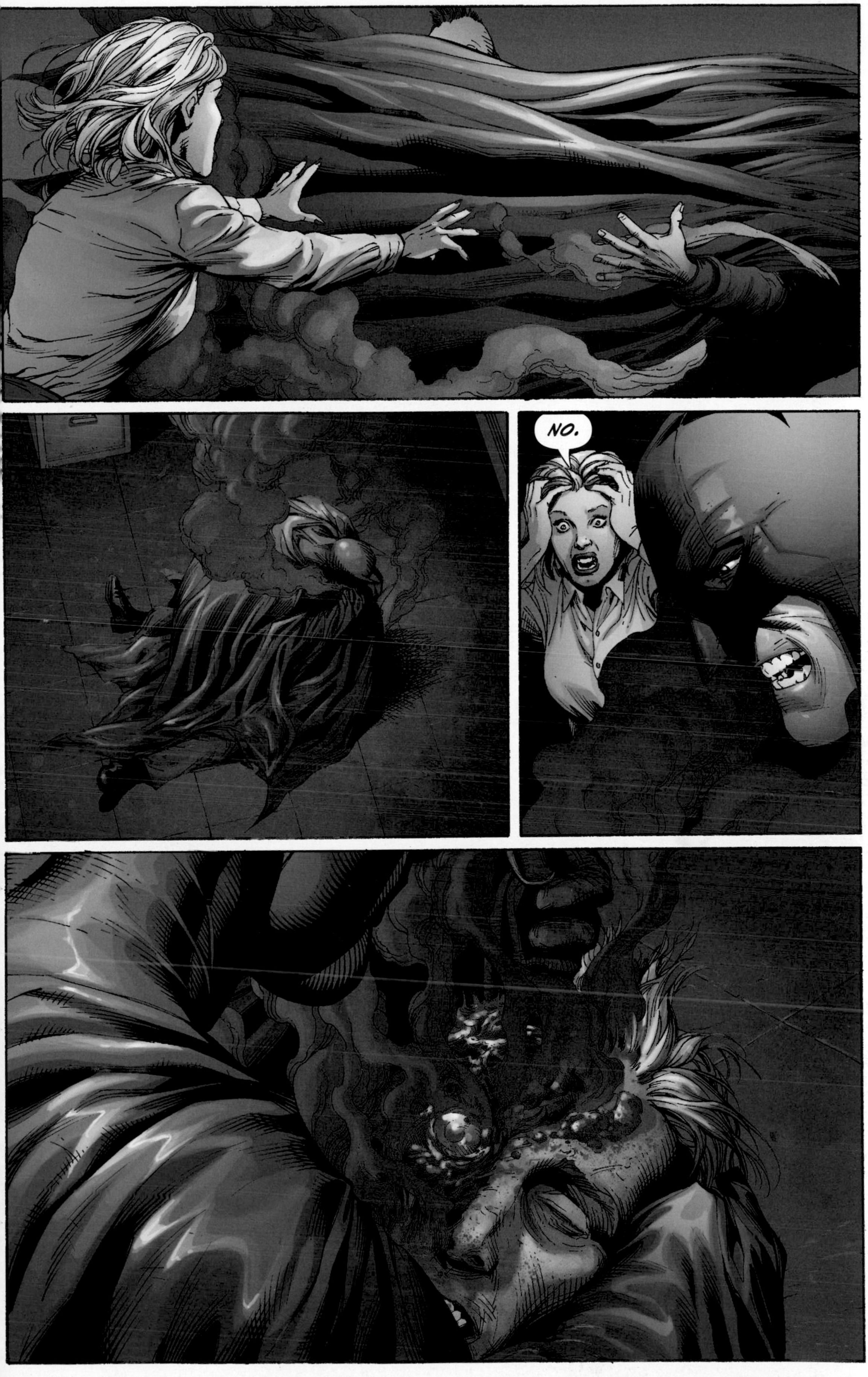
NO.

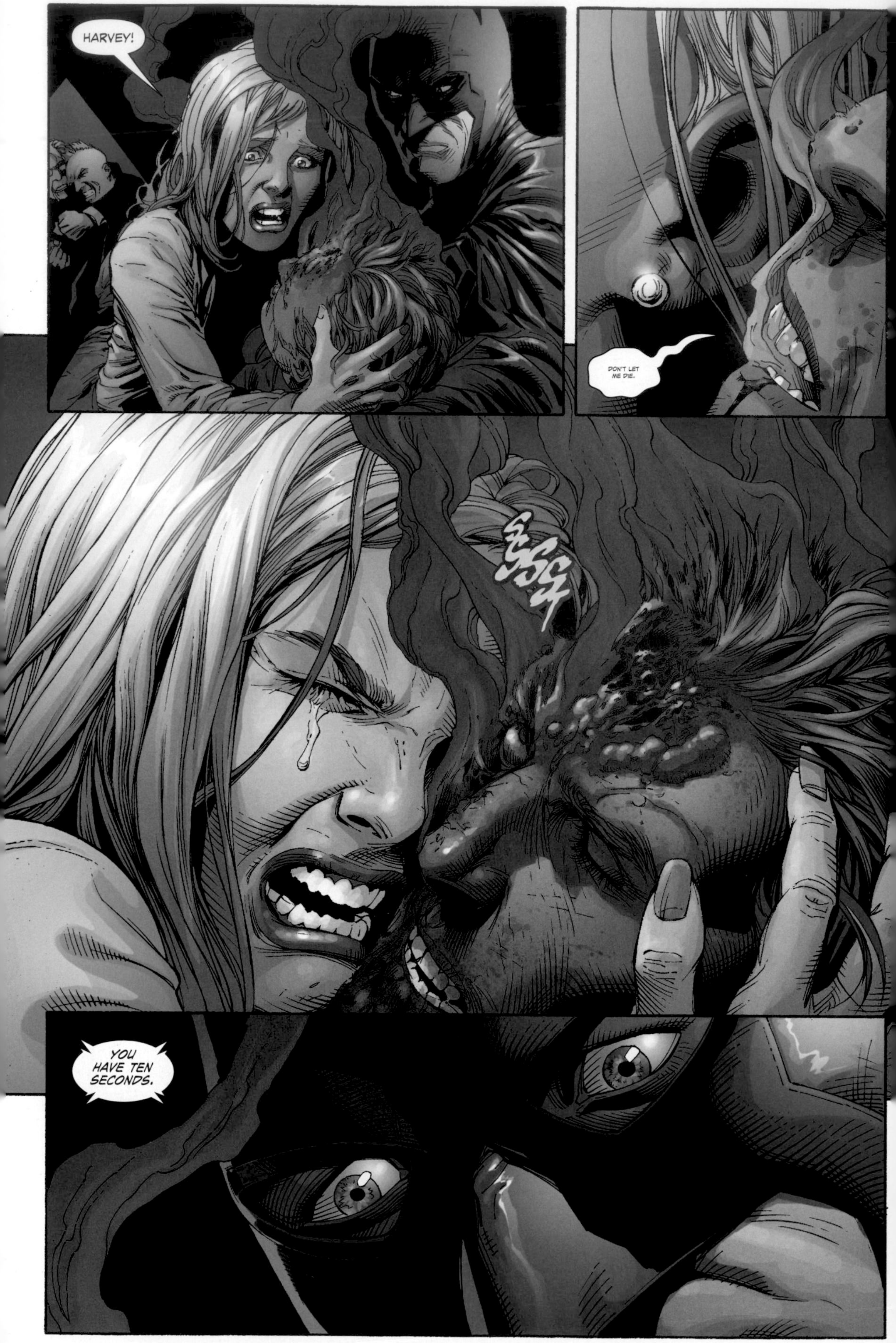
HARVEY!
DON'T LET ME DIE.
GSSSK
YOU HAVE TEN SECONDS.

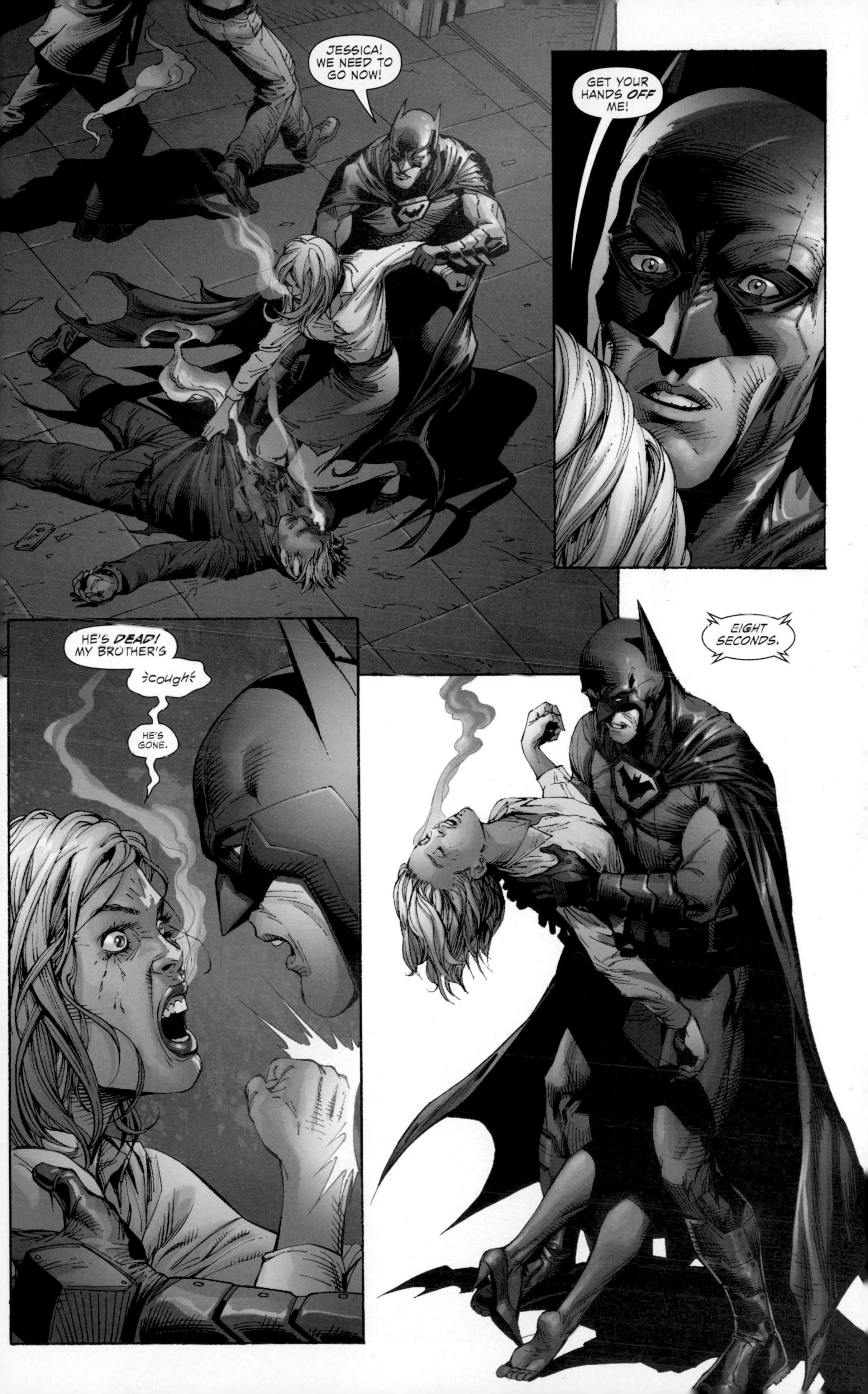
JESSICA! WE NEED TO GO NOW!
GET YOUR HANDS OFF ME!
HE'S DEAD! MY BROTHER'S
cough
HE'S GONE.
EIGHT SECONDS.

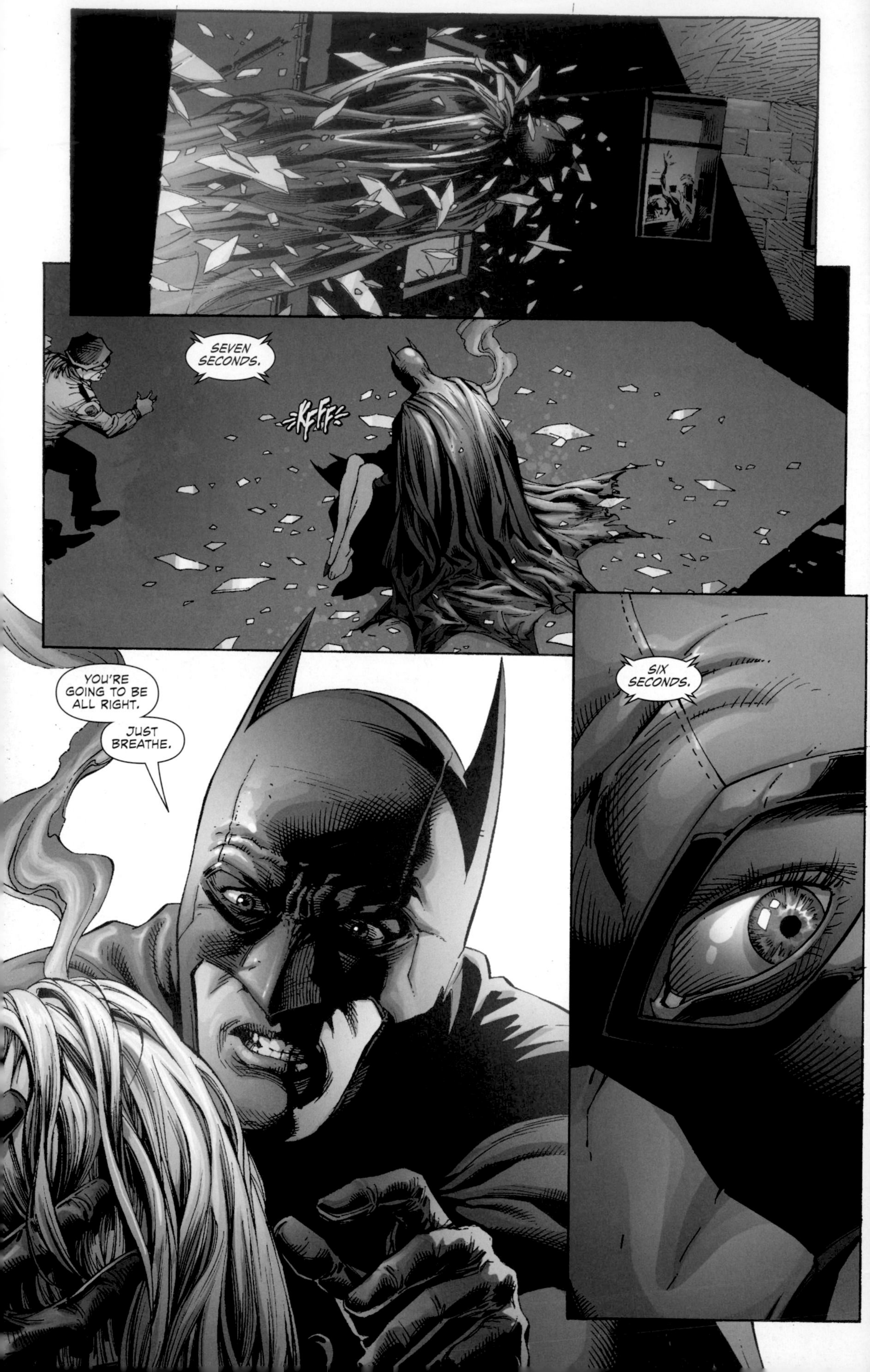
SEVEN SECONDS.
KFFF
YOU'RE GOING TO BE ALL RIGHT.
JUST BREATHE.
SIX SECONDS.

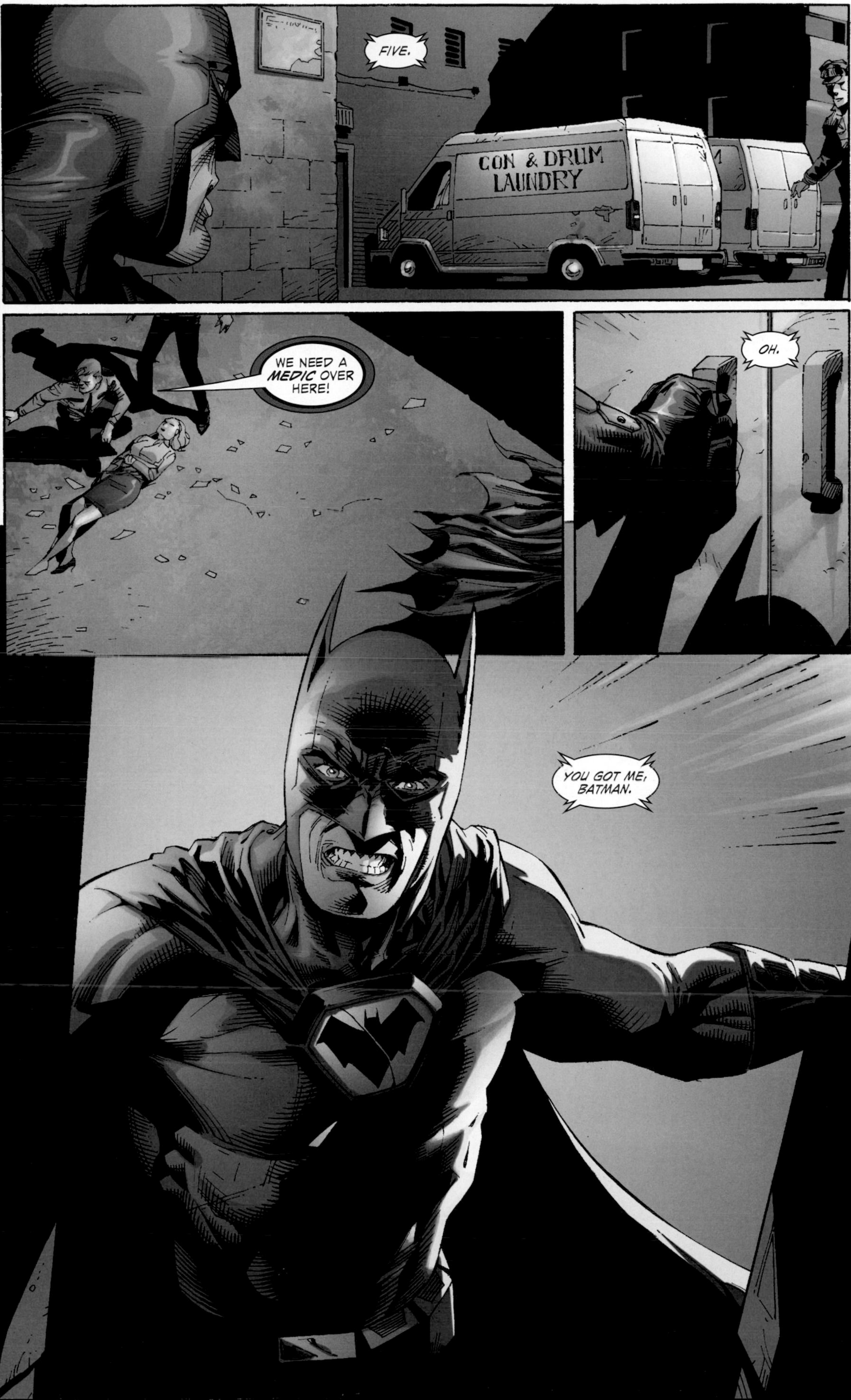
FIVE.
CON & DRUM LAUNDRY
WE NEED A MEDIC OVER HERE!
OH.
YOU GOT ME, BATMAN.

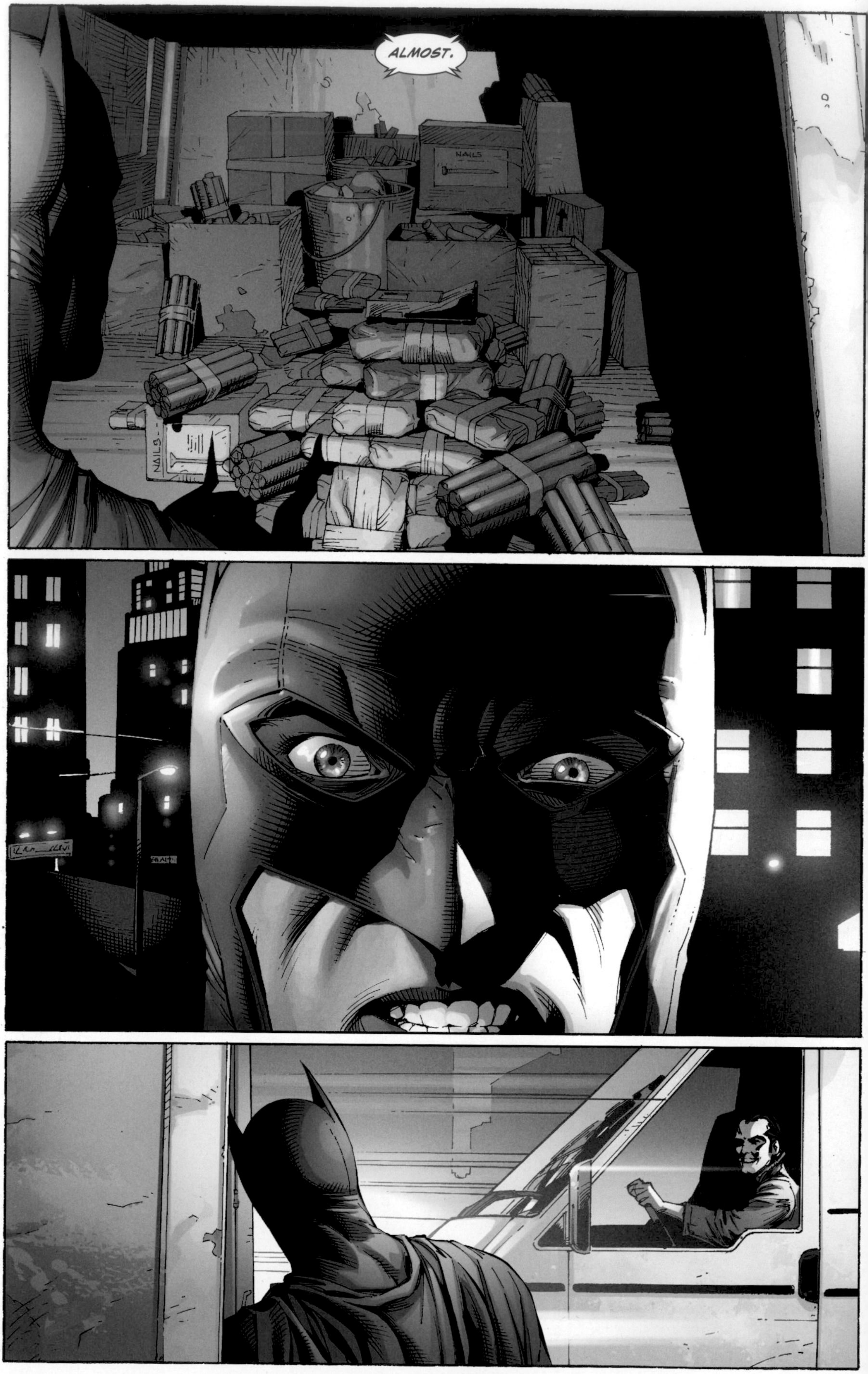
ALMOST.
NAILS
NAILS

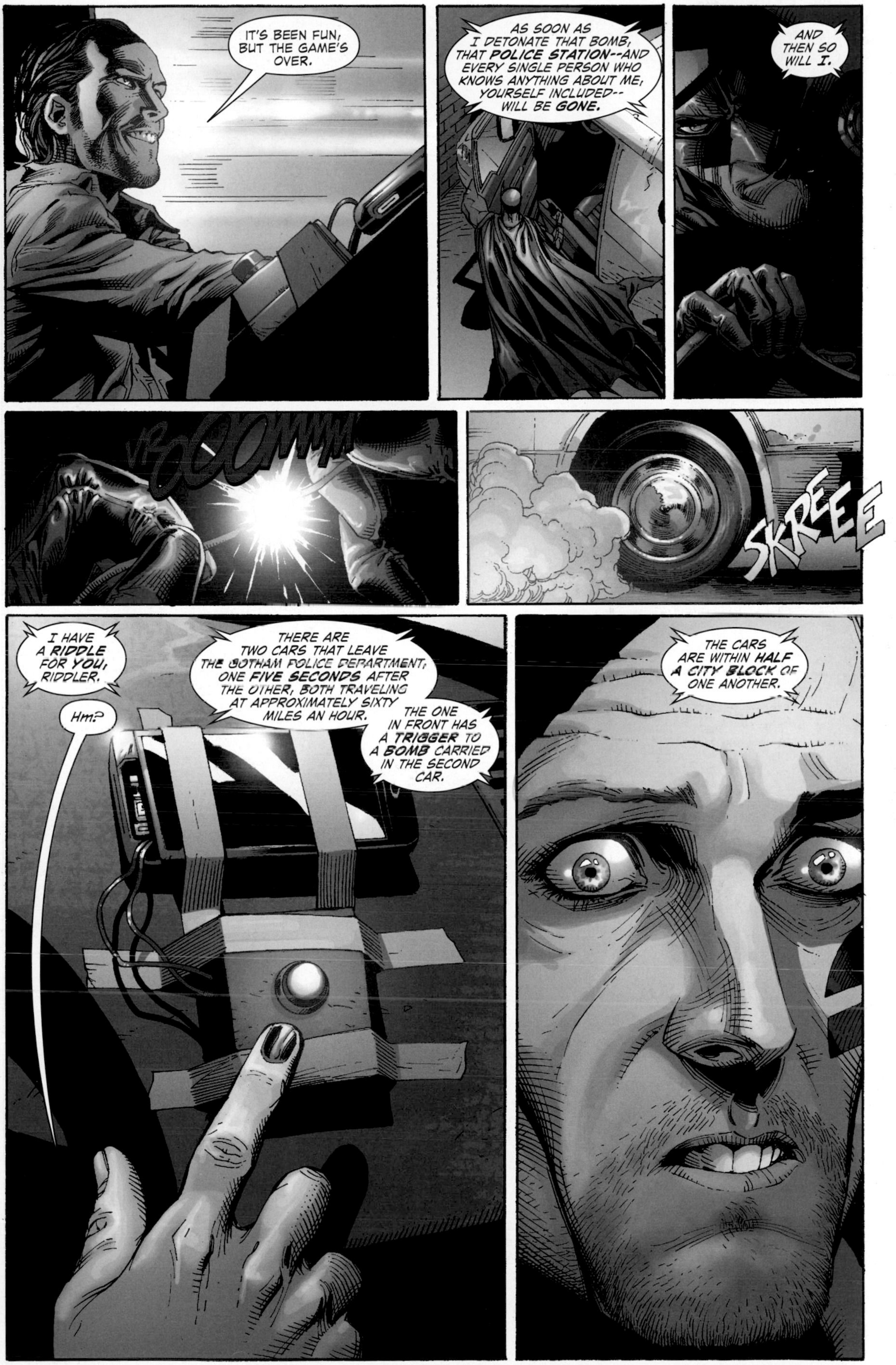
IT'S BEEN FUN, BUT THE GAME'S OVER.
AS SOON AS I DETONATE THAT BOMB, THAT POLICE STATION--AND EVERY SINGLE PERSON WHO KNOWS ANYTHING ABOUT ME, YOURSELF INCLUDED-- WILL BE GONE.
AND THEN SO WILL I.
VROOOMM
SKREEE
I HAVE A RIDDLE FOR YOU, RIDDLER.
Hm?
THERE ARE TWO CARS THAT LEAVE THE GOTHAM POLICE DEPARTMENT, ONE FIVE SECONDS AFTER THE OTHER, BOTH TRAVELING AT APPROXIMATELY SIXTY MILES AN HOUR.
THE ONE IN FRONT HAS A TRIGGER TO A BOMB CARRIED IN THE SECOND CAR.
THE CARS ARE WITHIN HALF A CITY BLOCK OF ONE ANOTHER.

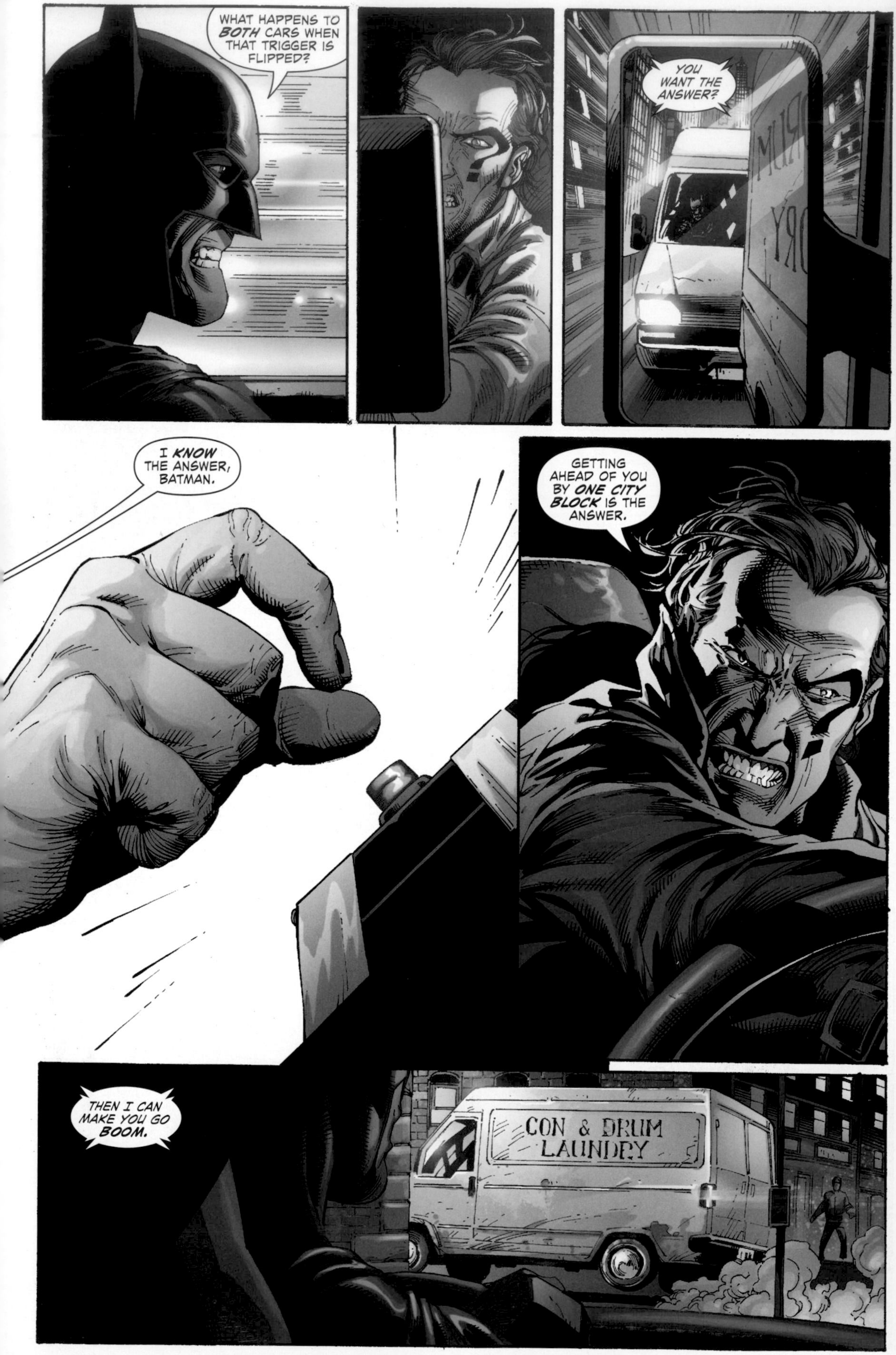
WHAT HAPPENS TO BOTH CARS WHEN THAT TRIGGER IS FLIPPED?
YOU WANT THE ANSWER?
I KNOW THE ANSWER, BATMAN.
GETTING AHEAD OF YOU BY ONE CITY BLOCK IS THE ANSWER.
THEN I CAN MAKE YOU GO BOOM.
CON & DRUM LAUNDRY

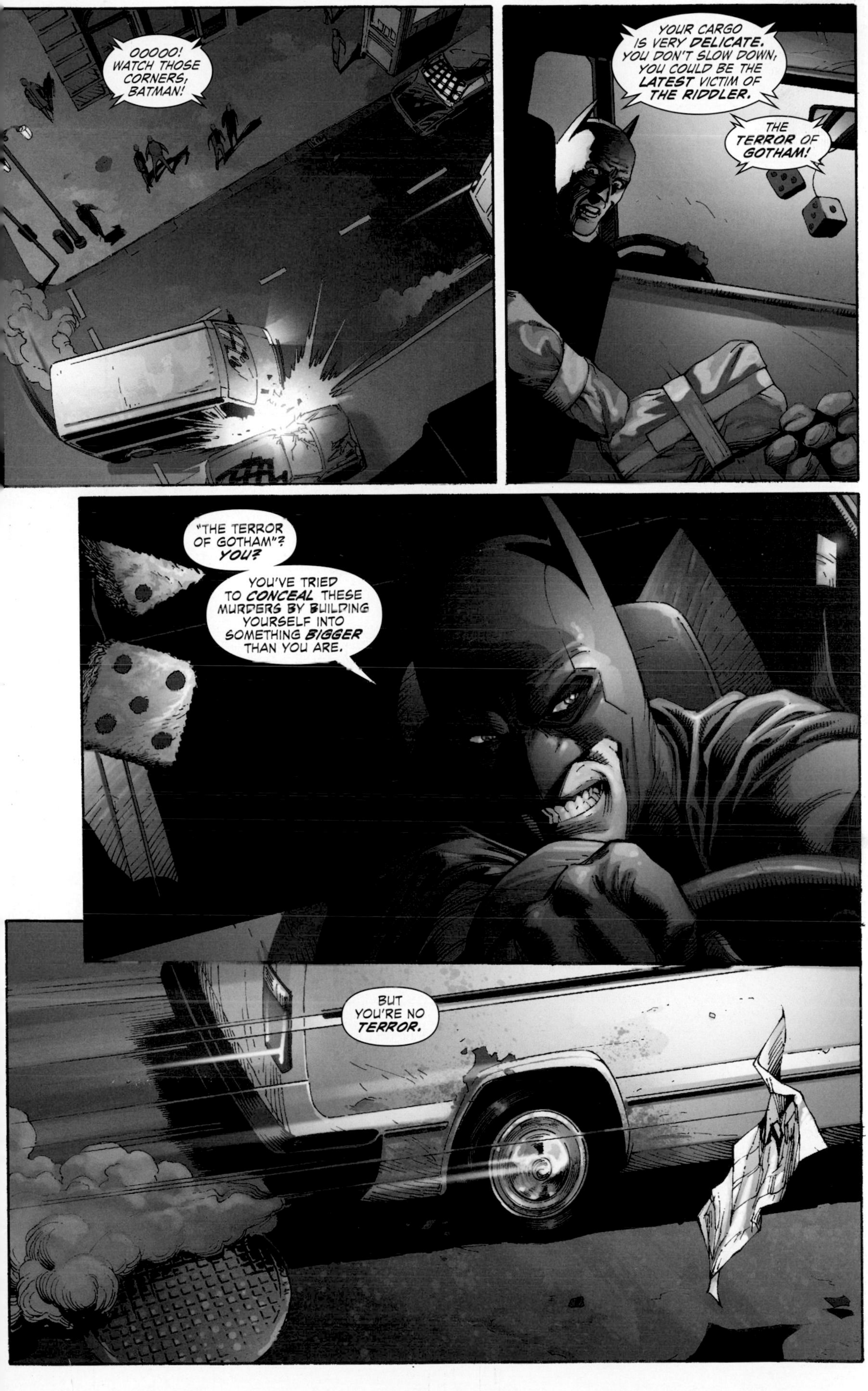
OOOOO! WATCH THOSE CORNERS, BATMAN!
YOUR CARGO IS VERY DELICATE. YOU DON'T SLOW DOWN, YOU COULD BE THE LATEST VICTIM OF THE RIDDLER.
THE TERROR OF GOTHAM!
"THE TERROR OF GOTHAM"? YOU?
YOU'VE TRIED TO CONCEAL THESE MURDERS BY BUILDING YOURSELF INTO SOMETHING BIGGER THAN YOU ARE.
BUT YOU'RE NO TERROR.

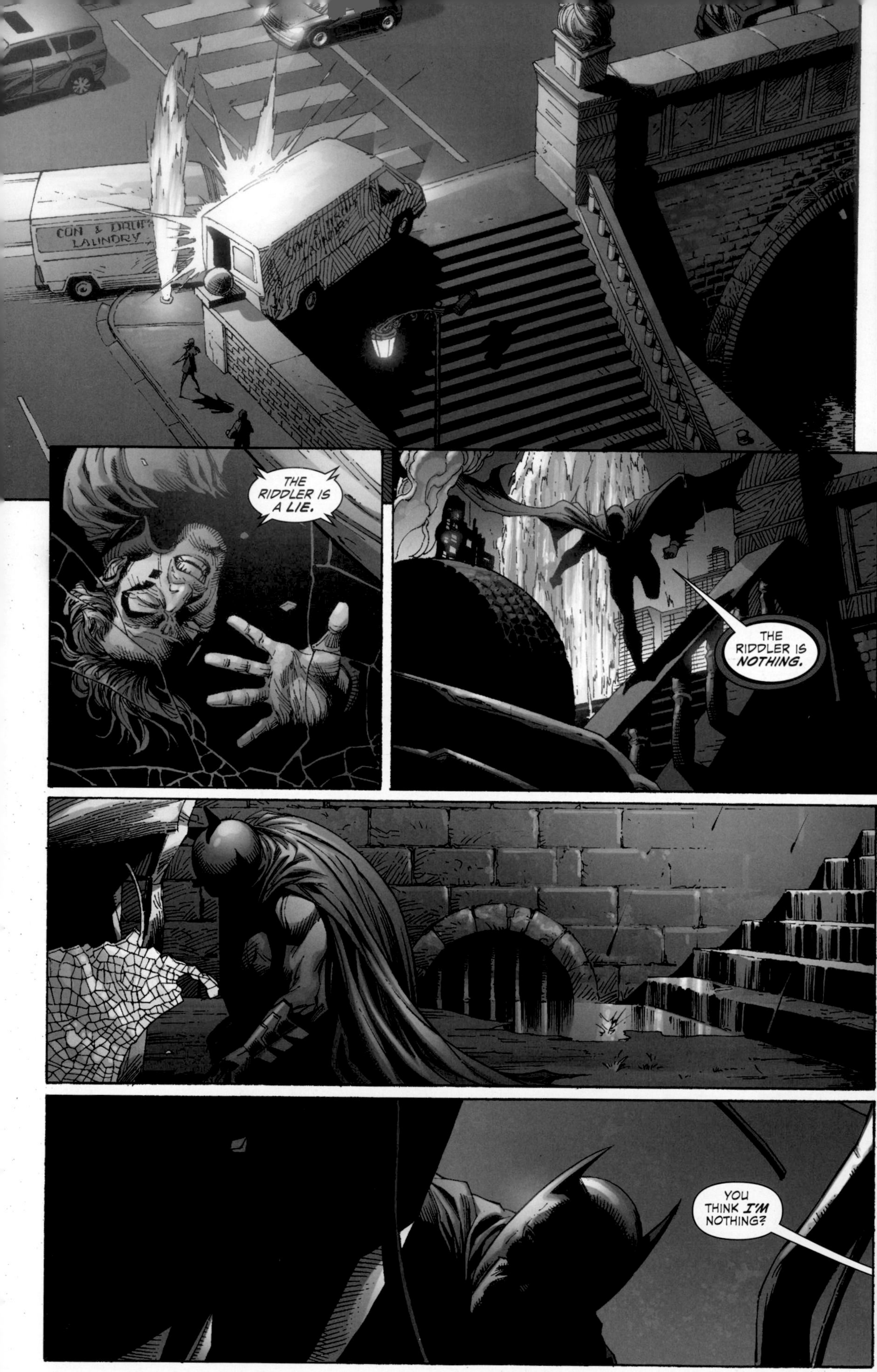
CON & DRUM LAUNDRY
THE RIDDLER IS A *LIE.*
THE RIDDLER IS *NOTHING.*
YOU THINK *I'M* NOTHING?

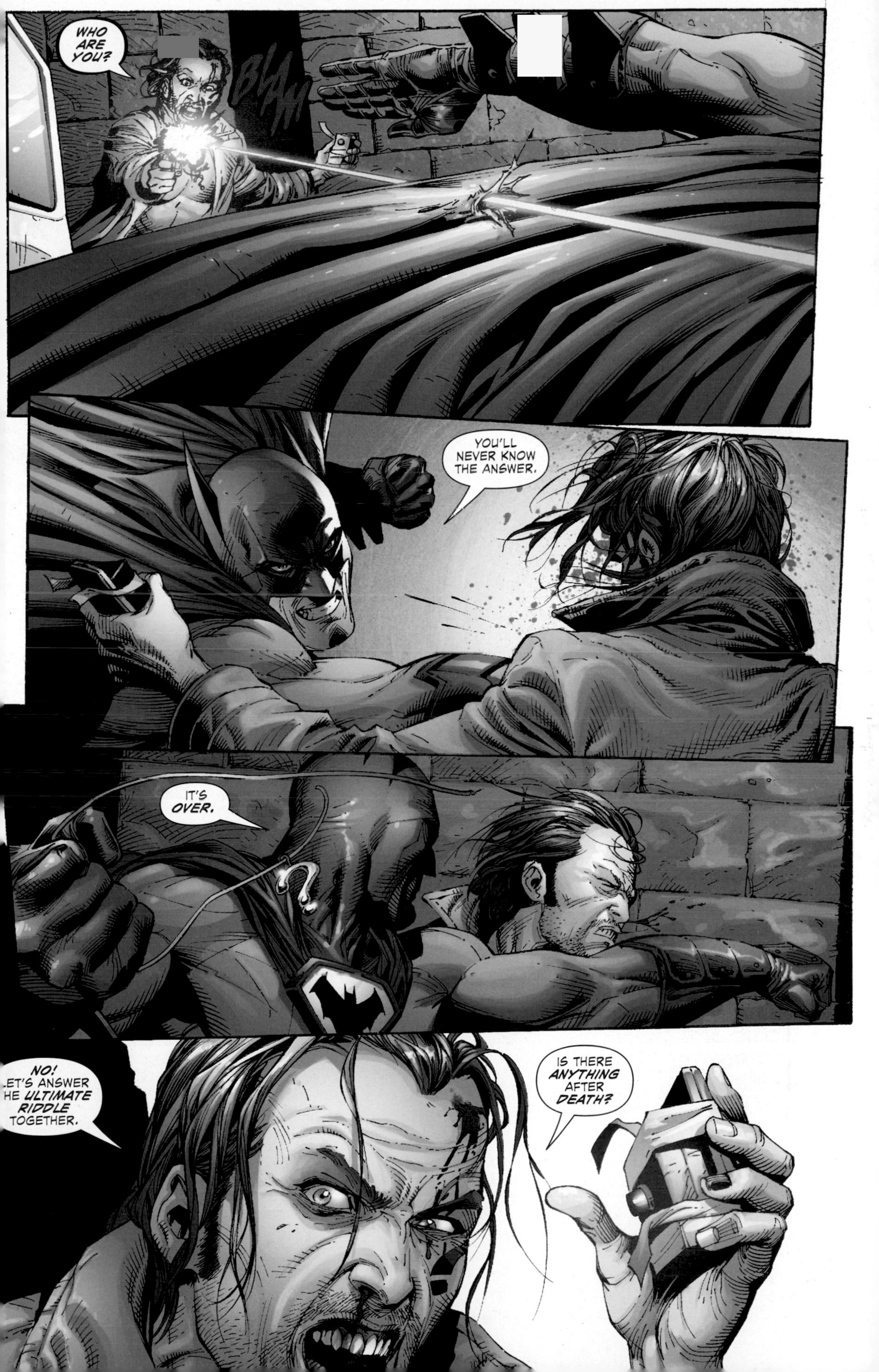

WHO ARE YOU?
BLAM
YOU'LL NEVER KNOW THE ANSWER.
IT'S OVER.
NO! ET'S ANSWER HE *ULTIMATE RIDDLE* TOGETHER.
IS THERE *ANYTHING* AFTER *DEATH?*

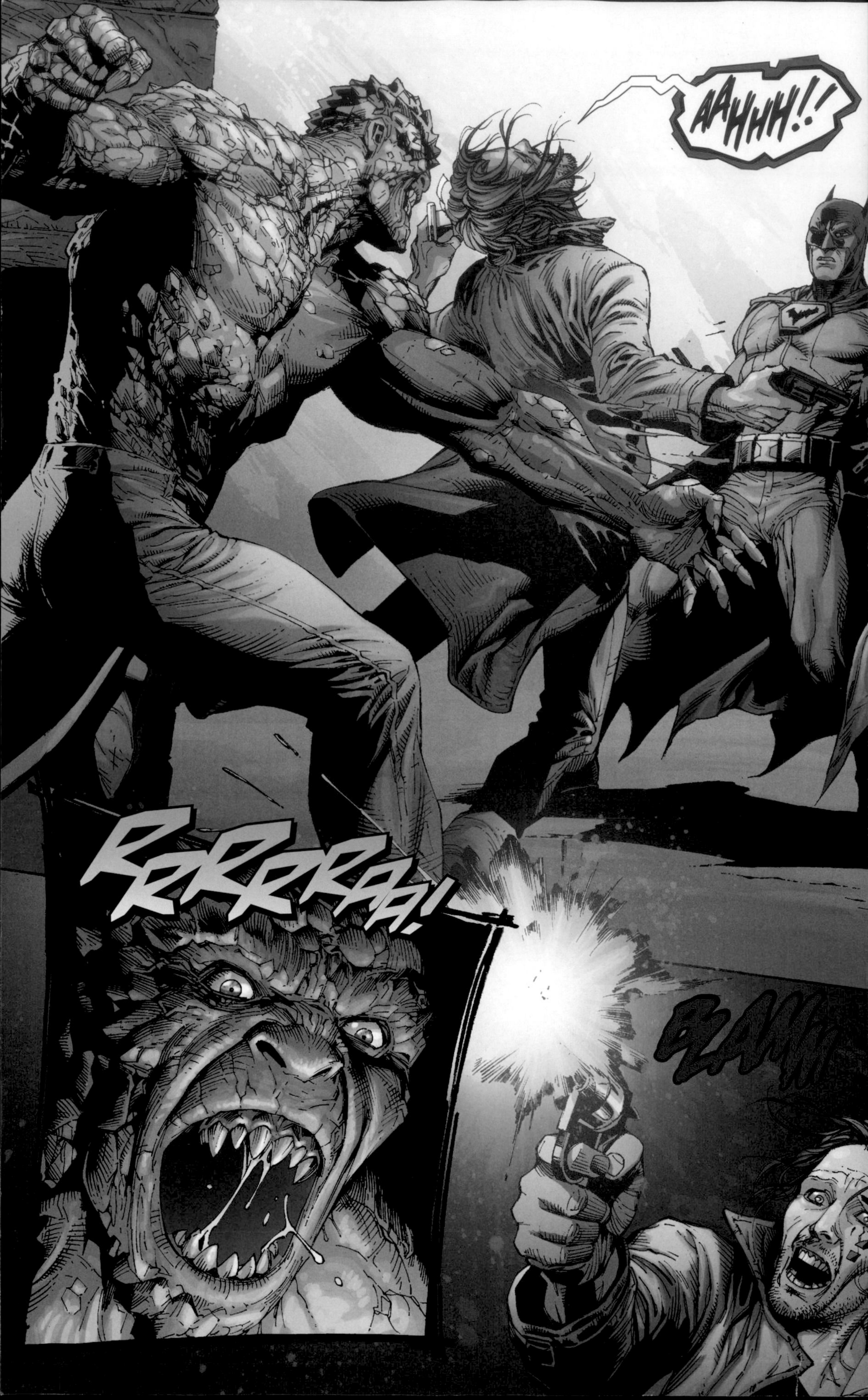
AAHHH!!
RRRRRAA!

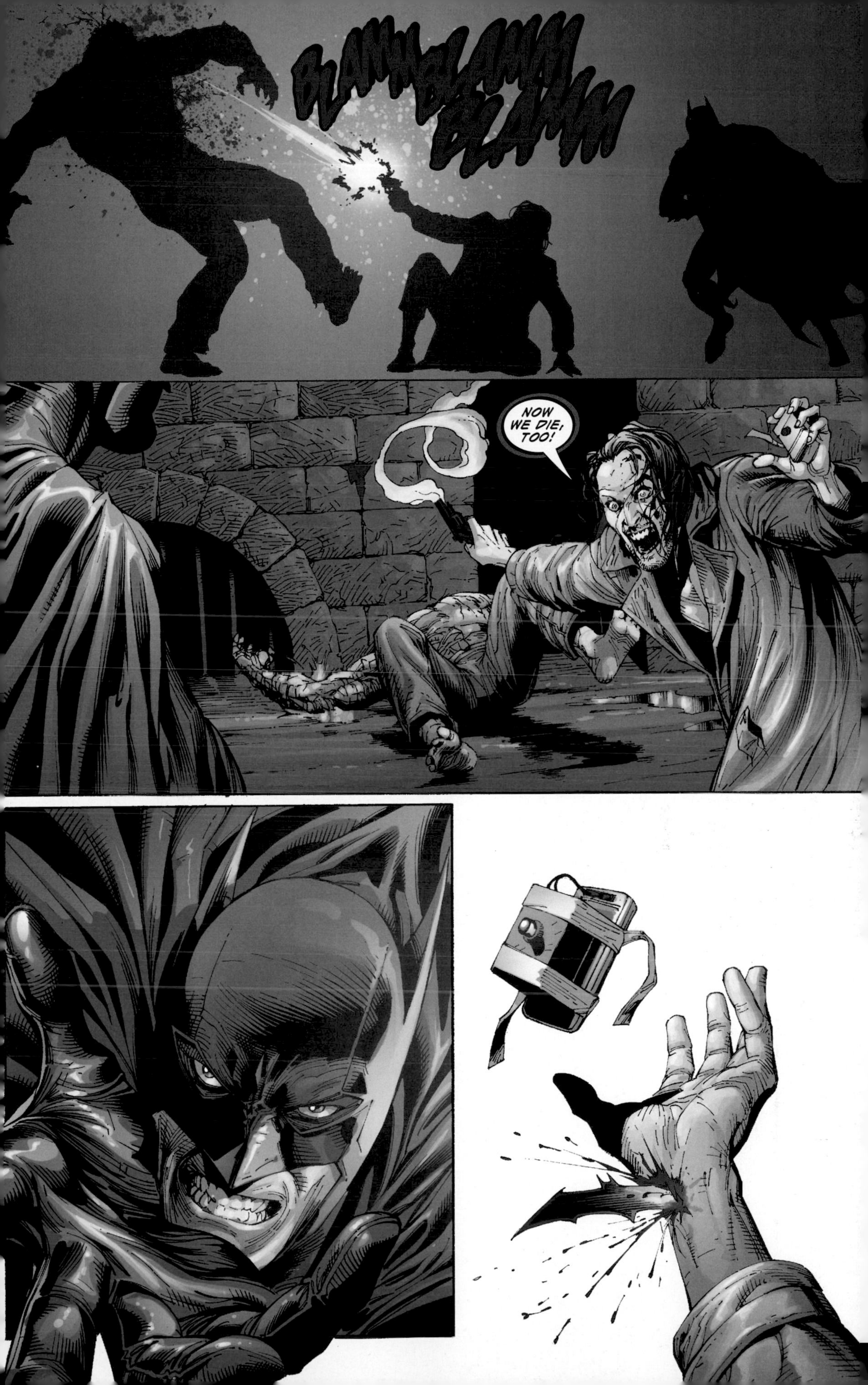
BLAMM BLAMM
BLAMM
NOW WE DIE, TOO!

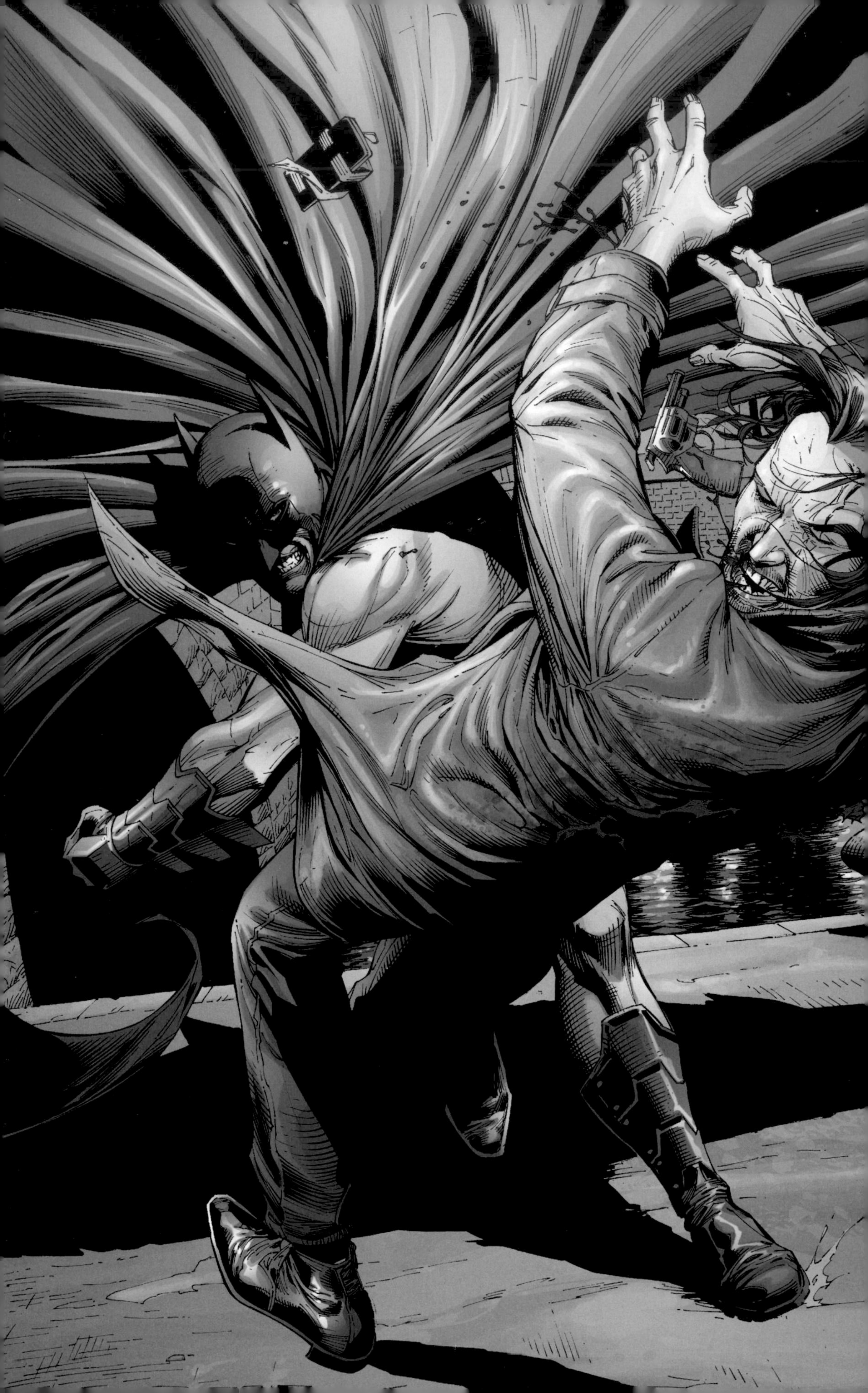

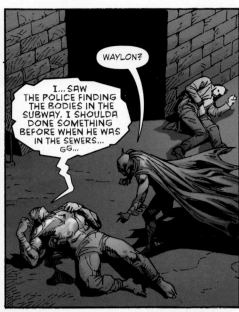

WAYLON?

I... SAW THE POLICE FINDING THE BODIES IN THE SUBWAY. I SHOULDA DONE SOMETHING BEFORE WHEN HE WAS IN THE SEWERS... GG...

...I DIDN'T WANT TO GO BACK DOWN THERE ANYWAY.

KK

"THE RIDDLER, WHOSE TRUE IDENTITY HAS YET TO BE VERIFIED, HAS BEEN CHARGED IN THE DEATHS OF 43 PEOPLE THIS WEEK..."

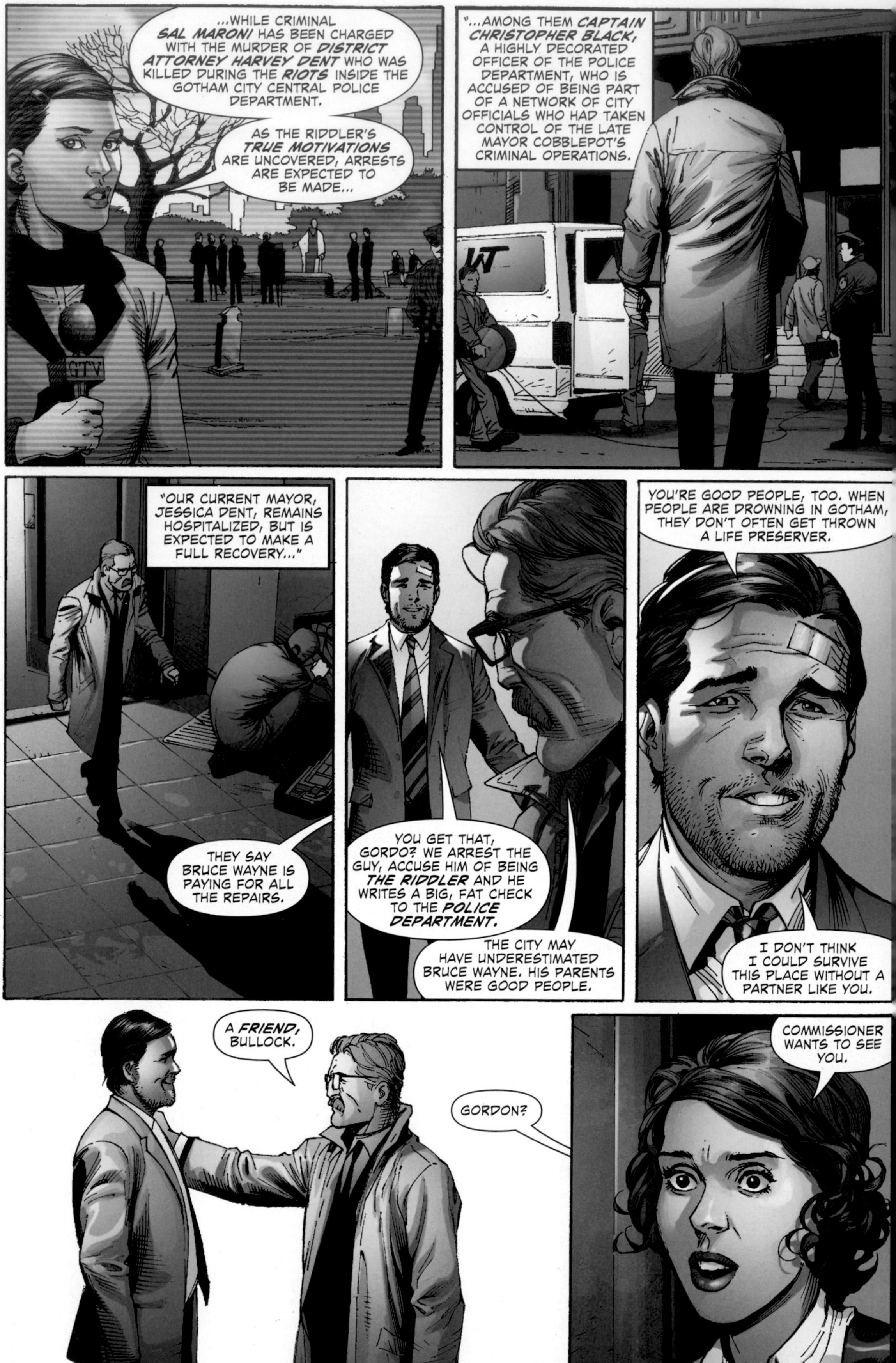
...WHILE CRIMINAL SAL MARONI HAS BEEN CHARGED WITH THE MURDER OF DISTRICT ATTORNEY HARVEY DENT WHO WAS KILLED DURING THE RIOTS INSIDE THE GOTHAM CITY CENTRAL POLICE DEPARTMENT.
AS THE RIDDLER'S TRUE MOTIVATIONS ARE UNCOVERED, ARRESTS ARE EXPECTED TO BE MADE...
GTV
"...AMONG THEM CAPTAIN CHRISTOPHER BLACK, A HIGHLY DECORATED OFFICER OF THE POLICE DEPARTMENT, WHO IS ACCUSED OF BEING PART OF A NETWORK OF CITY OFFICIALS WHO HAD TAKEN CONTROL OF THE LATE MAYOR COBBLEPOT'S CRIMINAL OPERATIONS.
"OUR CURRENT MAYOR, JESSICA DENT, REMAINS HOSPITALIZED, BUT IS EXPECTED TO MAKE A FULL RECOVERY..."
THEY SAY BRUCE WAYNE IS PAYING FOR ALL THE REPAIRS.
YOU GET THAT, GORDO? WE ARREST THE GUY, ACCUSE HIM OF BEING THE RIDDLER AND HE WRITES A BIG, FAT CHECK TO THE POLICE DEPARTMENT.
THE CITY MAY HAVE UNDERESTIMATED BRUCE WAYNE. HIS PARENTS WERE GOOD PEOPLE.
YOU'RE GOOD PEOPLE, TOO. WHEN PEOPLE ARE DROWNING IN GOTHAM, THEY DON'T OFTEN GET THROWN A LIFE PRESERVER.
I DON'T THINK I COULD SURVIVE THIS PLACE WITHOUT A PARTNER LIKE YOU.
A FRIEND, BULLOCK.
GORDON?
COMMISSIONER WANTS TO SEE YOU.

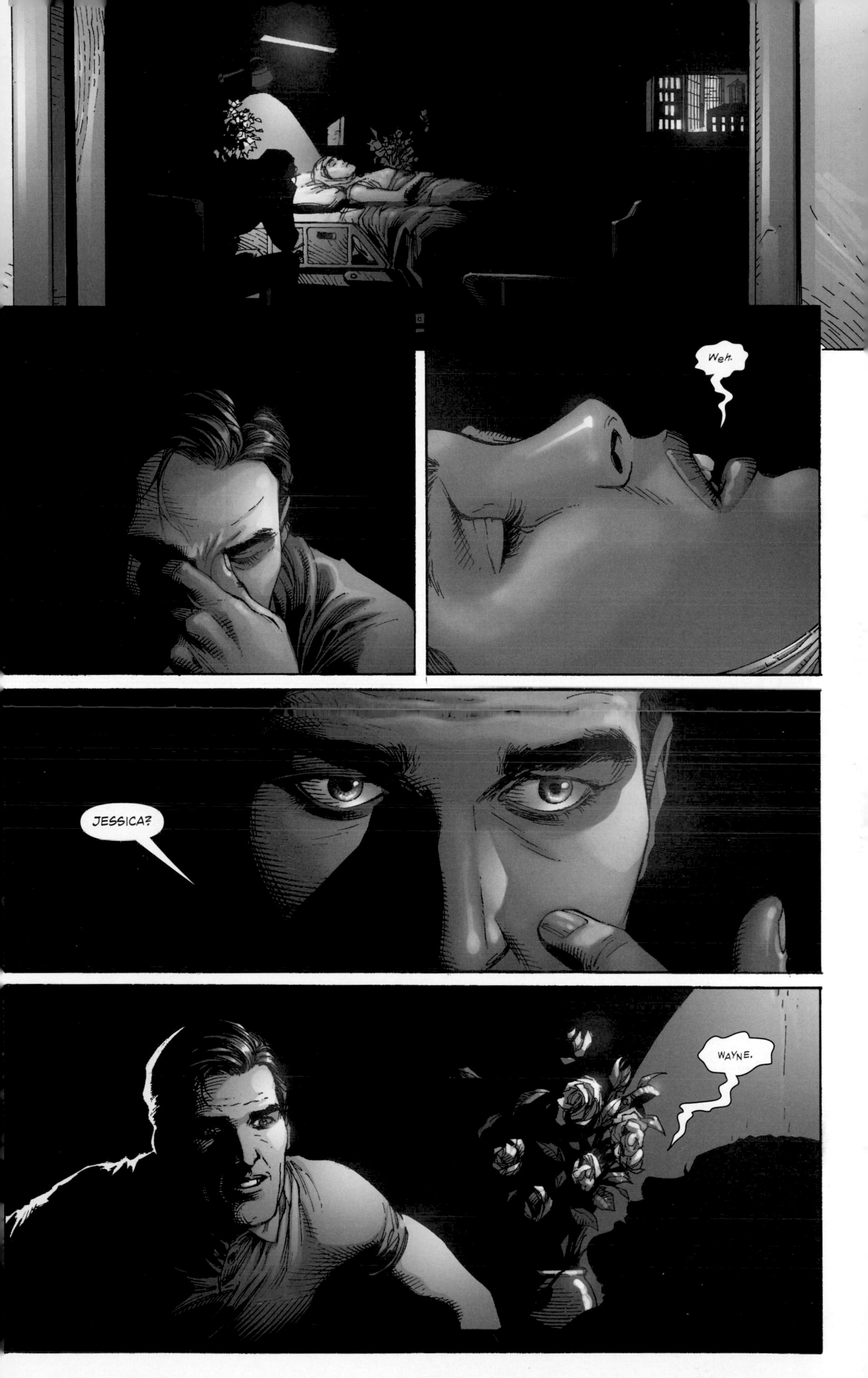
Weh.
JESSICA?
WAYNE.

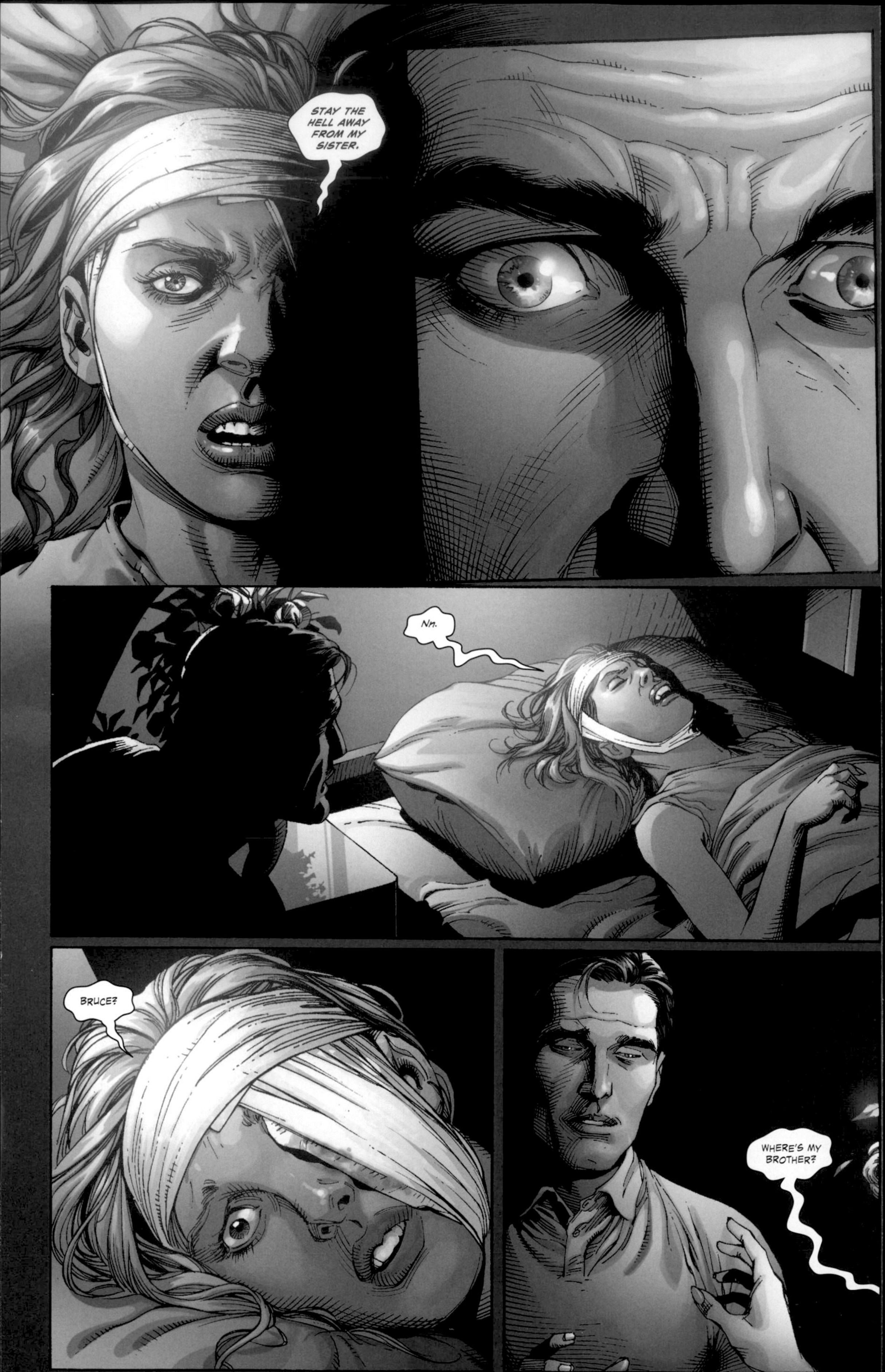
STAY THE HELL AWAY FROM MY SISTER.
Nn.
BRUCE?
WHERE'S MY BROTHER?

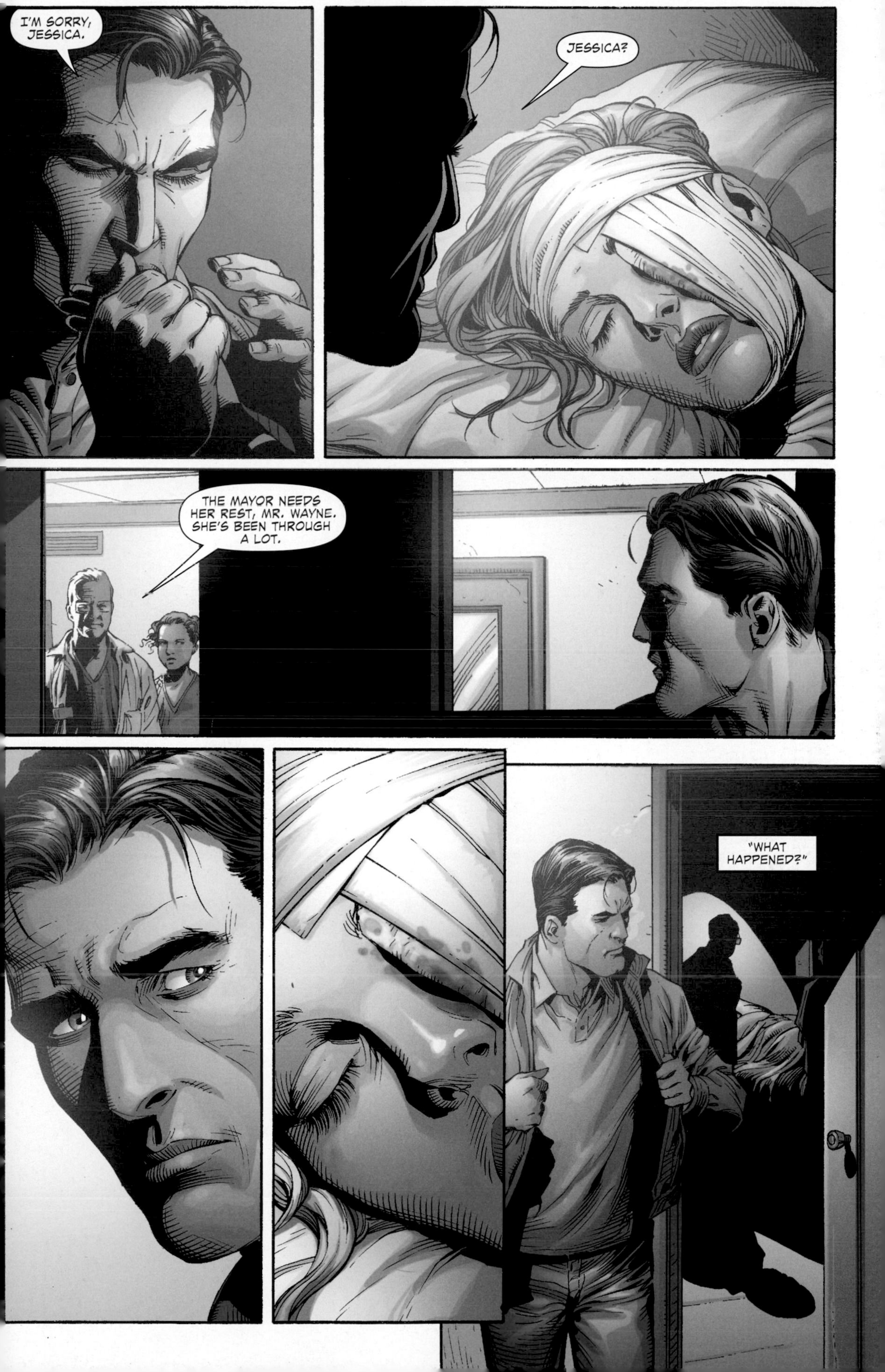
I'M SORRY, JESSICA.
JESSICA?
THE MAYOR NEEDS HER REST, MR. WAYNE. SHE'S BEEN THROUGH A LOT.
"WHAT HAPPENED?"

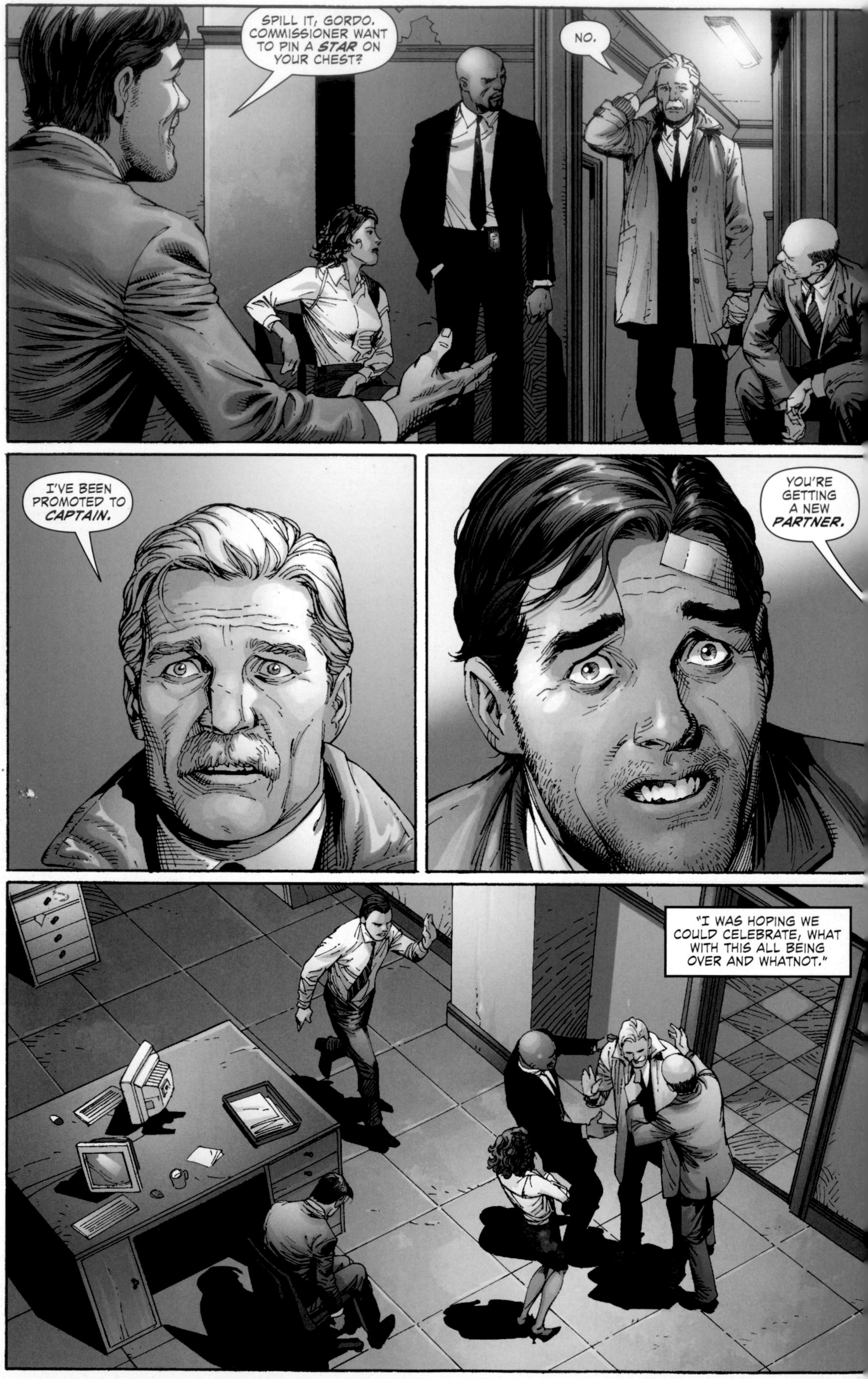
SPILL IT, GORDO. COMMISSIONER WANT TO PIN A *STAR* ON YOUR CHEST?
NO.
I'VE BEEN PROMOTED TO *CAPTAIN*.
YOU'RE GETTING A NEW *PARTNER*.
"I WAS HOPING WE COULD CELEBRATE, WHAT WITH THIS ALL BEING OVER AND WHATNOT."

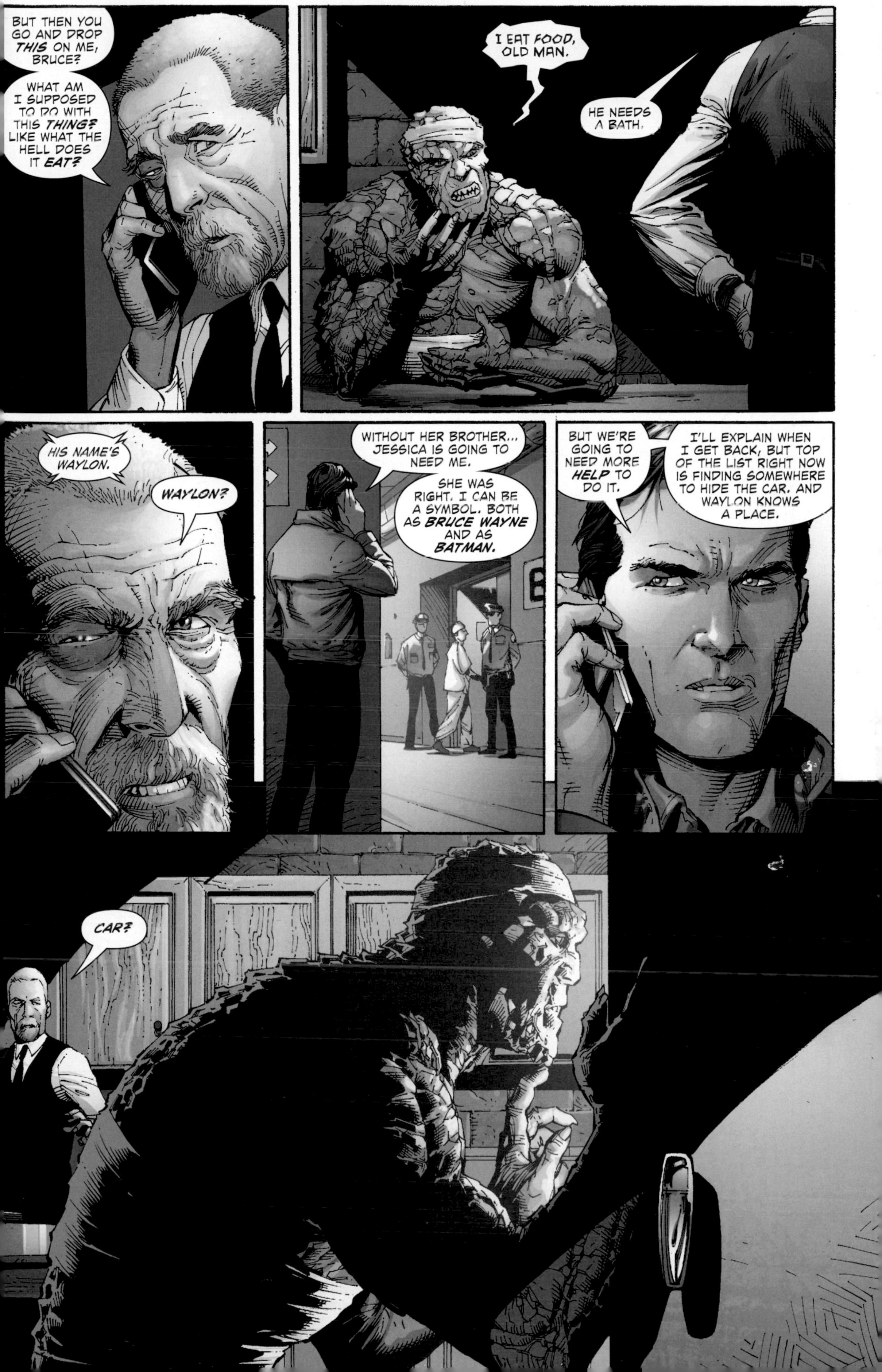
BUT THEN YOU GO AND DROP THIS ON ME, BRUCE?
WHAT AM I SUPPOSED TO DO WITH THIS THING? LIKE WHAT THE HELL DOES IT EAT?
I EAT FOOD, OLD MAN.
HE NEEDS A BATH.
HIS NAME'S WAYLON.
WAYLON?
WITHOUT HER BROTHER... JESSICA IS GOING TO NEED ME.
SHE WAS RIGHT. I CAN BE A SYMBOL. BOTH AS BRUCE WAYNE AND AS BATMAN.
BUT WE'RE GOING TO NEED MORE HELP TO DO IT.
I'LL EXPLAIN WHEN I GET BACK, BUT TOP OF THE LIST RIGHT NOW IS FINDING SOMEWHERE TO HIDE THE CAR. AND WAYLON KNOWS A PLACE.
CAR?

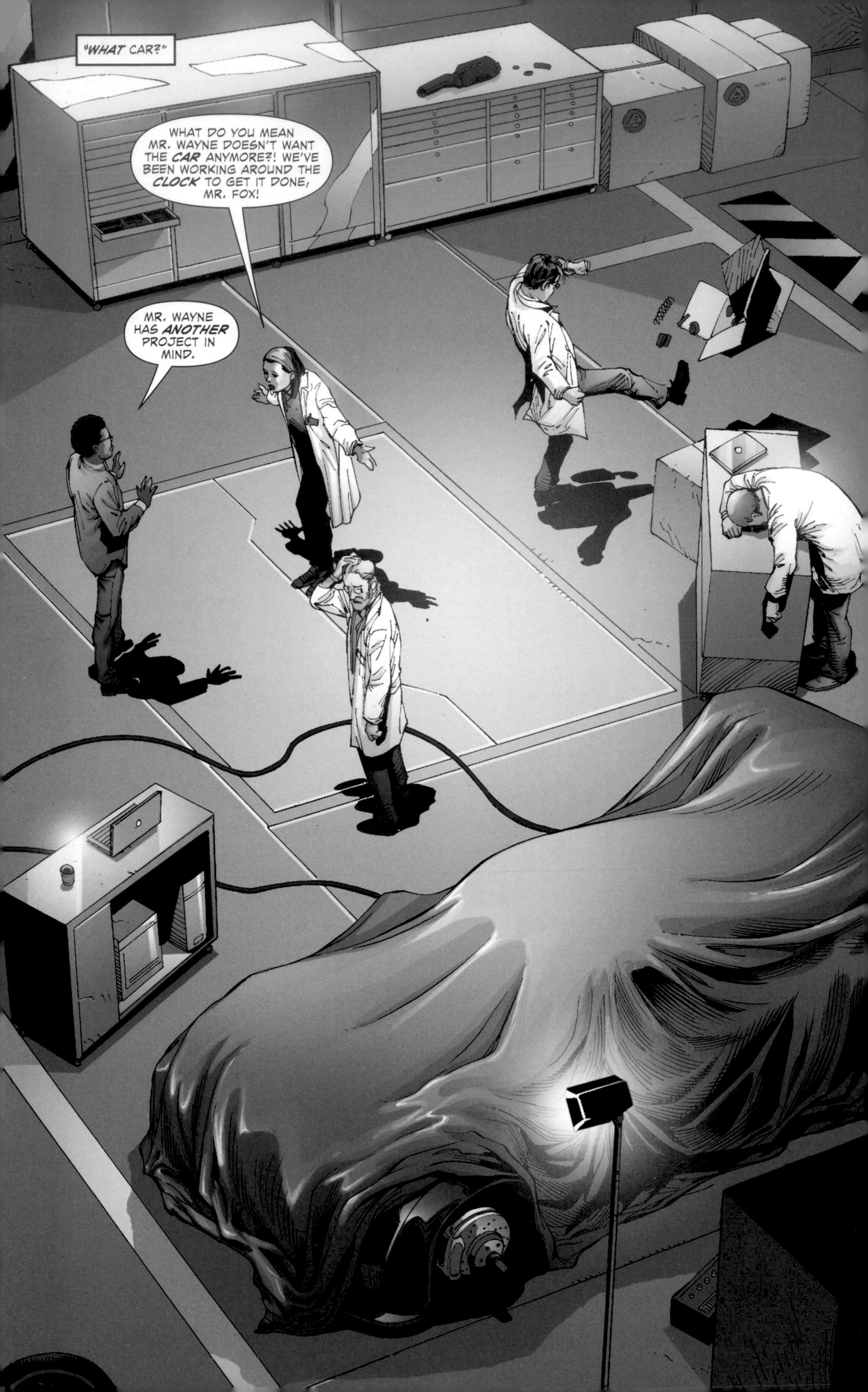
"WHAT CAR?"
WHAT DO YOU MEAN MR. WAYNE DOESN'T WANT THE CAR ANYMORE?! WE'VE BEEN WORKING AROUND THE CLOCK TO GET IT DONE, MR. FOX!
MR. WAYNE HAS ANOTHER PROJECT IN MIND.

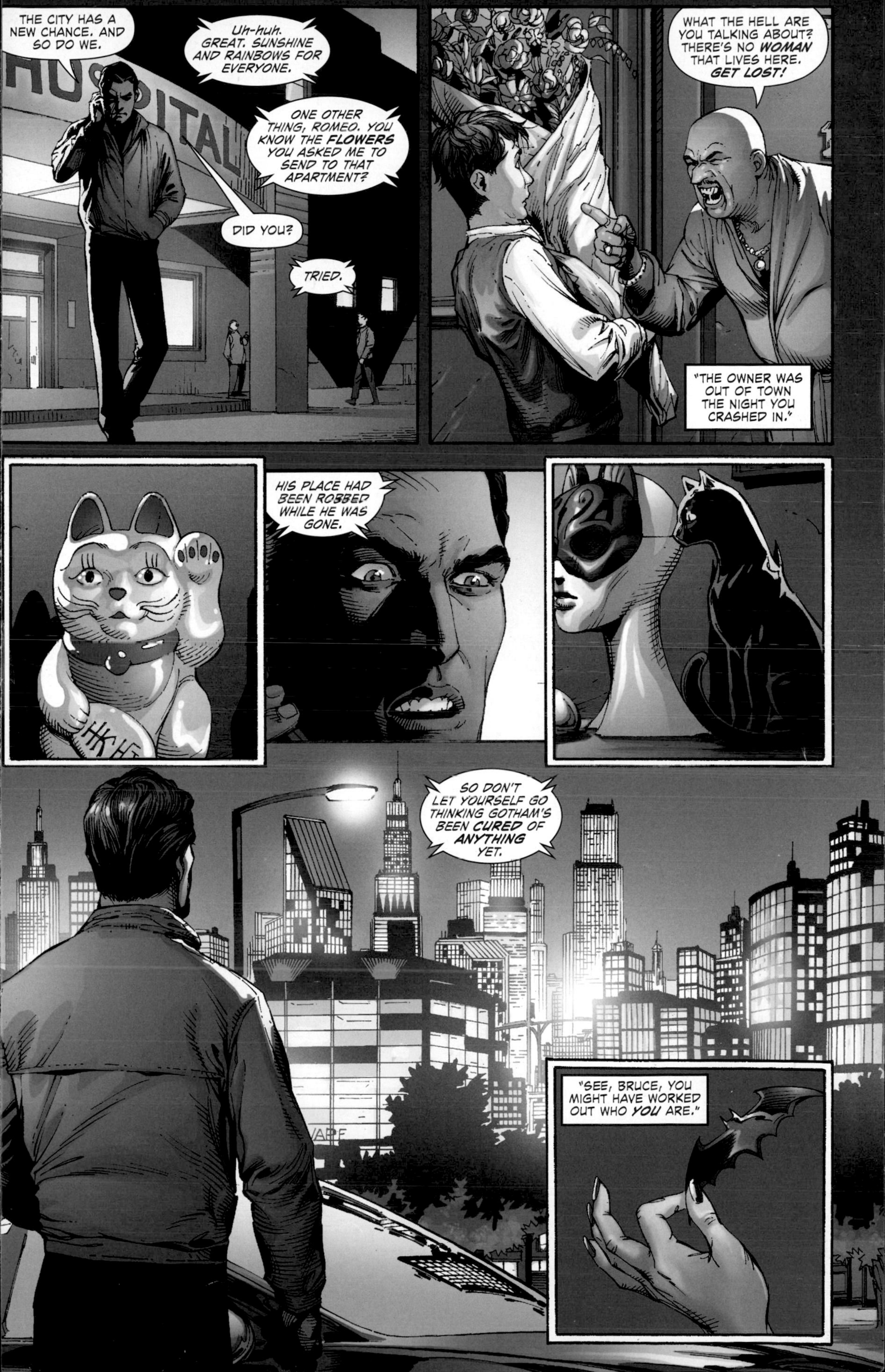
THE CITY HAS A NEW CHANCE. AND SO DO WE.
Uh-huh. GREAT. SUNSHINE AND RAINBOWS FOR EVERYONE.
ONE OTHER THING, ROMEO. YOU KNOW THE FLOWERS YOU ASKED ME TO SEND TO THAT APARTMENT?
DID YOU?
TRIED.
WHAT THE HELL ARE YOU TALKING ABOUT? THERE'S NO WOMAN THAT LIVES HERE. GET LOST!
"THE OWNER WAS OUT OF TOWN THE NIGHT YOU CRASHED IN."
HIS PLACE HAD BEEN ROBBED WHILE HE WAS GONE.
SO DON'T LET YOURSELF GO THINKING GOTHAM'S BEEN CURED OF ANYTHING YET.
"SEE, BRUCE, YOU MIGHT HAVE WORKED OUT WHO YOU ARE."

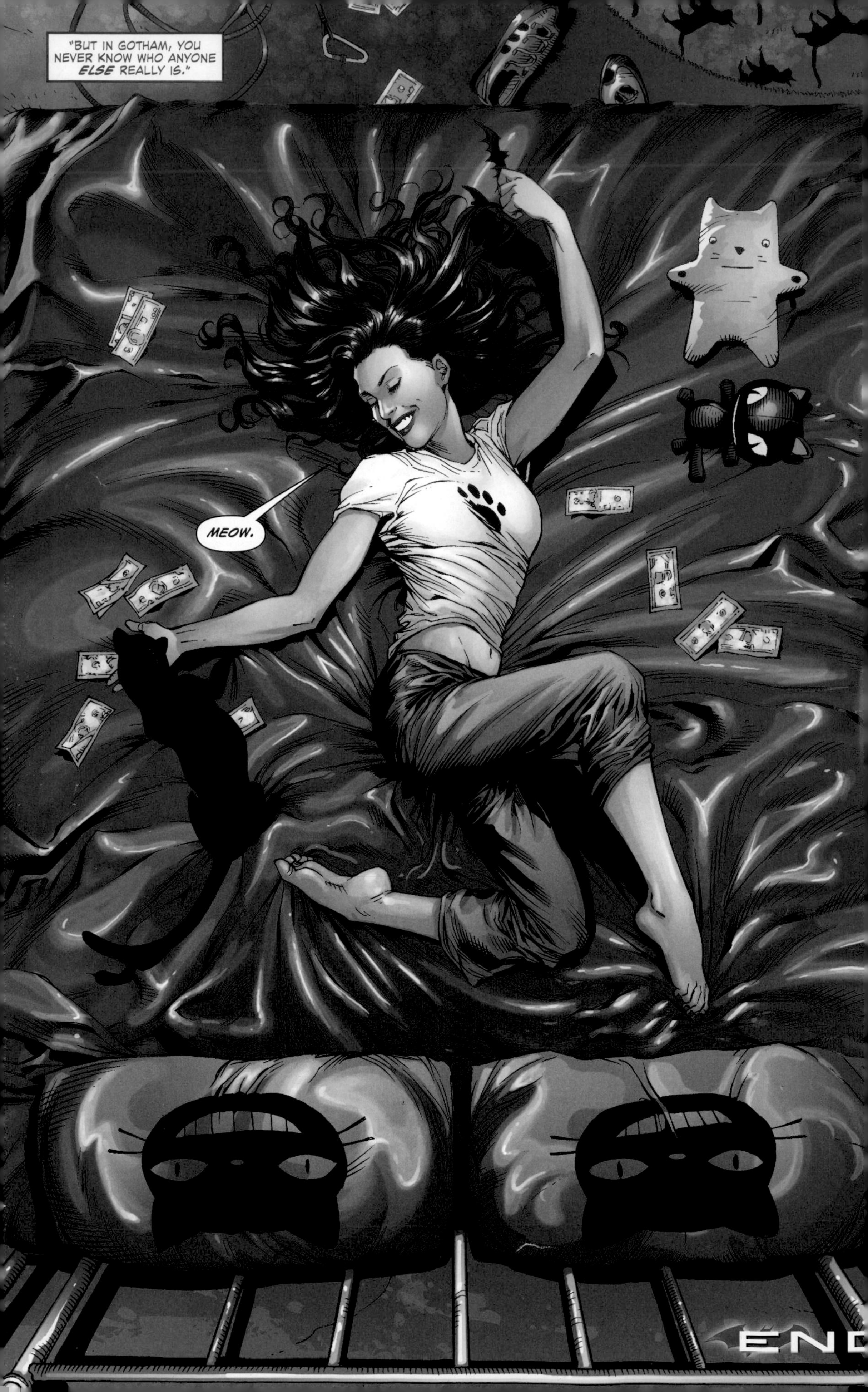
"BUT IN GOTHAM, YOU NEVER KNOW WHO ANYONE *ELSE* REALLY IS."
MEOW.
END